SEX IS NO EMERGENCY

Sex Is No Emergency by Dorothy Max Prior

First published by Strange Attractor Press 2025
Text © Dorothy Max Prior 2025

Typeset in **Avant Garde**, Helvetica Neue and Plantin
Design and layout by Alena Zavarzina
Cover design by Foz Creative

ISBN 9781913689810

Strange Attractor Press
BM SAP, London,
WC1N 3XX, UK

www.strangeattractor.co.uk

Distributed by The MIT Press, Cambridge, Massachusetts. And London, England.

Printed and bound in Estonia by Tallinna Raamatutrükikoda.

SEX IS NO EMERGENCY

Adventures in a Post Punk Wonderland

Dorothy Max Prior

Contents

"Like sexual desire, memory never stops. It pairs the dead
with the living, real with imaginary beings,
dreams with history."

Annie Ernaux, The Years

"You say that you want love
You want to want love
But love is more than some fucking four-letter word...
Are you afraid? Well, we all are.
Sex is no emergency."

Monte Cazazza, Sex is No Emergency

To Sons and Lovers

IN EVERY DREAM HOME...

Now I'm no longer a lone nomad, but one of a pair, wandering around London, taking refuge wherever and whenever.

I'm sitting on one of those high stools at Trader Vic's Tiki bar, downstairs in the Park Lane Hilton, wondering why so many men are looking over at me. I mean, I'm used to men in bars looking over at me, it happens a lot, and I *am* wearing a rather nice tight-fitting tiger-print dress and red stiletto-heeled ankle-boots, but there's something a little different going on here. The stares are long and hard. And there seem to be quite a few of us lone ladies sitting on bar stools here tonight. Then I remember: Trader Vic's has always been one of the best pick-up joints for upmarket ladies of the night. I cross my legs and smile to myself as I take a sip of my Singapore Gin Sling.

A man comes over. He's tall, dark and handsome, with a broad smile, dressed in a midnight blue suit, clearly made-to-measure, with an open-necked, dazzlingly white shirt giving the expensive suit a slightly dressed-down look. But dressed-down in that *I have loads of money so I don't need to wear a tie to get in to posh places* kind of way. "Well, hello there," he says. The other girls glance over, glare, then get back to their drinks.

But this isn't a pick-up, I know this person – although only vaguely. This is Dani, the Argentinian property dealer who masterminded my exit from 69 Exhibition Road, where I'd been living for the past six years. Me, my dearly beloved Andy Warren, and the other 20-plus inmates of this mouse-infested old wreck of a house had been bought out in a complex negotiation with the building's current owners and the would-be developers, and Dani had brokered the deal with breathtaking bravado. At some point during the process, Dani had found out that I had a new job teaching ballroom and partner dance, and had confessed that he felt awkward about being an Argentinian who couldn't tango – so would I teach him? Well yes, why not. And could he take me for a drink to talk it through? Well yes, why not. Especially as that meant a trip to Trader Vic's.

So let me tell you about Trader Vic's. The Park Lane branch opened in 1963, fast becoming the place to be for Swinging London's guys and dolls – it's still going strong now, two decades on in 1982. There's a main bar, a restaurant area, and a labyrinth of smaller rooms. It's a fabulous mash-up of pan-Pacific culture, embracing all things Polynesian, Hawaiian and Maori. I presume that all the Trader Vic's across the world have the same or similar decor: this one has lattice-work bamboo ceilings, rattan chairs with ludicrously high seat backs, and carved wooden masks on the walls. On the bar – and any other available surface – are a muddle of stainless steel cocktail shakers, pineapple ice buckets and Tiki mugs depicting the face of the archetypal first-ever human in every shape, size and colour.

The only other place that is anything like Trader Vic's is the Beachcomber Bar at the Mayfair Hotel. This is an even more over-the-top Tiki bar that features a pool full of turtles, with tropical rainstorms erupting every 20 minutes, water cascading down a rocky wall into the pool to a soundtrack of crashing thunder, the lights zinging on and off in mock lightning flashes. All conversation has to stop for a minute till the 'storm' fizzles out. The bar staff look mightily bored whenever this happens. I suppose a five-hour bar shift means fifteen storms a night, which is probably quite annoying. The staff often do an odd kind of 'musical statues' freeze when a storm starts. This all greatly amused Andy, who I took to the Beachcomber even before he moved into 69 Exhibition Road with me, and we subsequently took all of our friends and bandmates there at least once – El Trains singer Jay Strongman said years later that our trips to the Beachcomber started his life-long obsession with Tiki art and culture. He's even written books about it.

The Beachcomber served food as well as cocktails, but I gave up on the food after an unpleasant encounter with some spicy chicken wings. Andy and I had gone to the Beachcomber before heading off to the Scala to see the UK premiere of David Lynch's *Eraserhead*. I spent a lot of my time in the cinema turning green and running to the loo to throw up. Which people might have thought was a reaction to the film, but it wasn't. Mind you, the fact that *Eraserhead* protagonist Henry finds himself, in an early scene, carving a still-moving chicken oozing blood probably didn't help.

Somewhere along the way, and not just because of the dodgy chicken wings, Trader Vic's had taken over as the place to be for me and my friends. I think there came a point where the Beachcomber got swamped by tourists and loud hen parties from Essex, so we switched our allegiance – which is why I'm meeting Dani here not there.

So now I've signed Dani up to some dance lessons at the American school where I teach, Arthur Murray's in Kensington – which I feel slightly awkward about, as it's not cheap, but he laughs at the idea of me worrying about whether he has the money, or cares how much anything costs. In fact, he's on a mission to stop me worrying about money; to convince me to embrace the idea that money is there to be made, and if I want things they'll come to me. He's also now on a mission to find me somewhere to live. Not to rent, but to buy. This seems utterly ludicrous to me, but I humour him and agree to go and see some of the properties he's "working on".

Where I'm living right now, post-69 Exhibition Road, is at the Pirronis' house in Harrow. Dino and Bruna Pirroni are my ex-boyfriend and Rema Rema bandmate Marco's parents. They've adopted me, even though I'm no longer going out with Marco. They seem to like adopting homeless young people – Blitz Club founder Steve Strange once occupied the same small spare room that I'm now in. Most of my stuff is squirrelled away in their loft, but I do have a chest-of-drawers in the bedroom stuffed with whatever isn't packed away upstairs or at Andy's mum's house, and there is a broom cupboard next to my room that I use for things like the Vivienne Westwood SEX and Seditionaries clothes I rarely wear these days, bunged into carrier bags, or my 'exotic dancing' outfits that have been retired now that I have a respectable job as a dance teacher. I'd told the Pirronis that I'd only be there a few weeks, but it's been quite a bit longer than that, and I've no idea where I'm going to go next. But Dani is sure he's going to find me something soon.

The first few places he sends me to look at seem far too expensive, with an overwhelming amount of repairs needed.

For example, there's a whole top floor in Bayswater, very big but with water stains on the ceiling and ancient ripped wallpaper, which Dani says he can get for me for £35,000. How do I pay for that, I ask. You have almost a third in cash, he says – go talk to your bank. He's right – I have a £10,000 pay-off from 69. There are other options, too. He mentions a three-bedroomed flat in Brighton for £18,000 but although I like Brighton and visit regularly, there's no way I'd live there. I'm a Londoner through and through. Born, bred – and staying put.

I make an appointment with my bank manager. I'm expecting him to send me packing immediately, but he says, ah interesting – last time I spoke to you about your finances you were playing drums in some sort of punk rock band and now you have a proper PAYE job as a dance teacher. And you have a solid cash deposit. Things are looking up, he says – and now is the time to invest in property. Find somewhere and come back to me.

I speak to Dani – it might be possible, I say, but I don't feel like tackling massive house repairs on my own, I need something less ambitious. Dani has another idea, one that he feels will suit me better, and sends me off to Portobello Road. There, I get to see a one-bedroomed flat being created above one of the antique shops. It'll be all brand new: bedroom, living room, kitchenette, bathroom – you won't even need to decorate, says Dani. I could get more for it, he says, but I'll let you have it for £17,000. You have £10,000. You just need to borrow £7,000. Go back to the bank.

I don't. I don't know why. Some sort of fear of being a normal person, a property owner with a mortgage. Once a punk always a punk. It isn't quite the right time, I say to him. Now's the moment, he says – believe me, London is changing by the minute. It'll all be very different in a year's time. But no, I just can't. Can't pay, won't pay. Normalcy avoided. Phew – that was a close shave. Dani gives up on me eventually – although he does take his tango lessons, and we continue to meet up very occasionally at Trader Vic's.

It's Spring 1983, and I'm still living in Harrow, a year after leaving Exhibition Road. I offer rent money, which is refused, and apologies for still being there. Don't worry about it, say Dino and Bruna – we have the space for you, you can stay as long as you like. Which is why, I suppose, I'm still here. They treat me like the daughter they never had, or the daughter-in-law they almost had. They even take me away with them on holiday to Italy twice a year, where we stay in the tiny village near Pellegrino Parmense where Bruna was born. I have the occasional fantasy about living there, away from grimy old London, buying their broken-down old stone house in Villa Negri which – now that they've built a brand-new red-brick house with bathrooms and balconies, within sight just up the hill – is used for housing chickens. You can have the old house for £8,000, says Bruna's brother Aurelio. Gosh, I could buy it straight out, for cash! I don't.

One of my dance school colleagues, Vernon, lives in a house on Kensington Church Street, on the way up to Notting Hill Gate. It's a bit less shabby than 69 Exhibition Road, but is similarly a great big old house split up into self-contained bedsits. There's a lot of those in these parts. Vernon's room is large and airy, facing the front of the house. His showgirl friend Kim has a smaller room on the same floor facing the back. Vernon tells me that Kim is taking a job in a nightclub in Singapore, and needs someone to sub-let for a couple of months. Oh, yes please!

The room still has a lot of Kim's things in it, but I manage to squeeze in a drawer-full of clothes, my make-up and dance

shoes, and a transistor radio. It's a single bed, like the bed in the spare room at the Pirronis', with a nice black-and-white zigzag-print bedcover and lots of fluffy fake-fur cushions. Although it's ground floor at the front, the house is on a hill, so it's higher at the back, and I have a view of the garden with its big old plane and sycamore trees. These old houses are built like fortresses, so you can't hear any traffic from the back – it could almost be the countryside. Birdsong, squirrels, the lot. But you step outside the front door and hurrah – there you are, right bang in the middle of Kensington. There's a branch of Dino's for breakfasts; the Cherry Pie is just across the road, serving up cheap and cheerful dinners; and Jimmy's Wine Bar is around the corner offering very reasonably priced bottles of wine. Oh, and it's just five minutes' walk to or from the Arthur Murray dance school, which is on Hyde Park Gate. This is a lot different to the nightly hike back to Harrow on the Metropolitan line, followed by a horrid walk down deserted suburban streets. I'm a real city girl and always feel safer in bustling areas. I don't mind rough pubs and rowdiness, and can navigate my way through gangs of boozy blokes – in fact, I used to make a living doing just that, go-go dancing and stripping in East End bars – but the side streets around Northwick Park Station feel like real Ripper territory, and I walk home flinching at every twig crack behind me.

Back in London proper, I start going out more in the evenings. There are the trips to gay clubs or discos with my dance school colleagues – and my, oh my, what a lot of choice there is these days. There's Heaven and its sidecar, the Cha-Cha Club. There's the Copacabana in Earl's Court, or perhaps Wichity's or old favourite The Sombrero aka Yours or Mine on Kensington High Street, so staggering distance home.

Sometimes, I abandon my new workmates and meet up with old friends from the punk days. Ted Polhemus and Lynn Procter, who had been my portal into the ICA and the contemporary art scene, and who had also introduced me to the world of 'exotic dancing', have been interested long-term in the fetish scene – rubber, leather, piercings, whatever – so they're always happy to make a trip to Skin Two. Or sometimes I go with Andy and his new girlfriend Gill Smith who's keen to show off her growing latex clothing collection. Gill, by the way, is managing a band called The Smiths – which is a pure coincidence with the surname thing, but a very amusing one. Andy is amused, anyway. The Smiths come from Manchester and seem to spend a lot of time sleeping on the floor of her West Hampstead flat. Andy says the singer is a bit miserable, but the rest of them are alright.

Because of my working hours at the dance school – I'm often there until 11pm – I don't get out to see many bands.

And to be honest, there aren't many I want to see. When not distracted by esoteric electronica or other experimentations, my heart is firmly with disco and dance music.

Since starting work at Arthur Murray's I've become more and more engrossed in Latin music – especially the dance stuff from the 1930s to the 1960s. I've always liked jazz and swing – Cab Calloway and Louis Jordan have been on my radar for years – and this jazz connection led on to discovering Bossa Nova and Cuban music. But now that I know all the Latin dance rhythms, this has become a full-on obsession – there are no lines drawn between the music I use in my work and the music I listen to off-duty. I'm often to be found dancing a rumba round the room when home alone. Favourite band leaders include King of the Mambo Perez Prado with his wonderful 'huhs' shouted out to band and audience; and Catalan emigré to Havana, and then New York, Xavier Cugat. Then, there's Alfredito and His Orchestra with their fabulous 'Honeydripper Mambo'; Cuban star Celia Cruz with her songs about dancing dolls and female goddesses; and the tangos of Carlos Gardel, composer and singer of heart-wrenching tunes like 'Mi Buenos Aires Querido'. It's a whole new world.

Although most of what I do socially happens late-night, at clubs, there are also daytime possibilities on the days that I start work later. Andy and I take to meeting regularly for lunch – Pizza Express is a favourite haunt, but we do occasionally go wild and try somewhere else. The Chicago Pizza Pie Factory, say. Sometimes we meet on Saturdays after my dance class at the Pineapple Studios and we go to an exhibition or the cinema. We revisit old favourites, such as a Warhol double bill at the

ICA – *Flesh for Frankenstein* and *Blood for Dracula*, seen in Spacevision 3-D.

Andy Warren – former wife then slightly incestuous sibling then best friend and roommate at 69 Exhibition Road for six years – is now living back at the Warren family home in Balham and is firmly ensconced as bass player in The Monochrome Set. He and lead singer Bid had played together since their schooldays, although in 1976 he'd been enticed away from Bid to Beat on a Bass with the B-Sides, a band formed by art-school student Stuart Goddard, who later became Adam Ant.

Andy wavered between Bid and Adam for a while – at one point rehearsing with both of them, with me as the would-be drummer – until co-forming The Ants in 1977. That all came to a sticky end in late 1979, after a pretty dreadful time recording The Ants' first album *Dirk Wears White Sox*, and ever since then Andy has been happily back with Bid in The Monochrome Set. So far, they've made three studio albums: *Strange Boutique* and *Love Zombies*, both in 1980 on Virgin imprint Dindisc; and their latest, *Eligible Bachelors*, released on Cherry Red in 1982.

Since making that album, the band have been through a few changes, with lead guitarist Lester Square leaving, replaced by a female keyboard player called Carrie Booth, who also played with The Thompson Twins. This was the line-up that I'd seen – and indeed performed with as opening act – when they played The Ritz club in New York in December 1982. But now Carrie had left, and the band had a new lead guitarist, someone called Foz. Who's that, I ask. You know him, says Andy. He was in The Apaches. I do remember going to see The Apaches with Andy. We'd been put on the guest list by Apaches lead singer Simon Buxton, who was thrilled that punk royalty such as Andy from The Ants and Max from Rema Rema were coming to see *his* band play. Andy reminds me that Foz was the one who wouldn't hang out in the dressing room with us, saying he preferred to go out front and talk to the paying fans rather than lig backstage with the guest-listers. I'm also reminded that we then all went back to South Kensington in the band van, because The Apaches stored their gear at drummer Nick Wesolowski's family house in Thurloe Place, just around the corner from Exhibition Road. I still can't picture Foz. What sort of hair has he got?

Very short, says Andy – and that's because we gave him a sideways mohican when we were on tour, then he shaved it all off. Spring moves to summer. I've had another spell living back in Harrow with the ever- accommodating Pirronis, although I occasionally take up other offers, such as staying with Ted and Lynn in West End Lane, or with my Arthur Murray's dance partner Joe in Maida Vale, or very occasionally with ICA/ Eaton Square squat comrade Keith Allen who I've recently started seeing again, having reconnected at the Comedy Store – although I'm getting a bit uneasy about it as he's now in a proper relationship with someone or other, so I soon knock that one on the head. It is getting tiresome being a nomad and not having a proper home, reminding me of my pre-Exhibition Road days in the mid-1970s.

But now Kim's room on Kensington Church Street is up for grabs again, this time for a longer spell as she heads off for a nightclub residency in Hong Kong. I move back in. OK, it's her home not mine, and it's just for a few months – but still. Wherever I lay my hat...

Soon after, Andy invites me to a Monochrome Set party, which is at new drummer Nick's mews house, nearby in Chelsea. Yes, that's former Apaches drummer Nick Wesolowski, who when he's not at the family home in South Ken lives with his society girlfriend Lavinia Bunn, one of the Hickstead showjumping dynasty. Quite posh, is our Nick.

Someone comes up to me at the party and starts chatting. Medium height, stripey Breton fisherman top, very short hair, quite earthy features with full lips – the sort of face that you see in *Caravaggisti* paintings. I recognise him as one of The Apaches, bass player Wig I think, but no – this is Foz, who is now lead guitarist with The Monochrome Set. He's full of chat, talking quickly and moving from subject to subject with hardly a breath in between. Foz goes off to get a drink and I then speak to the former singer in The Apaches, Simon, who is delighted to now be a Monochrome Set insider via Foz and Nick. Simon has an upper-class drawl and talks in a knowing way about things I suspect he knows very little about. Theosophy, say, and the Golden Dawn. Elegant and eloquent man of the world with a niche interest in the esoteric is the persona he's chosen for himself – sometimes he pulls it off, and sometimes it slips.

A few weeks later, Simon invites me out to dinner, and makes it clear it's a date. What a novelty – I can't remember having been on many dates since my first one when I was 15, with my best friend Paul Elliot. We – me and Paul, that is – went to see jazz star Jon Hendrix, and had a nice enough time, but didn't even get round to kissing, which was a great relief as at the time I wasn't really into boys 'in that way'. But by now I've learnt that I like boys.

So, Simon has invited me to the Stock Pot in Earl's Court for an early evening dinner. Well, if it's a date, I'd better make an effort, I feel. I wear a strapless 1950s summer frock, black with yellow polka dots, paired with a little bolero cardigan – the type ballerinas wear – and my Anello and Davide gold pumps. When I arrive at the restaurant, I'm surprised that Simon has someone with him – Foz. Not quite what I was expecting, but I don't mind. After a pleasant couple of hours of food and chat, friendly rather than romantic (as befits a threesome dining together), I'm not sure whether I should say my goodbyes, or wait to see what happens next. I'm waiting for Simon to say something or do something but he doesn't, so I thank him for inviting me out, and stand up to go. Which way are you going? asks Foz. Oh, I'll walk back, I say, it's only about half an hour to Kensington Church Street from here. I'm going that way, says Foz. Simon looks as if he's going to say something, then doesn't. So off we walk, just the two of us, chattering away nineteen to the dozen as we weave through the back streets of Earl's Court and Kensington. We detour through Kensington Gardens, and as it's mid-July, it's still light at 9.30pm. The trees are dressed in their midsummer best, and the birds are in full flow, singing their little hearts out. By the time it gets dark, and the gardens close, it's clear that it's Foz and me who have been on the date, not me and Simon.

The new romance with Foz plays out in the little room I'm subletting from Kim – and in the parks and gardens of Kensington. We're particularly fond of Holland Park, with its shady walkways and screeching peacocks. Sometimes we venture further afield – to Kew Gardens, or to Richmond to walk the towpath, where we are overtaken by beefy male runners in weeny shorts. They are stallions and I am a pony, says Foz. We also spend a fair amount of time at Jimmy's Wine Bar, just around the corner from Kim's. Foz sometimes comes to meet me at Arthur Murray's, and we head out to a club. We often go to Feelings on Fulham Road, which is one of those supper club places where you have to buy a plate of food to be allowed to drink after 11pm. Crackers, cheese, olives if you're lucky. Maybe a saucerful of *patatas bravas*. They play Latin-Jazz music, nice mellow bossa novas and rumbas – and yes, even the Morris Albert classic 'Feelings' sometimes.

Autumn 1983 sees me back in Harrow – again. Kim has returned and reclaimed her room, and there are no other immediate options. Foz is living in a shared flat in Finborough Gardens in Earl's Court, so I spend at least one night a week there. We tour the local hostelries, or if we fancy going a bit more upmarket, have cocktails at the Costa del Sol. In the morning we breakfast at the Troubadour on Old Brompton Road – known as the folk-rock coffee house where Bob Dylan, Joni Mitchell and Paul Simon all played in the 1960s. It's still going strong in 1983 and offers a mighty fine Full English.

But as autumn turns to winter, Foz also finds himself homeless, and thus back living with his widowed mum and five siblings in their council flat in Churchill Gardens, Pimlico, on the north bank of the Thames.

Churchill Gardens was London's first ever social housing project, built in the 1950s, in tandem with the Festival of Britain. It was a showcase project – this was supposed to be the future. Nothing higher than six floors, the housing blocks built around green spaces, with shops, schools, a community centre and a playground. The playground here is a rather hazardous affair, constructed around a kind of concrete castle surrounded by enormous boulders – but still, it's the thought that counts. Like all council estates in Britain, it has lifts that smell of pee and often don't work – so you end up running up the stairs and arriving panting at the top. But apart from that, it's quite nice. The Foster family's fourth-floor flat overlooks the river, with a fabulous view of Battersea Power Station. One of the advantages of being here is that tenants don't have to pay for heating or hot water – all that comes in an odd kind of overflow arrangement from the Power Station that I never really understand.

Sometimes I meet Foz at Pimlico Station and we head to the nearby Tate Gallery to check out the Peter Blakes or whatevers in the general collection, or perhaps there's a special exhibition like the Richard Hamilton retrospective, *Just what is it that makes today's homes so different, so appealing?* We go to the Hayward to see the big Dufy exhibition – full of beautiful blues. Dufy Blue blues, that is. Or we go to the ICA. Late '83, there's an exhibition of photographs by Robert Mapplethorpe, which include some very racy stamen shots, and other sexual things of the human variety that cause a big stir, in these days of anti-gay AIDS hysteria.

Also at the ICA, in early 1984, is Derek Jarman's painting exhibition, *The GBH Paintings*, aka *The Last of England* (a title he'll also use for a future film) which I go to twice, once with Foz and once with friend and former musical collaborator Genesis P-Orridge – this second visit in order to meet up with and talk to Derek, who apart from the GPO connection, I also know from six or seven years ago, when he made *Jubilee*. As part of the Ants entourage, I occasionally found myself hanging around Derek's warehouse on Butler's Wharf or at the headquarters of Megalovision, producers of *Jubilee* and sometime managers of Adam and the Ants. Derek is now living on Tottenham Court Road, near Denmark Street. I'm not sure what has happened to the wharf warehouse. Possibly a victim of the redevelopment frenzy devouring London.

Much of those winter months is spent in art galleries, but there's also a lot of walking along the Embankment or sitting huddled on park benches, waiting for the pubs and wine bars to open at 6pm so we can get a few hours in each other's company in a warm place, drinking a bottle of red. As staying together at his mum's or at the Pirronis' isn't an option, Foz and I are edged into a weird pseudo-teenage romance situation. For Christmas 1983, Foz (who's an illustrator when he's not a musician) had drawn a card featuring a couple sitting sharing a bottle of wine, with '1984' written at the top, and both of them with fingers crossed under the table. Drawing cards (him) or making collages (me) for each other becomes something we do.

Early 1984 is a blur of wine bars and cafes and restaurants. Mildred's and Finch's and Sloanes. Picasso's and Dino's and Tarts. The Lone Star Cafe. The Perfumed Conservatory. Bistro Vino. We go to the cinema: to The Gate in Bloomsbury, the Classic in Chelsea, and the Coronet in Notting Hill. We see *Zelig*, and *Educating Rita*, and *The Draughtsman's Contract*. It keeps us off the streets.

Sometimes, we stay together at someone else's gaff. With Wig from The Apaches and his girlfriend Chrissie in Ladbroke Grove. With Nick and Lavinia in Ensor Mews. Now I'm no longer a lone nomad, but one of a pair, wandering around London, taking refuge wherever and whenever. Oh, where is my home sweet home?

Foz and I are both flat-hunting separately. Dani and the bank manager were right. London property prices have hit the roof in the past year or so. Never mind buying – even renting is nigh on impossible. Prices are ridiculously high, and some of the places I look at are disgusting dumps. Somewhere along the way comes the idea that getting somewhere together would be more economical than us each getting a place. I had quite fancied getting a nice little bedsit like Kim's, all of my own – but I reassure myself that it's going to be OK. Fingers crossed, like the Christmas card.

A couple of months later – April 1984 – we move into a basement flat at 44 Rosehill Road, Wandsworth. It's way cheaper than most places we've seen, and it's a whole flat, with a bedroom, a living room, a galley kitchen, and a bathroom. It has horrendous flowery curtains and swirly carpets, and a chintzy three-piece-suite, but never mind. The landlady (we call her Mrs Beastly, which is some approximation of her real name) is a bit old-fashioned, but she doesn't live on the premises, and we've managed to convince her that we are a respectable couple with proper incomes, and not the sort of people to have noisy parties. Which is true, actually – I'm out at work most days of the week, dancing and teaching and being the life and soul of the party at the Arthur Murray social gatherings. When your job is to party, you don't want to party on your own time. And Foz has given up on the beatnik look and taken to wearing English country gentleman clothes from a shop on the New King's Road called Hacketts, which sells tweed jackets, crisp cotton shirts and polished brown brogues. That helped keep up appearances when it came to flat hunting.

Home. We have a home. But although we have a perfectly good kitchen, in those first few months of domestic bliss it's mostly used for making the brunch that I eat before heading off to work. We're rarely home to make food on weekday evenings. I'm now teaching at two dance schools, Arthur Murray's in Kensington, and a more prim and proper English ballroom school in Marylebone. Foz often comes to meet me at Marylebone and we eat late-night at the Passage to India off Baker Street – or Vernon tags along too and we go to The Eagle or James' Wine Bar. If Foz is coming along to Kensington, that'll quite likely mean a trip to old favourite Jimmie's Wine Bar, or perhaps we go to a club with my workmates. But then there are the days when Foz stays home to write songs, which means sitting around all day in his green-and-white striped djellaba with a plastic cup on his head, guitar in hand, looking mildly surprised to see me when I arrive home at 11pm.

Our flat is on the Clapham Junction side of Wandsworth, and on days off we explore the area. French's on East Hill is an old-fashioned bistro that serves steaks and pies. Nearby Wandsworth Common has a duck pond and a restaurant called Neal's Lodge that does proper afternoon teas and Sunday roasts. Further afield, up the Junction, there's the Northcote Road street market, full of food stalls and bric-a-brac shops. Past Arding and Hobbs department store and up Lavender Hill, we discover Battersea Arts Centre, which is a magnificent old building with a theatre and a cafe – and something called the Puppet Centre, which you get to via a grand flight of marbled stairs, where there's a semi-permanent exhibition of puppets featured in film and TV – lots of favourites including Parker and Lady Penelope, Bagpuss, and the puppets from *The Dark Crystal.*

I did vow many years ago that I'd never again go south of the river, having been brought up in Gipsy Hill – which in the early 1970s was a scuzzy, deteriorating neighbourhood where incoming immigrant communities were crammed in to ever-smaller units in the big Victorian houses, and skinheads roamed the streets throwing stones at the brown-skinned foreigners and at glam rockers like me – but I was growing fond of Wandsworth. Yeah, I can do this. Once, when living in South Kensington, I defined London as anywhere within the Circle Line, but now was slightly reluctantly accepting that the next layer of the London onion was OK too.

After so many months of rootlessness, when we spent ridiculous amounts of time walking the streets of London or sitting in wine bars, we're grateful to now have somewhere where you could sit and do nothing, in your pyjamas all day if you liked. I'd forgotten how lovely it was to just kick off your shoes and relax in your own place – albeit one with swirly carpets and flowery curtains.

The decor might be hideous, but it has my books and records, and Foz's guitars and art materials. We're not allowed to put anything on the walls, but we fill up the mantelpiece and sideboard with our drawings and hand-made collages; our Paolozzi prints and our Man Ray postcards. We buy a yucca plant and a 1950s Ridgeway tea-set and Bob's your uncle: Home Sweet Home.

There's an upfront contempt here for English ballroom dance.
Think Studio 54 not Come Dancing.

"Love to Dance? Dance teachers wanted. Free training given to young, enthusiastic dancers." OK, well, let's see what's on offer – it'll make a change from topless go-go dancing and jumping out of cakes.

The glass-fronted Arthur Murray Dance Studio is tucked away behind the Strand. Sounds seep out into the street – the melodic guitar line and relentless snare beat of Shalamar's 'A Night to Remember'.

I push the door and go in.

Very snazzy! Wall-to-wall mirrors, beechwood flooring, glossy rubber plants. A main dance studio and a separate disco studio with an op-art floor, ultra-violet lights and a glittering mirror ball. Arthur Murray, who 'taught me dancing in a hurry' as the Cole Porter song would have it, was long dead and gone but his franchised dance studios lived on. They were massively successful business ventures in the States and it was hoped the same success could be had in England. The problem with this was the English. They had their own ideas about ballroom dancing – which was why the American company thought it better to train up their own teachers.

At the audition, I pull out all the tricks learnt from seven years of cabaret work and go-go dancing. High kicks in high heels, leggy lunges, and posey pliés. Hair tossing under the strobe lights, hips gyrating, snake-arms weaving patterns in the air. 'American splits' to end (full splits would be too difficult in this tight dress, and I'm not as bendy as I used to be as a gymnastics-mad teenager). I'm in! The training programme starts the following week.

I've done ballroom dancing before – my dad taught me a few basic steps in foxtrot and jive when I was a teenager, and then took me to his motor-trade Dinner and Dance dos to show me off. All a little strange, but there you go. And I'd trained in jazz and stage dance, learning the step-tap-step-kick vaudeville basics at Italia Conte's Saturday school, later graduating to Bob Fosse's *Cabaret* moves at the Pineapple Dance Studio – taught not by him, sadly, but by one of his raunchy female dancers, so the next best thing. But this is something else altogether. For eight weeks, three times a week, we spend hours on end immersed in American social dancing, learning to mambo, merengue and cha-cha (pronounced with a short-vowelled staccato punch – unlike the plum-in-mouth English cha-cha-chaaah to rhyme with baaah). We do the Latin Hustle and the Bus Stop. We learn the John Travolta line dance from *Saturday Night Fever* – choreographed by Arthur Murray's and at first taught exclusively in their schools. Then, there's the authentic

No.

16000 4

EXPIRES

18 FEB 83

ISSUED BY

GB

THIS IS TO CERTIFY THAT

DOROTHY PRIOR

IS A MEMBER OF THE

Pineapple

DANCE CENTRE LTD.
7 LANGLEY STREET LONDON WC2
TELEPHONE 01 836 4004

Arthur Murray, Franchised Dance Studio ®

58 HYDE PARK GATE,
KENSINGTON, LONDON, SW7 5ED
01-581 0382

Argentine tango, which is a world away from the regular ballroom tango: less bird-like head movements and more snake-like entwining and draping of the body – or more to the point, bodies.

There's an upfront contempt here for English ballroom dance with its silly bouffant hairstyles, frothy net dresses and fixed smiles. The American partner dance world favours flouncy blow-dried hair, tight Lycra dresses, and pouting lips. Think New York's Studio 54 rather than *Come Dancing*; Tina Turner not Peggy Spencer. Disco was sweeping the world, and the Latin-Jazz crossover had created the salsa craze in New York. Arthur Murray's were determined to capitalise on these trends, dragging the reluctant British away from their trad waltzes and quicksteps into the bump and grind of American-style dirty dancing.

After two months, the initial training programme ends and it's decision time. We are either offered a permanent job, or not. And yes – I'm in! I phone my agent, Bob at Gemini, and say I'd like to take a few weeks off from the 'exotic dancing' work. I don't go back.

I get whisked away to the Kensington branch of Arthur Murray's. "As soon as I saw you, with that pink dress and gold hair and blue eyeliner, I said to Chris: *we've got to have her*," Glenn, the senior dance tutor, tells me months later. "Camp as Christmas, and called Dorothy – I mean, *really*."

Glenn takes over the training of the group of four newbies who've been poached from the Strand. Monday to Friday, we arrive at the school at midday, train for two or three hours, maybe teach an hour or two, have a late lunch at the Cherry Pie on Kensington Church Street, then teach again from 5 or 6 till 10pm. If you have a free hour, you're supposed to practise, not rest. There's no staff room, no backstage – just a small closet for your outdoor coat and bag. Work, home, sleep, eat, travel, start again. Previous lives dissolve. Did I once have other lives? As a punk muse, a post-punk drummer, an exotic dancer working London's East End pubs? These days, all of life is played out on the Arthur Murray dancefloor.

The other apprentice teachers picked out for Kensington duties are the lovely Debbie, who has long black hair and a wide-mouthed smile; Geoff, a tall and lanky violin player turned dancer who Glenn flirts with constantly; and Joe, a beautiful blonde boy who Glenn also flirts with at every opportunity. Actually, come to think of it, Glenn flirts outrageously with me and Debbie too, and with Doris, the older woman who works on reception and turns out to be a lovely dancer – and indeed with anyone else who crosses his path.

The old hands here include the slinky studio manager Chris, who wears very tight fitting trousers that show off his perfectly-sculpted bottom very nicely, and very obviously has a jazz dance background; Vernon, a dapper man with a small moustache and a friendly smile who only works part-time as he is moonlighting from a very proper English ballroom school in Marylebone, run by a lady called Gwenethe Walshe; and the ageless Donald, who everybody calls Mother – a former merchant seaman who has been with Arthur Murray's forever, and makes a good enough salary to enable him to take frequent trips to Cairo or Marrakesh to enjoy romantic encounters with young gentlemen friends there. Then, there's Sharon, who supplements her short stature with immensely high heels; arrives with a new hairstyle each Monday morning (chignon, flicks, curly perm); and has never, ever been seen by anyone without a full face of make-up.

Perhaps she's just following the house rules to the T: when offered the job, we girls have to sign a contract saying we will

not be permitted on to the dancefloor unless dressed in a skirt and sheer, flesh-coloured tights or stockings, plus dance shoes with heels, coiffed hair, and lipstick. On one occasion I have a bit of a cold and stay in my civvies a little longer than usual – ski-pants and a turquoise wool sloppy-joe jumper. It's only 2pm and no clients have yet arrived, just us workers going through our moves. Our American boss Mr Shea – the only 100% heterosexual man in the place, an alpha-male who likes to make it known who's in charge – comes over to tell me to "buck up" and get myself out of "that ugly jumper".

Our students are a magnificent mix of the idle rich, the eccentric and the lonely: London misfits and mavericks who've made a home for themselves in our brash and breezy world of spontaneous applause, wine-boxed parties and line-dance demonstrations. The sensible young couples who want to waltz at their wedding take their special-offer introductory lessons then abscond to a respectable English school. Those who remain are the wild and whimsical, the widowed and the never-wed. There are the wives whose husbands travel and the husbands whose wives drink. Little men in olive green suits with too-short trouser legs, and long tall women wearing Yves Saint Laurent with the hem hanging down. The sons of Middle Eastern ambassadors attracted to anything glitzy, expensive and American. Solitary career women with well-paid jobs in the civil service who avoid a home life by coming straight here from Whitehall at 6.00pm and staying all evening. Oh, and people who just love dancing, and have the money to pay someone to partner them, those too.

The evenings are always busy, the dancefloor full. Specially compiled cassette tapes with two each of all the dance rhythms taught are kept on continuous play. Waltz, foxtrot, tango, cha-cha. Rumba, samba, mambo, merengue. Plus, swing of various tempos, the up-beat East Coast and raunchy West Coast versions; and disco, or swing hustle, or samba hustle. The Gibson Brothers' 'Cuba' is a current hot pick for samba hustle, and D-Train's brand new 'You're the One For Me' is our favourite swing hustle number. We have a turntable as well as the cassette decks, which is handy for playing new releases. I have the D-Train track as 12-inch single, extended version. And Arthur Murray's are keen on us using contemporary music as much as possible, even for the more traditional dances – The

Commodores' 'Three Times a Lady' is the studio's current favourite waltz.

The smaller back-room studio could be used for anyone wanting to work in a more concentrated way, but for most people, it's the main dancefloor that provides the atmosphere that they've paid their money to experience. On two evenings a week, 9 till 11pm, there are parties – hard work for the teachers as we're expected to dance continuously for those two hours, constantly changing partners so that no one feels left out, as well as doing dance demonstrations with other staff members, and starting off the line dances or conga lines round the ballroom. It is a relentless onslaught of fun and frivolity, everyone under the severest obligation to enjoy themselves.

But creating the dance demos with colleagues is a great opportunity for improving our own dance and choreography skills. Sometimes it's just a fairly low-key affair – a regular waltz or tango or whatever. Sometimes it's something fancier. Glenn and his partner Heather like to show off their lifts and drops in a rumba routine. When Glenn is teaching us lifts, he is as outrageously camp as ever. "One hand on the fanny, one on the tits and up she goes – flying tuna!" And then, on the descent: "Oh God, have you just shaved your legs? You've practically scraped the skin off my forearm." Occasionally, there are very special themed parties. The circus one, for example. Trapeze-girl tutus, red-nosed clown outfits, and white-faced Pierrots. I've been taking acrobatic classes at the Oval House Theatre, so that comes in handy as we put together an elementary tumbling routine that morphs into a samba. Or then there's the Ali Baba and his Harem Girls Arabian Nights special. Donald makes a splendid genie. I borrow a belly-dancing costume from a friend who works as a floor-dancer at nearby Cleopatra's restaurant, and hastily learn enough moves to get by. There's also An

Evening in Montmartre, for which we get taught the original Moulin Rouge Can-Can routine by someone who worked there for many years. Apparently, the routine is not written down and is passed on from one generation of dancers to the next. It feels exciting to be doing the very same steps that were danced in front of Toulouse-Lautrec – although, unlike the original Can-Can girls, we keep our knickers on.

Afternoons at the dance studio are usually quite easy going. The only people who like to come in the afternoons are the rare few who want to work seriously on their dance technique, together with a small number, mostly older people, who don't like coming out in the evenings, unless it's a party night. In this second group is Dick Payne, a cockney pensioner who always arrives early, and is thoroughly disappointed if anyone else is taking a lesson at the same time. Dick likes the dancefloor to himself, and this is because Dick likes to tango. If we have the place to ourselves, then we have sole control of the music and can put an endless succession of tangos on the turntable.

"Lovely dance, the tango," he'd say as we set off to the thumping beat of 'La Cumparsita'. He wasn't interested in the slower, more pensive Argentinian tangos. The tango as danced by Dick Payne has more in common with the Military Two-Step than the languorous dance of a Buenos Aires gaucho. He occasionally enjoyed a waltz or even a cha-cha, but push him too far with a mambo and he'd stop, feigning breathlessness and shaking his head. "Bugger that for a game of soldiers," he'd say crossly, sitting down until I agree to find a nice tango to put on. "That's better. That's what I call a proper dance." Dick had lost his wife, as they say, a few years ago. He lives in a small flat in Fulham near his son and daughter-in-law, who it seemed didn't have too much time to spare. His dance lessons are the highlight of his week, and he enjoys coming to the parties and impressing the ladies with his tango skills.

Dick's biggest rival is Archie Haines. Archie and his wife Doris take the train up to London for their double lesson every Friday afternoon. Dick always scowls as Archie totters through the door, arm-in-arm with poor dishevelled Doris. "He's here, then," Dick would say, with a curt nod towards the interloper. "Can't be short of a bob or two. You'd think they'd make a bit more of an effort."

Dick was always turned out smartly in a jacket and tie. The Haines's, by contrast, wear a dismal ensemble of jumble-sale clothes, Archie in crumpled Crimplene trousers and a drab beige jumper, Doris in a faded flowery frock and a nylon cardigan of indeterminate colour buttoned up to the neck. They are rumoured to be millionaires, and there was constant speculation about exactly where and how they lived. They rarely speak to each other, sitting side-by-side silently blinking like owls for at least half an hour before their lesson time.

The only facts known were that they owned a number of caravans on the South Coast, kept budgerigars, and were willing to spend limitless amounts of money on their dance lessons, signing up to any new programme that was offered.

On one particular Friday, a visiting big-wig from the American mother company is at the school for a promotional push that involves selling extra lessons to existing clients. As first-rate paying customers, the Haines's are summoned in to meet the big chief. Glenn and I, their teachers, go in with them. They clutch each other nervously, taking the offered seats without a word.

"Well now, Mr and Mrs Haines. It's a pleasure to meet you. I hear you're in the mobile home rental business," says the American with great gusto. Doris and Archie both turn to me and Glenn, and stare in panic.

"He means you let out your caravans," I say.

"Yeah, caravans. Don't we, Doris," says Archie, nodding furiously and rearranging his false teeth.

"And I hear you're making excellent progress with your current Silver Pathways Advanced Curriculum." More panicked looks.

"He's talking about your dance lessons," says Glenn.

"Well now," says the boss-man, "we feel you've made such good progress that we could move you straight onto Gold Pathways, converting your current lessons to the new programme".

I risk the wrath of Mr Big Wig by coming in with: "He wants you to buy more dance lessons."

"Yeah," says Archie. "Doris?"

Doris is already opening her handbag to get out her cheque book.

I feel like marching them out the door, telling them that they're being conned. But what's the point? Like everyone else who comes here, they want to be sold the big American razzmatazz dance dream. They want the girls with the Lurex boob-tubes and high-heeled Latin dance sandals, the boys with the jazzy shirts and Cuban-heeled boots. They want the parties and the boat trips down the Thames, the clapping after every dance, and the Showcase events at the Holiday Inn. And who am I to deny them life's simple pleasures? Doris and Archie are marched into the studio manager's office to close the deal, freeing Glenn and me to await our next booking. We've missed our meal break.

It's now seven o'clock on Friday evening – peak lesson time. Glenn's student arrives. It's Diana Harryhausen, one of Glenn's favourites, and she clearly adores him. They spend 50% of the time dancing, and 50% talking and giggling and discretely sipping gin in tea cups. Diana always has a small bottle in her bag. Diana's husband Ray doesn't really dance – he's more interested in making exquisite models of dinosaurs and fighting skeletons for feature films.

Ray is, though, signed up to the school, to keep Diana happy – I'm his teacher, but he skips lessons mostly, and just comes along to the parties occasionally. But he's here tonight! When we dance together, he apologises profusely for his lack of dedication to the dark arts of ballroom dancing. "I do try, for Diana's sake," he says, cautiously steering me to the edge of the dancefloor as Glenn and Diana gallop past in a mad-dash quickstep, laughing happily. He's quietly delighted when he finds out that I know about his 'dynamation' work on films such as *Jason and the Argonauts*, and relieved that he's allowed to opt out of the trickier dances and instead sit and chat to me about working with Raquel Welch in *One Million Years BC* or Ursula Andress in his latest film, *Clash of the Titans*. He's very discrete, but there are hints that he much prefers animated sea monsters to real live actresses. I also find out in our chat that he's a good friend of Ray Bradbury, one of my favourite authors, so that gives us more to talk about. Diana is looking over at us, wondering why we're not dancing, so with a soft sigh, Ray leads me off in a waltz, counting silently. "I'm so sorry, I can't dance and talk," he says.

The hour is up, Ray and Diana leave, and Glenn and I wait for our 8pm bookings to arrive. Who have I got? I really hope it isn't the Jordanian businessman who proposes marriage on a weekly basis, or Mr Cox, the creepy guy with a permanent hard-on who constantly asks me if I have a boyfriend. We all call him Mr Cock behind his back. Maybe it's Reg, the zoo-keeper who has invited me to spend a day behind the scenes at London Zoo feeding the snakes, or the young man from Algeria who has been sent along by his father to learn to dance, to better equip him as a man of the world, and to make him even more of an eligible bachelor.

Yep, that one. Farid. It is his second lesson and he is looking terrified. He is skinny and as pretty as can be: enormous soft-brown eyes with long lashes and a head of glossy black curls, his well-toned androgynous physique shown off nicely by skin-tight boot-cut black trousers and an immaculate white linen shirt unbuttoned at the neck to reveal a weighty triple-strand gold necklace – real gold, I'm sure. He's so obviously gay that the only sensible option is to conspire together to fool his father. I drag him round the ballroom so that he doesn't have to bother himself with anything as macho as leading a dance, and when his father pops in towards the end of the lesson to see how he's doing, I feign feminine coyness and flutter eyelashes accordingly. This all works very well, and his father signs him up for a year-long programme of dance lessons.

A firm friendship develops, and over the coming months – despite the school's ban on socialising with the clients – we follow our evening lessons together with outings to gay clubs. He is absolutely hardline about not touching alcohol, even refusing the cherry from my cocktail because it's been polluted, but he's a little more lax with the religious rules when it comes to sexual encounters – claiming that sex with boys doesn't count in his country.

Sometimes I stay with him in his Bayswater bedsit after a night out – platonically, of course, although he asks me lots of questions to shore up his knowledge about the opposite sex. On one occasion, it isn't merely platonic. Farid wants to know what sex with a girl is like, so I oblige, as a favour to a friend. His verdict: quite nice, but not as good as the real thing. Before the year is out, he is sent home to be married to a virgin bride lined up for him by his father, who by now is convinced that his son has learnt all that he needs to know about women.

Come 11pm on a Friday, lessons and parties done and dusted, we all (me, Glenn, Joe, Debbie, and whoever else might be up for it) pile into taxis and head off down to Heaven, under Charing Cross Station on the old Global Village site – which has taken off as the gay club to outshine all others. It's diametrically opposed to the old-school places of the 1970s which were all weak yellow lighting, flock wallpaper, and secret knocks on the door to get in.

Heaven is big and brash with a state-of-the-art sound system and sophisticated purple and pink laser lights. There have been interim places, like Bang on Charing Cross Road, that paved the way for a gay super-club, but Heaven really is the bees knees. As we burst through the door, we're greeted by the smell of poppers and the sight of a thousand bodies (mostly young and male) writhing in heavenly bliss to the sound of Miquel Brown's 'So Many Men, So Little Time'. The playlist pounds on: Rufus and Chaka Khan, 'Ain't Nobody', The Pointer Sisters, 'Jump', Midnight Star, 'No Parking on the Dance Floor'. We've spent all afternoon and early evening dancing, so you'd think we'd be too tired to dance any more – but oh dear me no, we dance and dance and dance until it's chucking out time. At least the studio is closed on Saturday mornings, so there'll be a lie-in...

+

Come Monday at midday, we reconvene at Arthur Murray's for our start-the-week training session, led by Glenn and Donald. After one of these staff sessions, we're taking a break before readying ourselves to teach when a conversation starts up about this weird new gay flu that's going around. It's turning into a bit of an epidemic, says Donald, who tells us that one of his close friends caught it and is now down the road in Brompton Hospital, with pneumonia. We start to speculate about what it could be. Thinking back to Heaven on Friday night, we remember the overwhelming smell of poppers everywhere. No one has previously had any worries about poppers – they're not even illegal – but perhaps we'd better stop using them. Who knows what they're doing to our bodies. Maybe amyl nitrate has a bad effect on the immune system. This seems logical – but why is it just gay men having the bad side-effects, we wonder. Could it be something else causing this weird flu?

As the weeks go by, the rumours intensify. There seem to be a lot of people catching this thing. Then comes some really bad news. Donald's friend has died. The pneumonia got worse, and he started to get all sorts of other things wrong with him. Basically, every organ in his body gave up, one by one. We're in shock. This doesn't sound like flu. But perhaps he was already ill with something else and didn't know it? Who knows. It isn't long before we learn that in America, this new illness has been named GRID, Gay-Related Immune Deficiency, although no one really understands why it is hitting gay men. A while later, scientists discover that the same immune deficiency syndrome has been detected in Haitians and in heterosexual women in America, so they rename it Acquired Immune Deficiency Syndrome, AIDS for short. This renaming and reframing doesn't stop the tabloids calling it the Gay Plague.

Everyone's floored by all this, but the dance must go on. Dance, dance, dance. Dance when you're broken open. "Life isn't about waiting for the storm to pass, it's about learning to dance in the rain," as poet Vivian Greene says. Or was that Rumi?

+

I'm now spending a lot of time with Joe, who started working here at around about the same time as me. We're often partnered together to do dance demonstrations at parties and showcase events, and we decide to take this a stage further, and make ourselves into a cabaret act, doing twisted versions of ballroom and Latin dance classics. But what shall we call ourselves? I'm called Max mostly, but had decided to revert to my given name, Dorothy, at Arthur Murray's. It's that old thing of wanting to carve out different identities for different aspects of my life. So, here I'm Dorothy, and we are – Dorothy and what? Dorothy and Joe? Nope. It doesn't take long for us to come up with Dorothy and Toto, as we both love *The Wizard of Oz*.

We work out a few different numbers – the first of which is a leopardskin-clad mambo, danced to Yma Sumac's 'Malambo'. We have one version of it for the dance school, but then there's a saucier take – with raunchy gyrating, bottom-pinching, and a swapping of leader and follower roles – that we have for cabaret appearances and other occasions. There's also a jive in which we're dressed as circus performers – me the trapeze artiste in a leotard and tutu, Joe as a clown (although I would have liked him to be a bear) which had grown out of a routine created for the school's circus-themed event. Then comes a tango, danced to Tom Lehrer's classic comedy song 'Masochism Tango', turned into a kind of Addams Family piss-take, utilising every tango cliché, which would horrify Argentinean purists. Just don't mention the (Falklands) war, which is in full swing right now...

+

A year on, the Kensington branch of Arthur Murray's has broken away from the mothership and turned itself into The Dance Club International. As well as all the usual classes and parties, the small back studio now gets hired out to choreographers and dance troupes. One afternoon we come in to find two smiley young men called George and Andrew rehearsing a routine with their backing singers and dancers, Pepsi and Shirlie – we learn that they are called Wham! They are so energetic and enthusiastic that they seem to almost bounce off the walls. They have a disco routine to their song, which is called 'Young Guns (Go For It)', but they like the partner-dance swing hustle which they see us practising in the main studio, and ask us to show them some moves. When the song's video – set in a disco – comes out, we're pleased to see that the swing hustle has made it into the mix.

More changes are afoot when my colleague Vernon starts to talk to me about getting some 'proper' dance teacher qualifications. He trained with and works for Gwenethe Walshe, a stalwart of the traditional English ballroom dance scene, and a leading light in the Imperial Society for Teachers of Dance, and he invites me along to meet her.

The Gwenethe Walshe school – famously the oldest ballroom dance school in London – is in the crypt of a Roman Catholic church in Marylebone. You go through the heavy door and down a very steep, twisting flight of stairs into a room that is as different as you could imagine to our Kensington studio. There, everything is light and bright and jazzy, with wall-length mirrors and little cabaret tables and chairs giving it a nightclub feel. Here, it's all brown wood, with a single row of chairs set against the wall, cream Anaglypta wallpaper, no mirrors, and low-wattage standard lamps. There is no reception desk, just a little cloakroom off the main space, mostly taken up by a cumbersome black Bakelite telephone.

In Kensington, the girls on the team are freely unbuttoned, with flowing locks, full make-up at any time of the night or day, and high heels. In Marylebone, the lady dance teachers are buttoned up, with just a slick of make-up, low-heeled teaching shoes, and hair drawn up into a tight bun. I always struggle to get my hair tied in a bun, but when I start taking my student teacher qualifications, I have my hair done by colleague Michelle – she also teaches at Ballet Rambert, so is used to prepping dozens of girls on exam days and has learnt to ignore wriggles and squeaks. Armed with hundreds of hair grips and an enormous can of hairspray, she wrenches and teases my long, thick hair into a solid knot, with not a strand out of place.

Miss Walshe herself is a petite, birdlike woman with a very loud voice. She enunciates every word, and her accent is hard to place. South African, perhaps? No, she's from New Zealand, but has lived in the UK for most of her life. How old she might be is hard to say: she has a trim figure and bright red henna'd hair, and is still dancing and teaching every day, but she often refers to her time training and working with Monsieur Pierre and Doris Lavelle in the 1930s – which must make her in her seventies. Miss Walshe is famous as the person who introduced Latin dancing to the English Ballroom societies; and for working with Monsieur Pierre and others to solidify the curriculum and exam system of the Imperial Society, for whom she is now a competition judge. She also, allegedly, kept her dance school – this very school – open right through the Blitz, simply turning up the music as the bombs rained down. The dance must go on.

Vernon has booked me in to take a lesson with him as a student teacher, and Miss Walshe watches us critically with her beady bird eyes as he puts me through my paces. Afterwards, she comes over to tell me that Vernon will continue to work with me, but she will take me on to work with her on the sections of the teacher training that are called 'Dancing as Man' (gentlemen trainee teachers are not required to demonstrate 'Dancing as Lady' with a partner, by the way). Vernon tells me later that this is a great honour as Gwenethe (as I'm now allowed to call her) won't work with just anybody. When I return for my first lesson with her, I find leading her a terrifying ordeal, but somehow get through it.

So I'm now moonlighting too, but in the other direction. I'm still a full-time employee of Arthur Murray's aka Dance School International, but on weekday mornings or Saturdays, I come in to Marylebone to continue my training, or to teach. I'm given a small batch of regular students by Gwenethe, who feels strongly that I need to learn to teach "the proper way" under her supervision – although when she sees how good I am at putting beginners at their ease, and getting them round the floor even on the first lesson, she begrudgingly admits that "the other place" (as she always refers to the Kensington school) do get some things right.

She's an odd bird, is Gwenethe. Very stern, but with hints of a wild youth. Wise and witty, mostly, but also embarrassingly racist in that completely unaware way that older white people can be, expressing obvious discomfort when confronted with people of colour outside of what she considers to be their natural habitat – dancing samba in a Rio carnival, say, or doing a merengue in the Dominican Republic. Gwenethe is well travelled, and credited with being the person who introduced the merengue and other Latin dances to Europeans.

Occasionally, someone would book a lesson over the phone, and when they arrived at the front door at the allotted time Miss Walshe would be appalled to discover that they were a person of colour. She'd show them in with a fixed smile, and come to get me from the staff cloakroom to introduce me, hissing in a stage whisper "They're as black as Newgate's knocker. I had no idea at all, so nicely spoken on the telephone."

Kwami, the gentleman I'm handed over to on this occasion, doesn't seem to have heard Gwenethe. I want to apologise, but feel it best not to say anything. He is West African, from a well-to-do family, and as a child was sent to a posh public school in England, from where he went on to Oxford to do a law degree. He's here, he says, because he feels awful about not knowing how to dance. Everyone looks at the colour of his skin, or hears that he is African, and assumes that this means he is a natural-born dancer, but, he says, he doesn't have a rhythmic bone in his body. Whereas you, he says – you were obviously born knowing how to dance. No, no I say – but I *have* been dancing since I was a small child.

And that's the thing, we agree – if he'd stayed in Africa, he'd quite likely have been dancing quite 'naturally'. We talk about the fact that 'natural' is not 'instinctive' – many natural things are in fact learnt. So, you can learn now, I say. He doesn't quite believe me, but we start at the very beginning (a very good place to start) and a few months later he's taking his bronze ballroom exam, and turning up at all the practice nights to get used to dancing with different partners. Gwenethe has taken to being over-welcoming when he comes to the school, smiling a little too brightly, I think to show him what a magnanimous and unprejudiced person she is.

Gwenethe also has a horror of any sort of disability or differentiating feature in the pupils. One of my regular bookings is a gentleman I call the Lavender Man. He always has a 9am appointment, an hour before the dance school officially opens. I don't know if this is his preference or whether Gwenethe encourages him to come at this time. Perhaps he likes to have the place to himself, or perhaps she is worried that other people would feel uncomfortable with him there.

The Lavender Man is the sort of well-groomed elderly white man that Miss Walshe encouraged to frequent the school. The problem – her problem – is that he's disabled by severe arthritis. The bell rings at exactly 8.50. Gwenethe lets him in, and I wait by the downstairs door as he makes the painful journey down the wooden staircase. He carries a metal-tipped walking stick, and wears highly polished leather shoes heeled with metal taps. On each step, he first places the stick, then carefully steps down with one foot, then the other foot, then a pause to catch his breath. Tap tap tap stop. Tap tap tap stop. As always, he is dressed in a well-tailored navy blue suit and immaculate white cotton shirt. The smell of starch from the newly-laundered shirt mixes with his distinctive lavender cologne to produce a clean, crisp cocktail that sweeps the musty smell of stale incense from the studio. The silver-tipped stick is leant against the wall: now he relies completely on me. I offer my arm, and together we make our way to the record player to choose a favourite dance disc. He goes for a selection of foxtrots by Victor Silvester. Like many of the older gentlemen who come for dance lessons, he doesn't want to be taught anything, just have the opportunity to enjoy a little social dancing.

Perhaps he once glided across the dance floors of London with debonair ease and grace – as he can no longer walk unaided, it's hard to tell. But there's something about his stance, despite being bowed over by arthritis, and the relaxed way he takes the ballroom dance hold – even though his left hand grips painfully and his right shoulder could hardly bear the pressure of my lightly placed hand – that gives an air of ease and familiarity.

After half an hour or so he says in his slow, slurred voice, "I think my time is finished," which would be my signal to fetch Miss Walshe, as he always calls her, to organise his departure. He thanks me before leaving, and as ever there is no mention of any plans for another visit, as he prefers to make all arrangements with Gwenethe. One day, he doesn't show up, and that is that. I never find out what had happened to him.

+

And so it all continues for a full-on couple of years. Going to Marylebone two mornings a week, plus Saturdays, on top of the work at Kensington, which is no longer full-time but still full-on. Training, teaching at two schools, taking my English ballroom and Latin dance teacher qualifications (I'm now an Associate of the Imperial Society of Teachers of Dance), doing the Arthur Murray parties and outings and Showcases in London and Birmingham.

Then, there's the occasional cabaret stint with Joe as Dorothy and Toto. And as if all that's not enough, I'm also going to regular dance classes at Pineapple or the Urdang in Covent Garden, or to the newly-opened Danceworks near Selfridges on Oxford Street. I take contemporary and jazz dance, but also ballet, making up for lost time as I hadn't done much of that as a child. As well as a regular weekly ballet class, I sign up for *pas de deux*, where you learn partnered balances, lifts and drops. The Royal Ballet teachers who lead the class do so with cigarettes on the go throughout – the fags placed in the ashtray on the windowsill of the dance studio for just long enough to demonstrate an elaborate Angel lift, then picked up with a nonchalant "your turn now" tossed our way.

Eventually it all takes its toll. Something needs to give. And it is just as I am worrying about what to do and how to handle it all that something surprising turns up out of the blue...

It has been hard to keep up with old friendships whilst working all hours in two jobs for six days a week, but I'd seen Genesis P-Orridge a couple of times in 1984. There'd been an outing together to meet up with our mutual friend Derek Jarman; and I'd been to see his band Psychic TV play at Heaven, right at the end of the year.

Gen has a proposal to make: would I consider joining Psychic TV? I was, after all, his favourite ever drummer. I'd made a record with Genesis and Alex Fergusson in 1980 – as a singer, rather than drummer, surprisingly. They had gone on to form PTV in 1981, and had asked me to be their drummer, but I'd stepped back then – and was subsequently drawn into this ballroom dancing maelstrom, so hadn't really been directly involved with the alternative music scene for the past few years – too busy waltz-ing and cha-cha-ing for much else. But now PTV have management and a record deal with the DJM label, and all sorts of exciting things on the horizon.

So it's crunch time. If I wanted to take up this new offer, I'd need to free up time. And it was better to free up evening time, as that would be what was more likely needed for band rehearsals and gigs. Kensington was a PAYE job, with American boss Mr Shea keen to keep tabs on his staff and control their activities. Work hours were fixed, students booked in by the company. Marylebone was freelance – you booked your own cohort of students in at times that suited, and you managed the money (most people paid cash) and took an agreed percentage of the lesson fees. And Gwenethe Walshe, despite the superficial strictness, was actually very tolerant of people having other lives outside of the studio, be it Ballet Rambert or Psychic TV – and she is surprisingly supportive. Of course, I'm a little vague about the type of music being played, and let her assume Psychic TV is some sort of carnivalesque ensemble. Which perhaps it is.

So I say my goodbyes to Arthur Murray – who had indeed taught me dancing in a hurry – and start in on a different sort of split life, as a buttoned-up dance teacher by day in the oldest and most respectable ballroom dance school in London, and by night the drummer with experimental multi-discipline art-tricksters Psychic TV.

New adventures are on the horizon, and off I go with a slow, slow, quick quick slow.

DOROTHY AND TOTO IN NEW YORK

People are being pulled in and out of dance partnerships, boys
with girls, then boys with boys, and girls with girls.

We are in New York for Christmas and expecting snow: skating at the Rockefeller Centre, cheery chestnut sellers outside Central Park, wind blowing in from an icy Hudson river. All of that. We'd come prepared, suitcases full of woolly jumpers. Instead, it's the warmest December on record. We stroll down Fifth Avenue with rolled-up shirt sleeves, only the neon Santas outside the department stores to remind us that it's almost Christmas day.

'We' are me and my dance partner Joe aka Toto – as in, Dorothy and Toto. Mr Shea, our boss at Arthur Murray's in Kensington, had set up this visit. It is a sort of working holiday. No pay, but two weeks at the Gorham Hotel on 54th Street (owned by a friend of Shea's) for practically nothing in exchange for a couple of showcase appearances at the Manhattan branch of Arthur Murray's, on Broadway. We are booked in tonight as special guests at their Christmas Eve party – all the way from London England, folks!

Broadway is – well, it's Broadway for quite a long way up. The bright lights of... *Cats. The Showgirl. Twice Around the Park.* You know the sort of thing. Further up, the theatres start to thin out, and it goes oddly dark. So where's this dance school, then? We can't see anything that looks like a dance studio. We're British and we haven't yet twigged that things don't necessarily occur at street-level in this high-rise city. Broadway runs the whole length of Manhattan Island and beyond, way out through the Bronx to Sleepy Hollow in fact, so we're starting to worry that we've misunderstood the directions, and will be following the Native American Wickquasgeck trail into the bleak beyond.

But no, the numbers are lining up. Eventually we find the building, a skyscraper with an electronic entryphone and steel doors. We're buzzed into an empty, blue-lit lobby. We look at each other. Spooky! As the steel doors close us in and we stand silently in a stark white room, it feels like we've been shut into a massive fridge. Ah, but it's not empty after all – a security guard appears from nowhere and wordlessly waves us into an elevator where we are whooshed to somewhere near the top. The doors open directly into a reception area festooned with candy-coloured fairy lights and a large tinselled tree standing in the corner, amplified into a triptych by the surrounding mirrors. A young woman in a tight red dress greets us with a big-toothed "Hi!" and introduces herself – she says Sherri or Cherry but I quickly forget which, and after asking her twice, give up. Sherri-Cherry shows us through an archway into the dance studio – a large room with one whole wall a solid plate-glass window, the lights of Broadway (the brightly-lit bit, anyway) and Times Square beyond it tinkling way, way below. Looking down is a bit scary, so we don't.

We are announced as we fall blinking into the room, and given a true American rip-roaring, whooping and whistling welcome, which makes us feel like gameshow contestants. Of course, they want to see a quickstep and a proper 'slow foxtrot' danced the English way, so that is what we do. Afterwards, there is eggnog and general social dancing: Joe's accent becomes more Brideshead by the minute; tossing a lock of blond hair from his face, charming the Manhattan matrons hung heavy with gold chains as he whisks them around the floor. I have, meanwhile, been cornered by the school's star teacher, a beefy hunk called Darryl, who wants to know if I'll do a demonstration dance with him. He assures me that I'll follow his lead easily, and offering his hand, guides me out to the centre of the room, showing me off with a flourish and a twirl in true Travolta fashion.

The music begins. Darryl doesn't so much lead as propel me in a King Kong grip as we dance what is supposed to be a romantic bolero to Marvin Gaye's 'Sexual Healing'. Perched on his right thigh for most of the dance, I am twirled and shuddered into submission – less ballroom dancing than all-in wrestling, greeted with tumultuous applause: USA 1, England 0.

We say our goodbyes, promising a return match after Christmas, and stagger out into the street.

The night is still young and there's plenty of time to party in this city that never sleeps, not even on the night before Christmas. We head off to the Village Gate, the legendary club where all of jazz royalty has played – John Coltrane, Coleman Hawkins, Duke Ellington, Dizzy Gillespie, Nina Simone (I could go on). It's where Lenny Bruce taught everyone *How to Talk Dirty and Influence People,* and where Yoko Ono did her first ever performance piece.

The club is run by Art D'Lugoff, a living legend in NYC. His daughter Sharon – who I know through British post-punk combo The Monochrome Set, as she's the girlfriend of former guitarist, Lester Square – works at her dad's gaff some evenings, and has kindly put us on the guest list.

Talking of The Monochrome Set, they're in town too. Bizarrely, as we'd walked into our hotel room, fresh off the plane from Old Blighty, the phone was ringing, and although I couldn't see any way that it could be for me, I'd picked it up. Three words: "Hello. It's Andy". Yes, Andy Warren – erstwhile roommate, best friend, and former lover – and bass player in The Monochrome Set. They've been touring the States this winter season, and it turns out it hasn't been a bed of roses. I get a five-minute resumé of the on-the-road tales of woe: snow drifts, broken vans, deserting crew members, cancelled gigs, and dishonest bookers. Hey-ho-ho-ho, rock and roll!

But here they were in New York City, playing The Ritz club on the 30th of December, and by the way: would Joe and I like to perform with them as a warm-up act? Andy pops round an hour later, and shows us how to order pizzas, to be delivered to our bedroom door. Pizzas delivered to the door? We'd never heard of such a thing. How exciting!

That was a couple of days ago. Now we've settled in. We've had a couple of days being regular tourists, visiting the Empire State Building, walking through Central Park, and mooching around Macy's. We're pleased our first slot at Arthur Murray's Broadway went well, and excited to be in Greenwich Village, which tonight has a summer evening vibe, despite it being December: music drifting out from open doorways; people on the streets drinking beer from bottles, which people never do in England, it's always pint glasses, indoors or out; and little stalls on street corners selling Middle Eastern foods like hummus and falafel, which they serve rolled up in flat bread. We also pass a Dolly Madison's Stall and a Chipwich Cart, each selling their rival versions of the legendary cookie-and-ice-cream sandwich. Ice-cream wars, American style!

And here we are, Bleeker Street – outside the legendary Village Gate. We ask for Sharon and she comes out to greet us. So let me tell you a little bit more about Sharon. She's a cool kitten, brought up with Nina Simone as her babysitter and the likes of Dustin Hoffman, Aretha Franklin and Sonny Rollins hanging out at her family home. She has all the confidence and pizazz that comes from being raised in such a fabulously arty ambience, and is both pretty and punky: wild brown curls, honey-brown eyes, and a low musical voice. When she's not waiting tables at her dad's club, she's sometimes a leopardskin-clad dancer in a troupe led by Lori from Kid Creole and the Coconuts.

This evening, the Village Gate has a show upstairs called *One Mo' Time*, a sassy and upbeat African-American vaudeville revue set in the 1920s, for which Sharon has got us guest tickets. After the show, we head off into the night, and on Sharon's recommendation go to a club called Danceteria, which has recently moved to 21st Street. It's a great big warehouse building that makes our London clubs, even Heaven, seem pretty small. The place is painted white with chrome fittings and lit with violet lights. There are DJs on different floors, with one floor dedicated to experimental music, one a more high-energy dance space, and the whole of the third floor a chill-out zone with big red sofas and videos projected onto the walls – a mash-up of kitsch found footage, video art, and films of bands. The dancefloor on the second floor is full of people of every persuasion. People wear string vests and peg trousers, vintage 1960s dresses with enormous pink daisy prints, bought from Screaming Mimi's, or brand-new branded sportswear boasting enormous Adidas logos. There are fringed cowboy jackets, and frilly tutus. Anything goes.

Sharon shows up after her Village Gate shift, and introduces us to some of her friends. There's Lori and various other members of Kid Creole's Coconuts, and there's another dancing girl called Madonna, who (like Sharon) is a bit punkish and very pretty. She has pouting lips, tousled hair, a tight top, and a tangle of rosary beads as jewellery – and on the dancefloor, all eyes are on her. Apparently she's a drummer as well as a dancer, which of course I approve of, and she has played in various bands, but has just made a single called 'Everybody' as a solo singer, and on the back of that has been signed by Seymour Stein of Sire (home to Richard Hell, The Ramones and Talking Heads) to make an album. Let's hope she's not making a mistake, giving up the dancing and drumming to be a singer.

After drinking and dancing non-stop for hours, we stagger back to our beds at around 5am. Later that morning, Christmas morning as it happens but it really doesn't feel like it, we get breakfast at Carnegie's Jewish deli on the corner of 7th Avenue and West 57th Street. The pastrami sandwiches are almost as tall as the Twin Towers of the World Trade Center (which we've yet to visit, but can see clearly from downtown). We drink away the rest of the afternoon at a bar called O'Neal's Backyard, which is – unsurprisingly for Christmas Day – very quiet. We're both pretty tired, so get an early night.

The next day, we're full of beans and ready for new adventures. We walk the city, eventually finding ourselves on the east side, close to the waterfront, and notice a rather strange thing – a cable car going over to an island. So of course we get on, and find ourselves transported to a very odd place. The island is really skinny – we can easily see over to the other side from our cable car – and it seems almost deserted. As we get out of the car, we see a sign saying Roosevelt Island. There are a dozen or more empty blocks that look like they might be part of an abandoned hospital, lots of scrappy grass, and piles of rubble dotted round the place. A few children are playing in the rubble and look over at us warily. We don't stay long, walking across the width of the island, which takes very little time as it's only about half a mile wide, then back again, before heading back over to Manhattan, somewhat bemused. What on earth was that? Back on familiar territory, we walk past a cinema and on an impulse go in. We find ourselves watching a film called *The Dark Crystal*, a fantasy tale featuring some rather lovely puppets, set in a strange land. It would seem strange lands are the order of the day. The story involves the retrieval of a magical crystal to break a curse, with a girl creature rescuing a boy creature, who says, "Oh you have wings – I don't have wings" – to which she replies, "Of course you don't, you're a boy". I nudge Joe and grin.

When we emerge, it's dark. We seek out Bogart's Piano Bar and while away a happy few hours drinking cocktails, before taking ourselves off to The Ice Palace, a gay disco on West 57th, just around the corner from our hotel. More dancing! Here, we're excited to see that people are doing some sort of version of the swing hustle, as featured in *Saturday Night Fever*, which we teach at Arthur Murray's in London. Except here, it's faster and more frenetic. People are being pulled in and out of dance partnerships, boys with girls, then boys with boys, and girls with girls. The dancers are swapping themselves in and out of lead and follow roles, happily switching without missing a beat. It's so exciting to see partner dancing done somewhere other than a dance studio, and how good it is to see gay boys and girls out on the razz together – this informal team of dancers look like an advert for an idyllic multi-cultural gender-fluid New York. The look here is more laid-back than at Danceteria, for the most part. Lots of tight jeans with sleeveless vests, or pedal pushers worn with skin-tight tops – although some boys wear diamanté necklaces and dangly earrings, and some girls sport butch black leather caps and motorcycle boots.

Another look, seen here and at other clubs: enormous baggy shirts covered in designs that mimic the work of hip new artist Keith Haring. Or maybe the shirts are actually designed by Haring. As a Warhol protegé, he happily moves from commercial design work to fine art and back again, resisting all pigeonholing. Haring had started out as a graffiti artist, working the subways. When we'd arrived at the airport and taken the subway through Queens to Manhattan, Joe and I had noted the fact that every subway car, inside and out, and most of the stations we'd whizzed through on the JFK Express, were covered in spray-can graffiti. Sometimes intricate designs in a riot of colours, sometimes a cruder monochrome scrawling of tags, as I learn they are called. But Haring was just as likely to be drawing his trademark outline-only dogs and humans and crawling babies in white chalk on empty poster boards, a novel take on this new craze, which is, we learn, all tied in with hip hop, along with the rapping tracks played in clubs, and the b-boy dancers on the street corners near Central Park.

There's one tune we hear everywhere – in clubs, on the streets, coming out from boom boxes or car radios – 'The Message', by Grandmaster Flash and the Furious Five, a no-holds-barred political protest song, but unlike all of those folksy protest songs from the 1960s, you can dance to it. If I can't dance, I don't want to be part of your revolution, as writer Emma Goldman didn't say. It's the 'Anarchy in the UK' moment for hip hop. What was an elite secret society, starting

ROOM PER	(LAST)	NAME	(FIRST)	RATE	ARR.	DEP.

WITH RM. NO.
RATE CARRIED IN RM. NO.
(WKLY)(MNTHY)
BILL GIVEN

ADDRESS

DAY $_____
RATE WK. $_____
MONTH $_____

C.TY   STATE

CLERK

DATE	REFERENCE	CHARGES	CREDITS	BALANCE	PICKUP
DEC 22	LDIST 120	B ☆ 5.10		☆ 5.10	c☆ 5.10
DEC 22	ROOM 120	c ☆ 55.00			
DEC 22	/ TAX 120	c ☆ 4.54			
DEC 22	NIGHT 120	c ☆ 2.00		☆ 66.64 ☆	c☆ 66.64
DEC 23	ROOM 120	c ☆ 55.00			
DEC 23	TAX 120	c ☆ 4.54			
DEC 23	NIGHT 120	c ☆ 2.00			
DEC 23	PHONE 120	c ☆ .80		☆ 128.98 ☆	c☆ 128.98
DEC 24	TAX 120	c ☆ 4.54			
DEC 24	NIGHT 120	c ☆ 2.00			
DEC 24	PHONE 120	c ☆ .80		☆ 136.32 ☆	c☆ 136.32
DEC 24	ROOM 120	c ☆ 55.00		☆ 191.32 ☆	c☆ 191.32
DEC 25	LDIST 120	c ☆ 14.45		☆ 205.77	c☆ 205.77
DEC 25	ROOM 120	c ☆ 55.00			
DEC 25	TAX 120	c ☆ 4.54			
DEC 25	NIGHT 120	c ☆ 2.00			
DEC 25	PHONE 120	c ☆ 1.20		☆ 268.51 ☆	c☆ 268.51
DEC 26	ROOM 120	c ☆ 55.00			
DEC 26	TAX 120	c ☆ 4.54			
DEC 26	NIGHT 120	c ☆ 2.00			
DEC 26	PHONE 120	c ☆ 3.20		☆ 333.25 ☆	

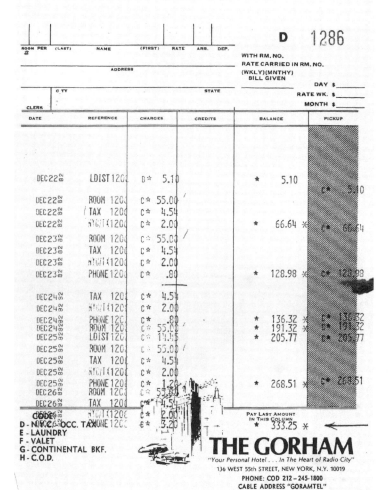

CODE
D - N.Y.C.C.-OCC. TAX
E - LAUNDRY
F - VALET
G - CONTINENTAL BKF.
H - C.O.D.

PAY LAST AMOUNT
IN THIS COLUMN
☆ 333.25 ☆ ←

THE GORHAM

"Your Personal Hotel . . . In The Heart of Radio City"
136 WEST 55th STREET, NEW YORK, N.Y. 10019
PHONE: COD 212 – 245 – 1800
CABLE ADDRESS "GORAMTEL"

out in the Bronx and spreading across the Five Boroughs of NYC, the voice of young Black America, has now been taken up by youth of all skin colours and persuasions, everywhere.

On other nights there are other clubs. We love, love, love the New York clubs. The Pyramid, Avenue A, The Red Bar, The Underground... The Paradise Garage is supposedly members only, but we're a good-looking couple from London England and we talk our way in by name-dropping madly. I'm a friend of a friend of a friend... Mostly we go clubbing together, but sometimes Joe heads off late night on his own to The Saint, the so-called 'Vatican of gay disco' which is a bit more hardcore and male-only, with balconies where you could make out whilst watching over the dancefloor. Or so I'm told.

We'd heard that HIV/AIDS – with far more cases here than in London – had taken its toll on New York nightclub attendance, but I don't see any evidence of that. All the places I go to are heaving. But I'm going to the mixed clubs, not the strictly men-only ones, and perhaps it's a different story for the bath houses and the Black Party leather scene, where unprotected sex with strangers is still the norm.

The idea of 'safe sex' hasn't really taken off yet. Even though AIDS awareness is much further down the line here than in London, people are still in the rabbits-dazed-by-the-headlights phase of knowing something terrible is happening, but not really knowing how to deal with it. And with raids on the gay clubs still a frequent occurrence – including an infamous one a few months back at Blue in Times Square that was believed to have been singled out because it was mostly frequented by Black and Latino gay men – there's something of a feeling that the AIDS epidemic is being used as just another stick to beat gay people with. Activists like Marsha P Johnson have been leading protests about police behaviour, and preparations are in place to up the ante for the Pride march next June, which will draw attention to the ongoing discrimination and harassment. And as the authorities had been so slow in dealing with HIV/AIDS, Larry Kramer had organised a fundraiser for the Gay Men's Health Crisis fund earlier in the year, which brought in 50,000 dollars.

As well as the moral panic about the so-called gay plague, there is also a whole 'city of fear' rhetoric going down. 1981 was apparently the year with the most felonies ever in NYC, and mayor Ed Koch is claiming that '82 is looking to top it. The newspapers and local magazines scream warnings to 'protect yourself against crime' and carry ads for super-locks and self-defence classes. Despite the warnings and horror stories about violence, Joe and I walk the streets day or night, separately or together, and never feel unsafe. We are staying in such a central location that we can walk easily anywhere, and only get the very occasional taxi. We feel invincible, and party on relentlessly, although it is true to say that a lot of the city is really run down. Many buildings are in a state of extreme disrepair, there are potholes in the roads that the taxis bounce over, and piles of rubbish on street corners. The legendary Washington Square – home to the Beat Poets and folk musicians of the 1960s, its cafes where people like Bob Dylan and Joan Baez made their name – is now a horrible mess of litter and sleeping junkies, although a few buskers and some of the old men who play chess can still be spotted amongst the debris. Best not to walk across it at night though, we decide.

You'd think we'd sleep through the day after all that night-time activity, but no – we want to take in as much of the Big Apple as we can. I'm keen to go to the art galleries, but Joe isn't that fussed. I do manage to drag him along to MoMA (The Museum of Modern Art), where he doesn't mind the

Rauschenbergs too much, but wrinkles his nose up at the first ever retrospective for a previously obscure artist called Louise Bourgeois, with her slabs of wood painted white, weird plaster 'dolls', and distorted phallic sculptures with provocative names like 'Fillette' hanging on meat hooks from the ceiling. Why? asks Joe. To which the only answer is, Because. He's happier when we head out to the East Village to seek out a gallery in a toilet called Loo Division, run by a drag queen called Gracie Mansion (a name she stole from the mayor's official residence). We never do find it, but we do track down Betsey Johnson's shop on Columbus Avenue, which boasts disdainful, gum-chewing sales girls in black basques and fishnets. A bit like the Yankee cousins of Jordan from the SEX shop on the King's Road, I remark – a reference lost on Joe, who had never been even remotely interested in punk.

Talking of which, I really want to go to CBGBs, the venue where Tom Verlaine, Patti Smith and Blondie all cut their punk teeth; but Joe won't come, so I end up going alone, and just loitering outside for a few minutes. It doesn't look like the kind of place to go to alone, and besides, punk is dead. Nothing to see here. Joe does come with me to the Chelsea Hotel, but when we get there, we can't think of any justification for going in, so just hang around on the pavement for a while, staring up at the windows, and watching people going in and out. We don't see anyone we recognise, but an old lady with some books in a shopping trolley comes out and gives us a small nod. Perhaps she's a famous artist – we never find out who she is. Meanwhile, back at the Village Gate, salsa is king, with dancing in the downstairs space at least a couple of times a week, often with appearances by legendary Afro-Cuban or Puerto Rican artists. Tito Puente is a regular. So, a few days after Christmas, fortified by supper at Vincent's Clam Bar in Little Italy, off we head to show off our salsa skills, honed at Arthur Murray's in London. Coals to Newcastle, you could say.

The dancefloor is a crush of bodies sashaying to the DJ's spicy mix of Cuban beats and Brazilian Bossa Nova. Joe heads off to flag down a waitress whilst I lean against a pillar. Someone appears next to me – someone who looks like an American Football player, and tells me he's up from the Bronx. He offers to teach me to salsa, and before I can answer, I'm led through the throng and held in the vice-like grip that seems to be a feature of Manhattan man's dance style. A large hand is placed on my left buttock. "Need to move yo ass more," he advises.

The music accelerates into a frenzied instrumental break, and I do as I'm told. I see Joe from the corner of my eye, now leaning against the pillar with an amused look on his face. After about 15 minutes my instructor releases me from his grip. "Good for a first time," he says.

I don't know whether to feel flattered or offended. I've been dancing and teaching salsa for most of the past year, but I don't think I should tell him that. Joe and I take to the floor and Mr Bronx looks on, surprised.

"Hey, you done this before!"
"Well, just a little. In London, but we do things a
bit differently..."
"London, England? Hell, that's something!"

The next morning, we're up early and decide that today's the day to head south – to see Wall Street (pretty nondescript), to gawp at the Twin Towers (which Joe won't go up – he says the Empire State Building was quite high enough for him), and to take a little boat out past Ellis Island to pay our respects to the Statue of Liberty.

This is a trip we both love. The view of Manhattan from the boat, imagining ourselves arriving in New York as part of the huddle of humanity that America embraced; seeing Liberty looming towards us, growing ever-larger as we get nearer; then going inside her and being ferried right up to her head, peering out to the world through the slits in her seven-rayed crown.

+

That evening sees us back at Arthur Murray's, to show off our Viennese waltz this time, rewarded with champagne cocktails. So refined, so wonderfully European, gasp the Manhattan matrons. Whilst on our way up to Arthur Murray's we'd done a bit of moonlighting, nipping into the Broadway branch of the Fred Astaire Dance School. We mention that we work for Arthur Murray's in London, but don't mention our connection to the school here. We're given a backstage tour, and told we'd always be welcome to do some hours here as guest teachers, if we wanted to – an offer we don't take up, but it's good to be asked. We hang out with dance tutor Darryl after the party, flitting from bar to bar, and end up eating tacos at 4am. It's one of our favourite things about New York – being able to get all sorts of interesting food at any time of the night or day.

The following night, 30th of December, is The Monochrome Set gig at The Ritz club, with our support slot. And in an interesting co-incidence – or perhaps it's meticulous planning – Bow Wow Wow will be playing The Ritz at midnight on New Year's Eve. Bow Wow Wow features guitarist Matthew Ashman and drummer Dave Barbe, who were in Adam and The Ants with Andy, so old and dear friends. The big bust-up following the recording of The Ants' first album, *Dirk Wears White Sox* resulted in Andy leaving to re-join schoolfriend Bid in The Monochrome Set, and The Ants splitting into two camps, with Adam in one and the rest of the band in the other, re-naming themselves Bow Wow Wow under Malcolm McLaren's management.

And here we all are now in New York, a big gathering of people from what we could call The Ants extended family. And this may not have been the best choice pre-performance, but where we gather is Chinatown for dim sum. With very full tummies, Joe and I decamp backstage to drink gin and tonics whilst putting on the slap, transforming ourselves into twisted cabaret duo Dorothy and Toto.

We'll be dancing to Tom Lehrer's 'Masochism Tango'. Dorothy will wear her Morticia Addams long black dress, with Geisha Girl make-up, and cigarette holder; poor little Toto will don his shabby dinner jacket and too-tight trousers, with greased back hair.

We had other party pieces – a leopardskin Mambo for example – but it was the Tom Lehrer number that was most often requested.

So now it's time to go on. The intro to the Tom Lehrer song kicks in, and off we go:

'*I ache for the touch of your lips, dear*
But much more for the touch of your whips, dear
You can raise welts like nobody else
As we dance to the Masochism Tango'

The audience applauds enthusiastically. Even in New York, the English Vice is understood and appreciated, it would seem.

Now it's New Year's Eve. Darryl has invited me to the Playboy Club for supper. I feel it isn't fair to go without Joe, but he apparently has a good offer from somebody-or-other that he hadn't told me about until now, so I say yes. And why not? Joe thinks it is very funny, me going on a date with this Action Man look-alike, muscles rippling under his wide-lapelled shirt, but I didn't think he had a leg to stand on, considering. "Swallow, don't spit" is his final word of brotherly advice as he disappears into the elevator, tossing the blond forelocks out of his eyes and grinning the sly Toto grin.

Darryl is, it turns out, a very nice person. I mean, a regular all-American guy, straight as a die, but a good guy. He saves me from being run over by the police car I step out in front of, sweeping me up into his arms in the nick of time. He opens doors and fetches champagne and picks out the very best titbits from the Playboy Club buffet supper. I do enjoy seeing the famous Bunny Girls up close, in the flesh (Look don't touch! And especially don't touch their tails, tempting though it is!) but find the place a bit tacky. For most of the evening, Darryl manages to restrain himself on the dance floor, keeping to a sedate bit of slow dancing like everyone else. Until 'Sexual Healing' comes on. Then it's no holds barred. A space clears around us on the dancefloor. Onlookers offer their smiling encouragement as I'm swept into submission once again.

Come midnight, we've escaped the Playboy Club and are at the Ritz for Bow Wow Wow. It's not really Darryl's cup of tea, but he politely applauds. Post-show, I say a quick hello to the Bow Wows before being whisked away.

I get back to the hotel at 6.00am. Both twin beds are empty, and I scurry under the covers just as Joe comes in.

The next morning, the first day of a new year – 1983 – and we're back at Carnegie's Deli. Joe takes a delicate bite of his enormous pastrami sandwich, the picture of nonchalance.

"How was it then?"

"Fine thank you."

"How was what's-his-name?"

"Darryl. He's very nice. He's from Kansas."

"How perfect!" Then, in a cartoon American accent, "*And your little dog, too, Dorothy.*"

"Don't be sarcastic. He's a nice person. Really."

"And?"

"And what? You know he's not my type."

"So did you?"

I concentrate on eating my chopped liver on rye. "Anyway, He's gay. Had him. Been there."

"Joe, don't be ridiculous. You haven't even been alone with him..."

"Toilets at the studio..."

"I don't believe you. I'd know. I've been to bed with enough gay men to..."

"Ha! So you did!"

There's no point in replying, so I call over a waiter and order a couple of beers. We clink bottles.

"Happy New Year" I say.

"We're not in Kansas anymore, Dorothy," he says.

"It's a far cry from Kensington, Toto," I reply.

+

What now? New Year's Day in old Blighty is dead as a doornail – but this is New York, New York.

We go down 7th Avenue, cross Christopher Street, pass the legendary Stonewall Inn, where Gay Lib and Pride started in June 1969. Riots kicked off following a police raid after 'a woman in masculine attire', identified later as Stormé DeLarverie, resisted arrest – the straight-from-the-horse's-mouth stories brought over to the UK in the 1970s by gay/trans theatre company Hot Peaches. We wander down through Greenwich Village, then, along Canal Street, and yes – shops and stalls are open for business. Chinatown's dim sum houses are open, the red balloons flying merrily above the restaurants, families out together for a celebratory meal. We turn up the Bowery and head to Elizabeth Street, where Sharon lives, dropping in to say hello. We curve up and through to East Village and St Mark's Place, where Andy Warhol lived when he first moved to New York, and where Lou Reed and the Velvet Underground cut their performance teeth at the Electric Circus. It was here that Warhol and Paul Morrissey had rented the upstairs space to open a psychedelic performance venue they dubbed *The Exploding Plastic Inevitable*, which had screenings of Warhol's films, and The Velvets as the house band, with guest singer Nico, dancers Edie Sedgwick and Mary Woronov; plus a whip-wielding Gerard Malanga, and performance artist and filmmaker Barbara Rubin, whose radically raunchy *Christmas on Earth* film was projected over a live Velvet Underground set at one of the EPI events.

I relay all this fabulous historical information excitedly to Joe as we stand outside what now appears to be a pretty mainstream restaurant called Dom's. He nods politely but I know that Warhol's Factory and the history of The Velvet Underground is of as little interest to Joe as hanging out at CBGBs and the Chelsea Hotel, or trudging around sculpture exhibitions at MoMA.

But that's how the cookie crumbles. New York, New York – it's a wonderful town. There's more than enough common ground to get us through our time here together. Dorothy and Toto's New York is walks in Central Park, and eating in Jewish delis and Italian clam bars. The New York that has captured both of our hearts is the New York of multi-floored discos in massive warehouses, and gay clubs in deconsecrated churches where boys and girls dance together all night long. We both love the Village Gate because we both love jazz and salsa music. And of course, we like to dance. Any sort of dancing will do.

I know, I say. Let's go dancing. Joe looks happy. Yes, let's. Where shall we go?

NIGHTCLUBBING

Skin Two is a secret pleasure garden.
It's escapism, pure and simple.
And that's what all of this clubbing feels like –
escaping real life.

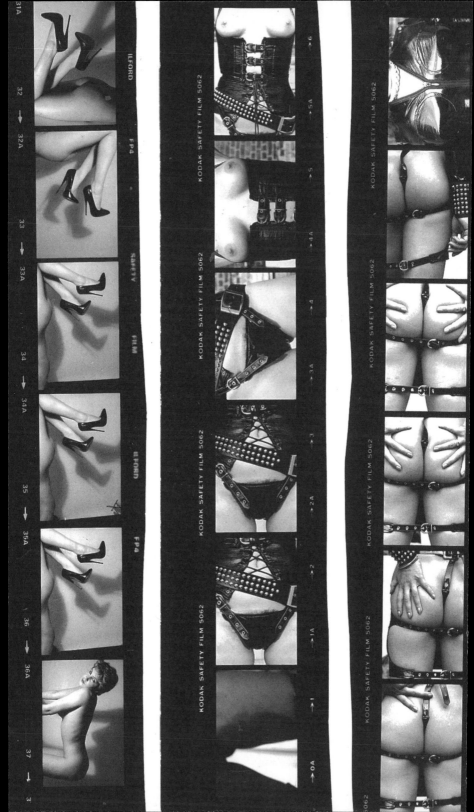

1983, and here I am. Not a drummer. Not a punk. Not even 'post-punk', whatever that might be. Something else altogether – a dancer and a dance teacher. I dance for a living, and I dance when I'm not working. I go to dance classes whenever I've got a spare hour, and in the evenings I'm out dancing in clubs.

London life – my life, anyway – has mostly shifted away from live rock gigs and back to pre-punk preferences – the gay clubs, the discos, and the pop-up themed nights.

Some of the old favourites are still going strong. Stringfellows, if you're feeling fancy. Ronnie Scott's, to dance salsa to visiting legends like Machito. Or the Sombrero, aka Yours or Mine, on Kensington High Street, which has a fabulous light-up dancefloor, like the one in *Saturday Night Fever*. People used to go there in the hope of spotting David Bowie, but now it has other associations. Adam and the Ants filmed their video for breakthrough hit 'Antmusic' here. And because the shoot ran late – I was only there to meet then-boyfriend Marco, Adam's new partner in crime – I ended up being drawn in as an extra, dancing on that fabulous flashing floor with two of my favourite female friends: former Ants manager, singer and muse Jordan; and Adam's girlfriend Mandy, who went on to play the Regency beauty in the 'Stand and Deliver' video, before going to drama school and emerging as actress Amanda Donohoe.

The Ants, the darlings of second-wave punk, have most definitely moved on in the past few years, away from the safety-pinned black-bin-bagged grit and grime of what punk rock had become by the late 1970s into a glamorous New Romantic world of pop stardom, peopled by dandy highwaymen and swashbuckling pirates and princes.

In fact, most of the original crowd had moved on to new things pretty speedily once punk became the nation's favourite four-letter word. People are now falling over themselves in their efforts to distance themselves from it. Steve Strange and Rusty Egan blazed the way for a hedonistic new club culture, starting back in 1979 with their Bowie night at Billy's in Soho, where they firmly shook off the shackles of punk, embracing glamour with gusto; then, on to Blitz in Covent Garden, Club For Heroes at Barracudas on Baker Street, and now Camden Palace in – well yes, in Camden, which seems all of a sudden to be the place to be.

Somewhere along the way there was another Steve Strange club in Covent Garden called Hell, which Steve ran with fellow Welshman Chris Sullivan. They were something of an odd couple – Steve dressed in a floor-length cossack and Chris Sullivan in an immaculate sharkskin suit. I rather liked Hell, with its shop-front entrance, little red velvet curtains, and steep stairs down to the inferno below.

In a direct reaction to the bleak black-and-white tawdriness of tower-block punk, the Blitz Kids – who never really called themselves this, but it became one of those handy bits of shorthand, so people did use it – created their own colourful space for experimentation, and defended it against nosy outsiders. Famously, Steve Strange once turned Mick Jagger away from Blitz – although he did let David Bowie in, and ended up appearing in his 'Ashes to Ashes' video.

And, unlike punk, where the people who managed the bands and designed the clothes and created the artwork for the gig posters and record sleeves and set up the clubs were a good few years older than the kids in the bands, within the Blitz scene almost everything was created in-house, by people who were under 21. Not just the musicians and DJs, but movers and shakers like Steve Strange and his right-hand woman Julia, and band manager Steve Dagger, and journalist and stylist Robert Elms – all hardly out of their teens. The clothes they wore – which could be anything from Weimar era evening gowns to Robin Hood outfits to Pierrot costumes – came from Oxfam shops, or were acquired from theatrical costumiers, or run up by one or other of the many St Martin's fashion students who went to Blitz.

Alternatively, clothes were bought at PX – a shop that was first in James Street, adjacent to the now-derelict Covent Garden Market, then round the corner in Endell Street. Here you could buy 'space cossack' tunics designed by Helen Robinson, or fabulous little hats created by Stephen Jones. Helen's partner in the business, Stephane Raynor, was one of the punk-era entrepreneurs who had jumped ship – he was the co-founder, with John Krivine, of Acme Attractions and BOY. Also on board was wheeler and dealer Roger Burton, who furnished the shop with steel cages salvaged from an empty

MI5 building; then kitted it out with ex-German army leather coats and flying suits acquired in job lots from warehouses in mainland Europe. Steve Strange and Julia (who'd later add a 'Princess' to her name) both worked at PX, and for a while it became the equivalent of Malcolm and Vivienne's SEX shop for this new crew of clubbers – a place to hang out, as well as to buy clothes. But it wasn't really for me. I'd popped in a couple of times to have a nose around, but had never bought anything. I'll pass on the space cossack look, I decide.

I'd instead gone back to wearing clothes from Johnson's, who still have their Kensington Market stall, plus a second outlet at World's End, conveniently near Malcolm and Vivienne's gaff. I like Johnson's Beat-Beat and La Rocka! ranges, and buy myself a black-and-white musical notes shirt and a circular-skirted dress with dancing stick figures. They still have a good stock of surplussed 1940s and 1950s garb, and I find some lovely silk 'tea dance' dresses there. Between Johnson's and the World's End, right on the bend as King's Road turns downmarket, there's a particularly good charity shop that always has a great supply of stuff chucked out by ageing It girls and debutantes who've outgrown their fancy frocks. For example, there's a gorgeous 1950s red voile dress embossed with white roses. And at the bottom of Kensington Church Street – very close to where the Bus Stop shop had once been, or perhaps it was even on the same site – was another great charity shop where I find a pink Chanel two-piece, a straight skirt and a boxy little collarless jacket with big round bobbly buttons.

So it's mostly, as ever, a 1950s/early 60s look for me, but with an 80s twist – there's a Fiorucci PVC raincoat here and some Katharine Hamnett zipped pedal-pushers (with that controversial little 'condom pocket') there. There are figure-hugging pencil skirts and soft jersey animal print dresses. Oh,

and although I've squirrelled away my clothes from SEX and Seditionaries, the Vivienne Westwood World's End pirate shirts stay in the wardrobe – often worn as dresses, cinched at the waist with a tight black-patent belt, and paired with high-heeled red ankle boots or my beloved gold leather Anello and David pumps. Yes, I think clothes are important, and I dress up to go out, but not in the way the Blitz generation do. I don't spend hours – days, even – shopping and planning and preening and posing, with a quest to outdo everyone else in the room.

The Blitz and beyond scene was mostly about dressing up and dancing to the music DJ Rusty Egan played: Bowie and Roxy and Kraftwerk; synth-based Euro-pop by people like Gina X or Telex; or perhaps something from Grace Jones or Japanese techno-pop maestros Yellow Magic Orchestra. I'd always had a soft spot for Rusty, after first meeting him at Rema Rema bandmate and boyfriend Marco Pirroni's house in Harrow. This was back in 1979, and I remember peeping out from under the bedcovers while Rusty rifled through Marco's record collection, looking for new tunes to play that night at Blitz. Maybe it's the shared Irish heritage, or the fact that he's a fellow drummer, or just his big smile and puppy-dog enthusiasm for life which was so different to the cool most people exuded – but whatever it was, we always gelled.

It wasn't all DJing and discs – there were new, young bands that came out of the Blitz scene, too. There was Spandau Ballet, whose first gig I saw there – or at least, their first gig under that name. They'd been called a few other things first. It was Robert Elms who renamed them, after seeing the phrase 'Spandau Ballet' scrawled on a Berlin wall. I don't know what I was expecting, but lead singer Tony Hadley could actually sing – plus, Gary Kemp's songs had a great pop sensibility, and the band was tight. And you could dance to it! We all did a kind of

membership card
name D.M. PRIOR
number 063
date 31.1.83
strict dress code essential · no admittance without card
5–6 falconberg court, charing cross rd., WC2

SKIN TWO

The **SCREEN** on Islington Green
01-226 3520
LATE NIGHT CINEMA CLUB
Member's Name MAX

Black & Beyond
Exciting and Unusual Leather Clothes by Michaelle
Sundays
Electric Ballroom Mkt.
mon - sat's phones
10.00 - 8pm. 01-485 1999

JAMES CUTS
is for you
114-KENSINGTON-CHURCH-STREET-W-8·
727-7033

PHOTO BY ROBYN BEECHE

The **CHA·CHA Club**
TUESDAYS 11.00 PM TILL LATE · MEMBERS £2 GUESTS £3
180 HUNGERFORD LANE · CHARING CROSS · WC2
THE CLUB FOR THE PEOPLE WHO DON'T NEED TO POSE

STRAND
CRAVEN ST
CHARING CROSS STATION
CINEMA
VILLIERS ST
ARCHES

TUES OCT 27 SPECIAL GLAMROCK PARTY

Cuts Club
276
Meard Street, W.1.

worlds end
430 KINGS RD
BORN IN ENGLAND

MEMBERSHIP CARD

THE LIFT

69/70 DEAN STREET, W1
01-437 6455/3278
Signature D. M. Prior
THIS CARD IS NOT TRANSFERABLE

Makers of Elegant Clothing for Men & Women.
Ready to wear and made to measure.

PX

S. Raynor & H. Robinson
57 Endell Street, Covent Garden, London WC2 Tel 01-379 6652

DO YOU BEAT OFF TO OFFBEAT SEX?!
DIRECTION ARROWS

DRESS FETISH
A MUST!

J. M.

AUG 23-19
WITCHITY'S
HIGH ST KENSINGTON.

two-handed partner dance that some people called slow jive or push-pull, but I saw as a simplified version of New York craze the swing hustle. I mean, people dancing together, and smiling, all dressed in pretty clothes – punk this was not, although perhaps closer in some ways to how punk started, in the gay clubs, than what punk later became.

Other bands that have come out of the Blitz scene are Boy George's Culture Club, and Steve Strange's Visage, featuring Midge Ure, who then joined Ultravox. Culture Club aren't really my cup of tea, and Visage I can take or leave, although I'm glad to see Steve – who I've known forever as he used to live in Marco's house – doing well. But I genuinely like the Midge Ure era Ultravox – 'Vienna' is a good old-fashioned pop tune, and deserved to be the big hit that it was. Depeche Mode, being from Essex, were viewed by some as outsiders – but insider Daniel Miller, who had started a label called Mute, certainly rated them, and signed them up. Their 1981 single 'Just Can't Get Enough' becomes a massive mainstream hit, but is also a favourite on the club dancefloors.

And you know, I like it all, it's fun. But I have mixed feelings. It doesn't seem *important*, in the way that the stuff that emerged in the mid-1970s – the first-wave of punk that spawned the Sex Pistols, Buzzcocks, and Subway Sect; and the industrial and experimental electronics scene, spearheaded by Throbbing Gristle and Cabaret Voltaire, felt not only important but vital. Is this an age thing? Now that I'm closer to 30 than 20, am I too old for youth culture? Or is it that it isn't as important? I don't think it's just a youth thing – both punk and industrial were dealing with, and making ironic commentary on, the world we were living in. Music, art, poetry, philosophy, and politics were all intertwined. Now, it seems more like avoidance – a Gatsby-style partying while the world crashes all around.

After Blitz and Club for Heroes close, everyone moves on to the bigger and brasher Camden Palace, formerly the Music Machine. I go here regularly with old friends and new – Andy Warren and Gill Smith, Fifi Russell and Carl Evans from Yip Yip Coyote, or dance partner Joe and other Arthur Murray's colleagues. By mid-1983, there's Foz to add into the mix, and he fits in happily with them all. I've stopped trying to keep the different strands of my life separate, and everybody parties together nicely – the only dilemma being that punk-era friends call me Max and dance-school friends call me Dorothy. But I'm quite used to having a number of different names, and will answer to anything.

Camden, it must be said, has really taken off in the past year or two. A lot of people seem to be hanging out here now rather than in Chelsea or Soho. Of course, there was always Dingwalls and the Roundhouse – popular venues for punk gigs, especially good for seeing visiting Americans such as The Ramones or Patti Smith (at the Roundhouse); and The Heartbreakers, Cherry Vanilla or Wayne-now-Jayne County (at Dingwalls). Compendium Bookshop was always worth a visit, to seek out copies of *Ambit* magazine, or to buy your Ballard or Bukowski – or perhaps nab something limited run like the poetry-prose mash-ups published by Iain Sinclair's Albion Village Press – mostly his own stuff – the punk DIY ethos spreading out to embrace not just fanzines but small-press literature. Compendium punched above its weight, getting people like beat legends William Burroughs and Lawrence Ferlinghetti in for readings and signings.

And now there is also 'Camden Market' as a place to be – this being a catch-all term for the various market spaces on either side of the canal, both new and established. The market at Camden Lock, near Dingwalls – the original Camden Market, in my mind – has always been a good source for quality second-hand stuff (from fur stoles to feather boas) but it has now also become a place to hang out, particularly at weekends. Towards Chalk Farm is the indoor market Oddities, where a year or so earlier Andy and I had our little shoplet called, with startling originality, Max & Andy, selling film and TV ephemera (*Man From UNCLE* books, *Thunderbirds* toys, *Romeo* magazines et al); with other stalls including Diana's 'definitely for the discerning' vintage clothes stall, The Candy Man 'old tyme sweeties' stall, and an interesting unit called Bunch of Artists who design their own T-shirts and sweatshirts which are sold alongside Crazy Colour hair dye and film posters.

Down the other way, close to Camden tube station, right opposite Inverness Street's fruit-and-veg market, the once tatty and downtrodden outdoor market has a new lease of life, as many of the post-punk designers and retailers look beyond Kensington or the King's Road for outlets. There are still a fair few stalls selling cheap nylon knickers and ladies' nighties, but they've been joined by people touting their Goth wares, so the place is ablaze with stalls selling red PVC trousers and black leather coats, Dr Marten's boots decorated with skulls and roses, chunky silver rings, and purple satin corsets. Plus, the Electric Ballroom also has stalls on Sundays – our friend Michaelle has one for a venture called Black and Beyond, which offers made-to-measure leather garments. Look, no seams at the knees, she points out – the best, softest leather, cut from one piece. Foz and I eventually both get a pair.

Having purchased whatever glad-rags are your particular thing – be it those shiny purple and black Goth claddings, rocker leathers with zips a-plenty, or a vintage ballgown in pink tulle – then of course you need to have somewhere to go and show them off. So it's off to the clubs of Camden, Soho or

Covent Garden you go. And my goodness, things in clubland are changing fast...

An interesting shift happening now is that instead of consecutive trends, things quite often happen concurrently. For the past year or two I've been working with anthropologist, writer and photographer Ted Polhemus on a book called *Pop Styles*, which has documented a million and one fashion and anti-fashion trends in post-war Britain – following neatly on, one from the other, for the most part, or operating as binary opposites – Mods and Rockers, say. But punk had then mashed everything together into one big ball of beautiful confusion – lesbian bikers in leathers and drag queens in SEX shop PVC happily mingling with rockabilly enthusiasts in peg trousers and soul boys with wedgie haircuts. The Blitz Kids continued that momentum – continued it and pushed it mainstream, with a handy TV camera inevitably watching from the wings. The river of time no longer flows in one direction, as things all happen at once, and people pick and mix between them. It's the era of the one-night wonder. Post-Blitz electronic pop nights, psychedelia nights, funk nights, rockabilly nights, Beatnik nights, hip hop nights... Ted will later coin the term "The Supermarket of Style" to sum up this new postmodernism.

Nowadays, there's a pretty fast journey from underground to overground. *The Face* magazine features a certain look or a commentary on style trends – the *Hard Times* ripped jeans issue, for example, or an article on the new/old working-class-lad trend for sportswear (Pringle, Fila, Nike, Lacoste) – and a week or two later, lo and behold the mainstream magazines and newspapers are reporting on it too. So things go from ultra-hip to high street very quickly. And channelling that pick and mix ethos, a lot of people chop and change how they look on a daily basis, dressing differently each night of the week for every different club night; or sticking with one club, but coming up with a new look each week to out-do fellow clubbers and catch the eye of one of the horde of photographers and documentary filmmakers hanging out in Soho who are hoping that by luck or judgement they'll capture the newest trend, the hippest trendsetter.

Because suddenly, everything is documented. In the 1970s, whole swathes of trends and bands and art happenings existed without ever being properly documented. Take my band Rema Rema – no live footage at all, despite being a cult success. It used to take a while for things to filter through, but now there's a TV documentary or a book of photos about any and every pop and counter-culture phenomenon coming out almost concurrently with the start of the thing itself. Plus we now have this new thing, MTV, which plays pop videos all day long, with an occasional short fashion or music news item thrown in. There's a demand for sound-and-vision content, with many hungry mouths to be fed. I get drawn into this cultural commentary thing when Ted introduces me to a guy called Charles – very posh, he is – who is producing a new TV show called *Riverside* – a BBC2 arts programme aimed at young people. They're looking for a presenter, and although I don't get the lead job, I'm invited to be a researcher and contributor, presenting items on the new youth tribes.

There are some crossover points for these 1980s tribes. When Andy Czezowski and Susan Carrington, who'd previously run The Roxy, open a new club in Brixton called The Fridge, the launch party attracts a lot of punk and post-punk faces – various Ants and Banshees and Sex Pistols and other seventies stalwarts – mixed in with Blitz Kids, plus the Brixton Rasta locals, and Latin and African music fans. The Fridge is an exception, a genuine meeting point – partly due to

Andy and Susan's pull, but also because it reaches out into the local Brixton community with its themed nights like the Gold Coast Club, where I get to practice my merengue and bachata dance steps with people who can really, really dance. But more typically, once an opening night has been and gone, each new club then falls into its respective niche.

The story of 69 Dean Street illustrates this well.

The entrance to this legendary venue is not actually in Dean Street itself, but in Meard Street, which is a dark and somewhat creepy rat-run between Dean Street and Wardour Street, with number 69 the corner building, next to a short terrace of decrepit 18th century townhouses. These houses are populated by Soho ladies of the night who dangle out of the windows; and the street is a hangout for drug dealers and strip-club managers – although these days, likely to be joined by queues of people dressed any-which-way, trailing back in opposite directions. There, in this run-down alley, we find two doors, one leading to the upstairs venue, and one to the basement, home of Gossips, formerly Billy's – hence the two queues.

Our occasional sort-of-punkabilly band The Weekend Swingers had played at Gaz's Rockin Blues in 1980, which at the time was a new rockabilly, swing and jazz night held at Gossips. The band was a just-for-fun venture with me on drums, Andy Warren on bass, and Marco Pirroni on guitar – joining forces with rockabilly enthusiasts Jay Strongman and Paul Stahl to play a set of cover versions with a Cramps-like sensibility. In 1983, Gaz's Rocking Blues is still going strong, rocking up a storm every Thursday – one of the few weekly clubs at Gossips to survive more than a few months. Now that I know how to jive and swing dance, I enjoy showing off my moves here, amused by the unconventional way some of the rockabilly boys lead. One, for example, clicks his fingers and shouts "Go!" when he wants you to spin. Meanwhile Jay Strongman, former lead singer of both The Weekend Swingers and its successor The El Trains, has gone on to become one of the most sought-after DJs of this new London clubbing scene... More on him anon!

Steve and Rusty started their Tuesday Bowie night here at Gossips way, way back in 1979, when it was still called Billy's – before moving on to the Blitz club in Covent Garden, allegedly because the Gossips boss, a bona fide Soho gangster type, wanted to double the price of the drinks.

Perry Haines, who like his friend Steve Strange is a multi-tasker, also ran a night here for a while, called *i-D*, the same as the magazine he co-founded with *Vogue*'s former art director Terry Jones: branding across different artforms and media is becoming much more of a thing these days. This was before setting up the Dial 9 for Dolphins night at The Embassy. He played 'dance music' – a curious catch-all name for the disco, hip hop, soul and new-fangled 'house' music that has sprung up of late in the USA. New York No Wave bands like James White and the Blacks, and Ze Records star Cristina, also find their way into the mix. Like a lot of the Blitz Kids, Perry was a student at St. Martins, allegedly coining the term 'New Romantic', which some people might never forgive him for.

By 1983, there's something different on every night of the week at Gossips. A new night on Mondays, called Alice in Wonderland, embraces the new-wave psychedelia that's springing up. I became a teenager in 1968, and can remember the first wave of psychedelia well, so all this late 1960s revival stuff feels odd. Kensington Market and its new rival Hyper Hyper, which is right across the road on Kensington High Street, are full of 60s stuff these days. I'll skip this one, I decide. I still have a blue satin trouser-suit and an embroidered velvet bomber jacket at the back of my mum's wardrobe, but feel pretty sure I'm not going to drag them out. I'm much happier with the 1950s – the decade I was born in, but was too young to remember much about, so it feels suitably distanced. I'm OK with the early 60s – capri pants, ski trousers, Mary Quant and Beatle boots – but nothing after 1965, thank you very much. New boyfriend Foz, on the other hand, is quite a bit younger than me so missed psychedelia first time round, and embraces the revival with gusto. He's a Syd Barrett-era Pink Floyd fan, and had often worn his mum's flowery chiffon blouses onstage in a one-man bid to turn his band The Apaches into a psychedelic group. Oh, and when his seamstress mum got fed up having her blouses nicked, she started buying double quantities of fabric so she could run up matching mother-and-son flouncy blouses...

Upstairs at 69 Dean Street – which you get to in a terrifyingly rickety lift that only takes two or three people at a time, depending on how big their hair is – is the Gargoyle Club. In the 1930s, this was the hangout for Noel Coward and Tallulah Bankhead and their set; then, the meeting place for painter Francis Bacon's Soho Group, before becoming a strip club hosting the Nell Gwynne review – named for the King's mistress who apparently once lived at this very address. The Gargoyle has been host to various once-a-week nights over the past three or four years, including mixed-gay club The Lift on Thursdays, which I go to regularly with dance partner Joe. It has as its mantra 'boogie leads to integration' which I'm happy to endorse.

The Gargoyle Club now also hosts The Batcave. Despite, or perhaps because of, the cheapo-cheapo decor – fake cobwebs, toy spiders and all – the place always feels cosy and welcoming. More like a kids' Hallowe'en party than a de-Sadean den of iniquity. Quite a lot of the people do, though, look like extras from *Nosferatu*. I mean, the pale skin, heavily-shadowed eyes and blue-black hair combo has been a thing right through punk, from The Damned's Dave Vanian onwards – but an awful lot of next-generation dark young things seem to have emerged recently, adopting that Gothic look.

So here on this Wednesday night in early '83, here's a throng of girls dancing together to DJ Hamish MacDonald's mix of T.Rex, Cure and Cramps tunes, and they all look like Siouxsie Sioux circa her Top of the Pops appearance for 'Spellbound' – PVC jerkin, leather miniskirt, London Leatherman studded bracelets. All, to a woman, with big black hair almost covering their eyes, although you can just make out that those eyes are painted black, black, black with no delineation between eyeshadow and eyeliner and mascara, just two great blocks of black. But no, yes, hang on, can it be? Yes – one of the Siouxsie Sioux lookalikes *is* Siouxsie Sioux.

I occasionally go along with Andy to see bands who all seem to have the word 'sex' in their names: Alien Sex Fiend, Sexbeat, Sex Gang Children. Was there one called Alien Sex Children? Maybe not, but there should have been. Of course Andy, being the original bass player of Adam and the Ants, is something of a demi-god in Goth circles, The Ants and The Banshees being the two most fêted punk bands for this tribe. And it's the original *Dirk Wears White Sox*-era Ants that Goths most relate to, rather than the New Romantic Adam. Andy spends much of the evening standing with his back to the wall, cigarette in hand, fielding questions from devoted fans, many of whom have now formed bands of their own. Although my former band Rema Rema is far less famous than the Ants, it has a fair amount of kudos here, gaining Brownie points for being the first signing to 4AD, who also release records by Bauhaus, Cocteau Twins and The Birthday Party, all of whom are rated highly in these circles. The Birthday Party are great live, I must say – no doubt the true punk successors, regardless of the 'Goth or Not-Goth?' debate. The singer Nick Cave is as wild and shamanic as Johnny Rotten, howling and rolling on the floor, and guitarist Rowland S Howard has a great look, with an odd heart-shaped face and big eyes, and an intense distorted and discordant guitar sound. But they don't hang around for long, declaring they hate London, absconding to Berlin then splitting up.

Before leaving town, Nick Cave is sometimes to be found at The Batcave, hanging out with fellow Australian JG Thirlwell aka Foetus, and American No Wave star Lydia Lunch – she of Teenage Jesus and the Jerks and 8-Eyed Spy. I think those three are cooking up some sort of collaboration...

The Immaculate Consumptive, with Marc Almond in tow, is what later emerges, but sadly they only ever play in America, so I don't get to see them. Marc, by the way, is an extraordinarily busy bee – not only still making music as half of Soft Cell, but also forming Marc and the Mambas, and guesting with both Psychic TV and Coil.

By the end of the year, it's not only Nick who has left town. Whilst he and his gang head east to Berlin, Jim Thirlwell goes west to the US of A. To be honest, I feel like doing the same. I agree with Nick. London is wasted, horrible. It's lost its pizazz. It's as ruinous as it was in the 1970s, but now with added greed and consumerism. Most of the old warehouses, taken over by artists to become galleries and studios, are going or gone. Tooley Street near London Bridge is being redeveloped. Butler's Wharf is being requisitioned. Covent Garden is being turned from an artists' playground into a new commercial hotspot. There are a few squats left in Camden and New Cross – the epicentre of the anarcho-punk thing that is the alternative to the Bright Young Things of the Blitz-and-beyond – but that's about it.

But where would I go? Maybe New York. I did so love the New York nightclubs. I try Darryl, the dance teacher I'd met at Arthur Murray's. I write, offering my services at the Broadway school, but the letter comes back with a Return to Sender stamp. Oh well. I even toy with the idea of moving to Northern Italy, where Marco's parents Dino and Bruna come from. They've taken me to Pellegrino Parmense a number of times, and I love the place and the people, and especially love all the outdoor festivals, with their *pasta frita* stalls and local bands playing waltzes and tangos and paso dobles, where I'm whirled round the wooden dancefloor by old farmers who are astounded that an English girl can dance 'their' dances. Who needs nightclubs when there's an artichoke festival to go to? But really, what would I do there? Become a farmer's wife? I don't think so.

So no – it's back to Blighty and the Batcave. Away from the Italian sunshine and clover pastures, and back in to that rickety lift, heading up to the dark and gloom of The Gargoyle.

Olli Wisdom, the Batcave co-founder, was one of the gang of wide-eyed young kids who followed The Ants around. He now has a new band, called Specimen. When Andy and I had first got to know him, he was playing in The Unwanted – a punk outfit that were for the most part unremarkable, although they did do a cover of Nancy Sinatra's 'Boots', which was kind of funny. Olli, like so many others, including my then-bandmate Jay Strongman, ran a stall when he wasn't fronting a band. But whereas Jay sold pristine 1950s pegs in Kensington Market, Olli's stall in Beaufort Market on the King's Road was stuffed with black PVC, fishnet and chains. Although it's not quite my thing, I do have a soft spot for Specimen. Maybe it's because they are so much better than The Unwanted. Maybe it's because Olli is always so sweet and smiley when you speak to him, his real-life personality in sharp contrast to the ghoulish *Grand*

Guignol theatrics onstage. Plus, the band have a good guitarist in Batcave's other main-man Jon Klein, and an interesting and visually arresting keyboard player called Jonny Slut – probably not his baptismal name – whose ripped and torn fishnet shirt and 'death-hawk' mile-high spiky hairdo become the defining look of Goth.

By mid-1983 the Batcave has outgrown The Gargoyle and moved on to sleazy old gay club The Subway in Leicester Square. And with the release of *The Hunger* – starring David Bowie as a vampire, opposite Catherine Deneuve, and a soundtrack that includes Bauhaus' 'Bela Lugosi's Dead' – Goth is most definitely hitting its heights. (Or should that be plumbing its depths?)

But I never make it down to The Subway. I'm fine with proto-Goth bands Bauhaus and The Cure; and – like The Cure's Robert Smith and Pete Murphy of Bauhaus – I was brought up Roman Catholic and am still drawn to all that fabulous iconography. I understand the obsession with all things dark and devilish, but I've decided that Goth really isn't for me. I've chucked most of the black out of my wardrobe; and as more Goth bands come to the fore – from Killing Joke to UK Decay to Sisters of Mercy – it becomes clearer and clearer that this is not my bag.

+

1983 sees new ventures a-plenty in clubland. Another gay venue, Stallions, is hosting fetish club Skin Two, which opens its doors one Monday night in January. The entrance is in a cobbled courtyard that you reach through an alleyway just off of Soho Square, so it feels quite naughty and secretive even before you get in. Dress code is strictly rubber, leather and PVC. Luckily,

I have a cupboard full of this stuff left over from my days as an 'exotic dancer', most of it bought from She n Me in South Kensington (although SEX sold much of the same stuff). So the thigh-high wet-look leggings, shoulder-high matching gloves and strappy conical-breasted basque get a new lease of life. It does feel a bit like fancy dress, as this look is no longer really me, but I'm happy to play the dressing-up game occasionally.

Skin Two is the brainchild of David Claridge, who, rather bizarrely, has another life as Roland Rat, a much-loved children's TV puppet character. Of course, when the tabloids get hold of this juicy bit of information and make the connection between these disparate worlds, it causes a bit of a scandal, and Skin Two gets rebranded as Maitresse – but that's all to come. For now, Skin Two is a secret pleasure garden. It's escapism, pure and simple. And that's what all of this clubbing feels like – escaping real life. Avoidance. Avoiding Thatcher, the AIDS worries, the political unrest, the threat of annihilation any minute now by a nuclear bomb.

Never mind, ignore it all – let's party on. *We're nightclubbing, bright white clubbing. Oh, isn't it wild?*

The Mud Club in Leicester Square, hosted by Philip Salon and Tasty Tim, also opens its doors in January 1983 and soon becomes a favourite haunt for me and dance partner Joe. We're here to dance, dance, dance – that's it. It has two regular DJs who play very different sets. Upstairs, Tasty Tim plays kitsch classics; whilst downstairs my friend and former bandmate Jay Strongman plays cutting-edge funk, imported from the USA.

On Thursdays, the very busy Jay can be found DJing at Whisky A Go-Go (abbreviated to WAGG, then becoming The Wag) on Wardour Street, which is now run by Chris Sullivan and Ollie O'Donnell, who formerly collaborated on Le Beat Route, around the corner on Greek Street. The Whisky A Go-

Go had also run something called Club Left for a while, a 'lounge' night hosted by Vic Godard, who – with manager Bernie Rhodes' approval – had ditched the old Subway Sect, donned a tuxedo, and recruited a new line-up of swing-savvy musicians to back him in his new career as a jazzy crooner. Which was, well – interesting I suppose – but let's face it, Vic will never be Frank Sinatra. Not even Matt Monro. A lot of the old Blitz and Gossips crowd turn up at The Wag when Jay is DJing, including Steve Strange and Princess Julia, Boy George and Marilyn, and hairdresser James Lebon from Cuts.

James Cuts (as most of us call him) has decided it's time to move in on this nightclubbing lark – whilst still plying his trade as a hairdresser, thank the Lord, because nowadays I won't let anybody else near me with a pair of scissors in hand. James sometimes uses me as a model – a dancing model, that is – in shows he is involved in at the Hippodrome, or the March 1983 Anthony Price event at Camden Palace. It was James who'd persuaded me to get rid of all the Crazy Colour and the weird poodle perm I'd had done at Antenna, the rival salon down the road from James' joint These Are Cuts on Kensington Church Street. Where Antenna went in for lavish be-ribbonned extensions, as modelled by the likes of Haysi Fantayzee, James was really into simplicity. It's all about the cut, and never mind the frou-frou adornments, says James. When we're doing the pre-show run-through at the Anthony Price event someone, thinking I'm out of earshot, says something about dyeing my hair pink to give me more impact under the lights, and James explains, in his wonderful booming bass voice, that it's taken him the best part of a year to get all the crap out of my hair, and there's no way we're going back. So here I am, my natural strawberry blonde hair cut shoulder length, bottom edge as chunky as a paint brush; with a razor-sharp fringe that you could use as a ruler, it's so straight.

As well as doing these sort of club-cum-fashion show type things, James also, for a while, starts up his own night. Really and truly, everybody's at it. It's called The Language Lab, and gains a name as the capital's first dedicated hip hop club. He does a lot of work as a stylist in the USA, so keeps up with what's going on over there, bringing back suitcases full of rap releases.

As 1983 moves into 1984, things are on the move again. I still regularly go to Heaven with my dance school mates, but if I'm with old friends from the punk days, we're more likely to be found at the Café de Paris in Piccadilly for Anne Pigalle's *Nuit de Mercredi* – which is bringing a little bit of Montmartre to London.

Or then there's Der Putsch, which opened in 1983, and by 1984 has overtaken SkinTwo, aka Maitresse, as the place to be for those serious about all things rubber and leather. The club, held in a wine bar in Northumberland Street, is strictly members-only, run by a couple called Steve and Sadi – both young and good looking, and both very serious about fetishism and S&M. Der Putsch has strong links with *AtomAge*, the rubber people organisation and magazine, and has a strict 'no tourists' policy – many people on the scene feel that SkinTwo opened itself up to too many gawpers. The impeccably dressed (in latex, of course) Sadi always has an entourage of men following her around who'd do anything to kiss her thigh-high boot or get a taste of her whip. The club also rides high on the hipness scale. It prides itself on its high-quality graphic design and limited-edition merchandise, with Der Putsch T-shirts – created in runs of just 100 – taking off as objects of desire.

The fetish and S&M scene is still relatively underground at this point, but we are reaching a cusp.

Rewind a few months to late 1983. Holly Johnson, formerly of Liverpool band Big in Japan, has a new venture called Frankie Goes to Hollywood, a collaboration with Paul Rutherford who is billed as 'backing singer and dancer'. Both are openly gay. ZTT Records signs Frankie after the label's co-founder Trevor Horn sees the band play an early version of their song 'Relax' on TV show *The Tube*. After various attempts to record the song, none of which Trevor Horn was happy with, he bypasses the band and constructs a more electronic-based version, turning a catchy indie band song into a clubbing classic. ZTT co-founder Paul Morley then comes up with a marketing campaign that he calls "a strategic assault on pop". The accompanying video is set in an S&M club, featuring an orgy of leathermen, dominatrices and drag queens, and sees Holly manhandled, stripped of his sensible jacket and tie, and made to wrestle a tiger – all on the command of a toga-clad Roman emperor. It was inevitably going to get banned, and Morley knew it. Frankie appear on *Top of the Pops* in January 1984, after which Radio 1 DJ Mike Read announces that he considers the track to be "distasteful" and says he won't be playing it. So then comes a BBC ban, which ignites curiosity – and 'Relax' soars up the charts, reaching number 1.

So at last we have it – another of those cultural big-bang moments. Frankie Goes to Hollywood are the thing that brings together many of the disparate elements of post-punk culture: crazy non-stop nightclubbing, the expanding gay scene defiantly defending its lifestyle choices in the face of the emergence of HIV and AIDS, the growing fetish scene, the re-styling of indie bands into electronic synth-pop ensembles, and the birth of exciting new sounds masterminded by a new breed of studio producer who uses all means at his disposal.

The future is here. Hit me with those laser beams.

TAKE FOZ

All things considered, it was almost inevitable
that Foz would eventually join The Monochrome Set.

Well, there has been a lot of speculation about 1984 and how closely it would resemble Orwell's vision, and now here we are. To be honest, by the time the clock strikes midnight on New Year's Eve, we're all pretty fed up with all the Orwellian references. Yes, yes, there are CCTV cameras everywhere, and this is very 'Big Brother', and there is a great deal of double-think going down in the House of Commons – but enough, already.

Foz and I see in the New Year together in Notting Hill, staying at former Apache bandmate Wig's flat, which is shared with his girlfriend Chrissie – for we are nomads, wandering the streets, hanging out in the wine bars and cinemas of Kensington and Chelsea, and occasionally staying over with friends. I am once again homeless and living with the Pirronis in Harrow; and Foz has left his Earl's Court flat and is back living with his mum in Pimlico. On a grey and dreary New Year's Day, we wander along a deserted Portobello Road, kicking through the litter and the discarded vegetable trimmings from yesterday's street market, wondering what the year will bring. It's a Sunday, but doesn't New Year's Day always feel like a Sunday and then some?

The year gets off to a shaky start. January sees Britain battered with hurricane force winds – not so great for hanging out in London's parks or walking the Embankment. Plus, no more ha'pennies! The teeny coins are 'demonetised' by chancellor Nigel Lawson in February. Every time I see that word written down I read 'demon-etised' rather than 'de-monetised'. Still, there's some good news when ice skaters Torvill and Dean win gold at the Winter Olympics. On 12 March, the Miners' Strike begins, and that's going to be a defining feature of this so-far rather dreary year. Margaret Thatcher had been re-elected in 1983 with an increased majority, and she was sharpening her claws and teeth, ready to do battle with miners' leader Arthur Scargill. Then, in April, extraordinary scenes unfold just up the road from my old flat on Exhibition Road, when hostages are taken at the Libyan Embassy, near the top of the street, close to Hyde Park. Yvonne Fletcher, a policewoman standing outside the building, is shot and killed by a gunman inside; and 11 other people are also shot, although they survive. Diplomatic relationships with Libya are broken off, leading to a longstanding animosity between our countries which would have repercussions for many decades.

Well OK, yeah – I suppose it does all feel rather *Diamond Dogs*.

Two events at the ICA seem to capture this dystopian mood perfectly. In early January, Einstürzende Neubauten, the Berlin industrial band who'd made their UK debut to great acclaim (in certain quarters, anyway) in 1983 – return to the UK. The *Concerto for Voices and Machinery* features special guests Genesis P-Orridge, Stevo Pearce from Some Bizzare and the always-entertaining Frank Tovey of Fad Gadget. Industrial noise and chaos a-go-go, but it's a health and safety no-no – they only play half of their planned set before the show is halted, because of the damage being done to the venue's stage with their drills and jackhammers. That and the fact that the whole place is now full of smoke and debris from the smashed-up piano and the broken bottles chucked at the whirring concrete mixer. The power is switched off – not the first time the ICA have pulled the plug on something they don't like that's going on inside their own building! The damage to the stage isn't accidental, we find out later – the band are trying to dig through it into the tunnel system underneath the venue, which allegedly goes all the way down the Mall to Buckingham Palace.

Then, in February, a new exhibition by Derek Jarman opens: *The GBH Paintings (The Last of England)*. Derek's paintings are big, bold canvases – rich, tactile layers of reds and rusts and blacks that are plastered on so thickly that the paintings are almost 3D rather than 2D. Well, of course they *are* 3D. You forget, if you just see paintings reproduced on the page rather than experiencing them for real, that they are tangible physical artefacts. Objects of desire. Derek has lots to say about the current state of England – particularly the demonising of AIDS victims and the anti-gay venom seeping through the country. This is the real plague, says Derek, who has been 'out' forever. He's the first person I know to use the word 'queer' with pride, turning the insult on its head.

+

By April, Foz and I are living together in Rosehill Road in Wandsworth – not that we're there that much. I'm kept as busy as can be with my two dance school jobs, and Foz is busy with The Monochrome Set, who are now signed to Blanco y Negro, a Warner Brothers subsidiary managed by Geoff Travis of Rough Trade and Mike Alway of Cherry Red.

After Foz had joined in early 1983, The Monochrome Set had toured extensively in Europe and Scandinavia, as well as playing across the UK. I didn't really know Foz then – although I had met him a couple of times when Andy and I had gone to see his former band The Apaches – otherwise known as Les Apaches, to give them a dash of Gauloise glamour. Although that backfired when they'd turn up at a venue and the sound guy would say, "OK then, which one of you is Les?" For their first gig, at The Bridgehouse in Canning Town, they got billed as Leather Patches – the audience expecting a heavy metal band rather than a group of effete young New Romantics. The Apaches all proudly sported "Too Old at 20" badges – which they perhaps got in a job lot from Better Badges on Portobello Road where Foz worked part-time – so naturally felt obliged to disband when they left their teen years behind them. That and the fact that singer Simon Buxton was being urged to go solo by a record company interested in him. When Simon quit, Foz and the others did briefly consider carrying on without him, and indeed auditioned Tony from the Soul Boys – a band doing the same circuit as The Apaches who had Ants/Bow Wow Wow drummer Dave Barbe's brother Louie on drums – as a possible singer, but it didn't happen. However, a few of the tunes that Foz came up with around that time did eventually see the light of day – one becoming The Monochrome Set's 'Andiamo'.

After a couple of false starts, playing a gig or two with bands he wasn't that interested in, Foz joined forces with a disparate bunch of London-based musicians, a loose collective of people of Irish and African heritage, who busked a punky Afro-Celt set in the old market place at Covent Garden, and outside Metro stations in Paris – guitars, mandolins, hurdy gurdies and all. I didn't witness any of this, but I got to hear Foz's "down and out in Paris and London" stories as soon as we started going out together.

I don't know if I ever knew what name this odd-bod ensemble went out under. Perhaps they didn't have a name, being a busking band. I do know Mervyn Africa had something to do with it all.

Then, in late 1982, Mike Alway got in touch with Foz to talk to him about joining The Monochrome Set. He met with the band, who were about to tour the USA with keyboard player Carrie Booth on board rather than a lead guitarist. That was the fateful tour where everything went horribly wrong, and I ended up meeting up with Andy and co in New York, then doing a support slot at their Ritz club gig with my dance partner Joe.

Foz hadn't joined at that point, but did very soon afterwards. Mike Alway was keen to get him in, and Foz had a whole raft of other connections with the group. Andy and I, of course, knew The Apaches; and there were additional links through Monochrome Set driver-cum-tour manager Dave Harper, and TMS roadies Longfellow and Mark Alleyne, who both knew him well. Plus, Foz's former Apaches bandmate, Nick Wesolowski, was now permanently in the band on drums. He'd done a stint in 1982, but then a guy called Morris Windsor did the USA tour, jumping ship somewhere along the way, and Nick joined up properly with Foz at the beginning of 1983. All things considered, it was almost inevitable that Foz would eventually join The Monochrome Set.

At this stage, the band were riding high on the indie success of studio album *Eligible Bachelors*, the third and last one made with original guitarist Lester Square, recorded with Tim Hart of Steeleye Span; and Mike Alway was also putting together a compilation of all the early demos, radio sessions, and Rough Trade singles that would go out on Cherry Red under the name *Volume, Contrast, Brilliance Vol. 1*. Once Foz was on board, Tim Hart was once again secured to work with the new line-up, and some demo tracks were laid down as the first try-outs for the Blanco y Negro record deal. These didn't get used at the time, but eventually saw the light of day, years later, on *Volume, Contrast, Brilliance Vol. 2* as 'Cilla Black' and 'The Greatest Performance Artist in the World.'

Foz played his first live gig with The Monochrome Set on 5 February 1983 at the London School of Economics. The line-up was Bid on vocals and guitar, Andy on bass, Foz on lead guitar, Nick on drums – and Dave Harper on percussion, although Foz later said that this seemed to mostly involve him playing a riding boot with a feather.

After that: Europe! Belgium, Italy, France – including the legendary Bains-Douches club in Paris. A couple of weeks back in Blighty, then it's off to Scandinavia – Denmark, Norway, Sweden. It's whilst on a boat crossing the icy waters of Sweden that Foz gets his infamous haircut. Of course, it's Andy's idea. Foz is short of money, so Andy says he'll pay Foz if he can give him a haircut, and is free to do anything he likes. Go ahead, says Foz – and soon finds himself with an east-west Mohican. Bizarrely, it catches on – by the time they reach Stockholm a number of fans are sporting sideways Mohicans. All of this I get told about by Andy, who seems to find Foz a source of constant amusement.

When Foz and I start going out together in mid-1983, Andy is not too happy about it. Apparently, I deduce, I'm not supposed to go out with anyone he's in a band with – even though Andy and I are no longer living together, and haven't been lovers for quite a few years now. Being Andy, he never quite explains or talks about it, but it's obvious from his behaviour. He's off-hand with Foz in the studio; and makes it clear he doesn't want to come out with us – so I just see them separately. After a while he thaws, little by little. He occasionally calls Foz and invites him out to see a band – the Psychedelic Furs, say, who both of them are independently friends with. "I've asked everyone else and no one else is free tonight," says Andy. And who could refuse an invitation like that?

By 1984, when Foz and I are living together, Andy has realised that it's not just a passing whim, and is reconciled to me and Foz being a couple – so we regularly go out together to clubs or gigs and Andy even comes round to our Wandsworth flat sometimes.

+

Foz and I settle in to life together in Rosehill Road, and I meet more of his friends. I already know The Apaches, but there is also an Apaches associate, a high society DJ called Mark Farmer. We sometimes go to posh events where Mark is DJing. I'm getting less and less good at handling late nights, so on more than one occasion find myself a nice sofa to doze on. There's a photo of me in *Tatler* or some such rag, doing just that. Another of Foz's friends is about as high society as you could get – Pauline Astor, who is indeed the daughter of Lord Astor (he of the infamous Profumo scandal, which of course must never be mentioned in front of Pauline's mother, Bronwyn).

Foz is also good friends with a bass player called Steve Marshall, who he's known for many years. Steve – unlike the public school boys in The Apaches – is, like Foz, from a working-class background, and when Foz first meets him is living in a council flat in Battersea. It was there that Foz first encountered Dave Harper and Dave Knight, spotted perched on bunk-beds, dressed in matching stripy beatnik tops and berets. The brace of Daves had formed a band called Five or Six, which had a fluid line-up but sometimes included Dave Harper's brother Simon, and Ashley Wales – who would later, like Dave Knight, join forces with Karl Blake in Shock Headed Peters. Mike Alway had signed Five or Six to Cherry Red, with whom they recorded a number of singles and albums, and like The Monochrome Set, Eyeless in Gaza, and Tracey Thorn, they ended up on the label's 1983 compilation album *Pillows and Prayers*. An album which also featured the Naked Civil Servant himself, Quentin Crisp.

Steve, until recently, had worked for the now-defunct Fetish Records. He was right-hand man to Rod Pearce – and although still a teenager when he started the job, had the grand title of 'label manager'. Fetish had its office in Denbigh Street in Pimlico, just round the corner from Churchill Gardens where Foz's family lived, so that was handy.

In its short life, Fetish Records certainly made its mark. Pearce founded the label in 1978 and reissued Throbbing Gristle's debut release *The Second Annual Report* after its initial pressing on the group's own Industrial Records had sold out. It was re-pressed using the original metal plates, handed on to Steve by Genesis P-Orridge, and using money Rod had made through releasing the Devo bootleg *Workforce to the World – Live on Site*. Artists on the label, other than TG, included UK industrialists 23 Skidoo and Clock DVA, and numerous New

York No Wavers like 8-Eyed Spy, The Bongos, and Bush Tetras. Not a bad line-up! It was also home to graphic designer Neville Brody, who was both art director and lead designer for the label, whilst at the same time becoming art director for *The Face* magazine. Neville's distinctive cover art added to the desirability of Fetish Records releases.

As well as playing bass (he'll eventually join both Gene Loves Jezebel and The Woodentops) and working for Fetish, Steve ends up DJing (using the name Marine Boy) at Dial 9 for Dolphins, a club night set up by Rod's friend Perry Haines. Steve, who seems to get everywhere, is also friends with Peter Kent from Beggars Banquet, who a year or two previously had invited Steve and his then-girlfriend Angela Jaeger to do some demos. I think Angela came after Danielle Dax in Steve's life – it was quite hard to keep up with Steve's romantic liaisons. He was a very good-looking boy, pioneering that famous overgrown mullet cut from Antenna later adopted by Perry Haines' band King. Angela, a native New Yorker who had been in the UK for quite a few years, was a member of Pigbag and had also sung with The Pop Group and Bush Tetras. Steve roped in Foz, and the three of them recorded a version of Angela's song 'Larchmont' – an angular funk track boasting jangly guitars.

I get to meet Angela in early 1984, and take a shine to her immediately – she's smart and strong-willed and very easy to get on with. And it's good to talk to someone who is bridging the gap between UK post punk and the New York No Wave scene. Angela now had a new venture, Instinct, with her husband, The Pop Group's Simon Underwood, and they were signed to ZTT – although that wasn't going as well as might be hoped.

Foz meets my friends Ted and Lynn, Fiona and Carl from Yip Yip Coyote, and the many and various people working at both the dance schools that I teach at. The Monochrome

Set extended family is our shared territory, and this includes current members Bid, Andy and Nick, and their various wives, girlfriends and associates; plus former member Lester Square, and Lester's girlfriend Sharon D'Lugoff who seems to be to-ing and fro-ing between Manhattan and Brixton these days. There are also the band's tour managers and roadies: the aforementioned Dave Harper; Longfellow aka Spider, who I'd known for yonks as he was The Ants roadie too, and used to have a windowless basement room at 69 Exhibition Road (one that Adam Ant rented for a month or so but never moved in to); and Mark Alleyne and his girlfriend Kay, who came into the Ants/TMS scene a little bit later.

Mark is a soul boy turned punk of Trinidadian heritage who looked white, so was often in the company of racists unaware that they were sounding off to 'one of them'. They soon discovered their error, as a punch landed unexpectedly. I can't remember when I first met Mark, but I do remember Andy and I going round to his Kilburn flat and forming an impromptu band, with me playing 'drums' on Mark's pots and pans. Mark would go on to front Mark Antony and the Centurions – more on that venture anon! As he's a friend of both Andy and Marco, we'd sometimes all meet up at the Pirronis' restaurant on Tottenham Court Road, and get fed for free; perhaps afterwards going round the corner to visit Andy's madcap friend Nicky and her flatmate David (who's dating a barman at Stallions). Their house at 60 Grafton Way seems to have replaced 69 Exhibition Road as the portal that everybody has to pass through at some point.

Andy has also befriended a Canadian-Italian DJ and journalist called Gabriella Bregman, who he met when she interviewed The Monochrome Set for Ottawa-based *TransFM* magazine. She frequently travels to England, often en route

to see family in Rome, and when she's here, Foz and I go out with her and Andy to one of the inevitable old favourites, like Pizza Express in Coptic Street. We also take her to the Pirronis' restaurant – of course, they are always glad to meet fellow Italians, and her family are also restaurateurs, so there is lots in common. Afterwards, we nip down the road to Bernigra's for some proper traditionally made Italian ice-cream.

The social circle is ever-increasing. We spend time with designer Michaelle and her partner Debden, who live in Camden. Debden helps Michaelle with her leatherwear business, Black and Beyond, but has his own cottage industry too, making Sacred Heart of Jesus plaster-of-Paris statues painted with camouflage patterns or day-glo psychedelic designs. He begs to borrow my RE/Search books on JG Ballard and William Burroughs – which I'm reluctant to lend and never get back. Never mind.

+

Having toured pretty relentlessly in 1983 – abroad and across the UK – The Monochrome Set are not on the road much in 1984 as the focus is on recording, but there are a few London gigs, mostly on the college circuit, and a couple of summer balls at Oxford and Cambridge universities. These are weaved in and around studio time, with a new album – their first for Blanco y Negro – underway, Foz pleased to be trying out his new strawberry-coloured Gretsch Atkins Super Axe, bought from Denmark Street with his record company advance.

This album, *The Lost Weekend*, is written and recorded throughout 1983 and 1984 – produced by John Porter, and mixed by Ben Rogan – but there are all sorts of delays, and it doesn't get released until 1985. The title references Billy Wilder's film about an alcoholic writer. Film had always been an inspiration for the band, as in songs such as 'Alphaville', 'Ici Les Enfants du Paradis', and of course 'Goodbye Joe', their homage to Warhol superstar Joe Dallesandro that had been covered a couple of years back by Tracey Thorn.

Although Bid is the band's main songwriter, other band members do contribute and the new album features a fair few tracks written or co-written by Foz, including 'Take Foz', 'Letter from Viola', and 'The Twitch'. As Foz doesn't sing, he tends to write instrumentals – as in 'Take Foz', loosely inspired by Dave Brubeck's 'Take Five'. 'The Twitch' is an odd little ditty – an attempt to establish a new dance craze: Let's Twitch, everybody! 'Letter from Viola' is interesting – Bid having run with a song based on a break-up letter written to Foz by a soon-to-be-ex-girlfriend, the eponymous Viola, listing all the reasons why they needed to part. It's a squirmy sort of song, I feel – although funny with it.

Foz's cover design for *The Lost Weekend* features a surreal beach scene, using a photo shot by Nick, done on a day trip to Brighton. By the time Foz has finished with it, the sky ends up rendered in bloody reds and oranges, the Pier a reversed-out electric white glare, the beach a moonscape blue-grey – and the people waist-deep in the water are only just visible... Everyone got very cold in the freezing water, but one must suffer for one's art, yes?

In October '84, there's another Monochrome Set gig at London School of Economics, where Andy was once (very briefly) a student – although I don't think that's why they keep going back there. The band decide they'd like extra drummers to join Nick Wesolowski on their opening number, so I'm roped in for the rollicking intro to THE Monochrome Set, Monochrome Set, Monochrome Set, Monochrome Se-e-e-et. There are also some backing singers on-hand for the night – three lovely punkish girls called Siobhan, Sara and Keren, all fluffy hair and big smiles and ra-ra-skirts, looking a bit like a 1980s version of The Shangri-las. They try to persuade me to sing with them, but I keep insisting I'm a drummer not a singer. Oh but you do sing, they say, you made a great single as a singer. Come on, give it a go. But no. I mean, it's true, I did make 'I

Confess' with Genesis P-Orridge and Alex Fergusson a few years back, but that was a one-off. Well, other than the backing vocals I did with the El Trains... I'm weakening, but I hold out. No, can't sing, won't sing.

So that's the story of how I don't join Bananarama.

Around about this time, Foz gets his first publishing deal – with a cheque arriving in the post. Money for writing songs, hurrah! So that's what he does: spends whole days writing songs, as happy as Larry to be paid for doing what he loves the most. Towards the end of the year, The Monochrome Set release a single called 'Jacob's Ladder' – the first to be taken from the new album, although that's not out yet. Foz's friend Angela Jaeger has contributed some wonderfully angelic backing vocals on this and other tracks. The 12" version has a lovely *Book of Hours* inspired cover designed by Foz, printed in lush blues and greens and golds, with a free poster inside featuring Bid dressed as an Indian prince, resplendent in turban and pearls. Plus, there's a postcard that says "Take home a real turkey this Christmas". Well, that's a novel sales pitch.

January 1985, and there's another major shift. I'm contacted by Genesis P-Orridge, who has a proposal. After a few phone chats, we agree to meet up on 1 February at The Monochrome Set gig at the University of London Union. It's quite a gathering that night: Genesis and his wife Paula; Madcap Nicky and David; and inevitably, Fiona and Carl from the Yip Yips – to name but a few. My dance partner Joe and I, under our cabaret name Dorothy & Toto, have revived our Masochism Tango act, performed with The Monochrome Set in New York, which acts as an opener for the band.

And here's a thing. Gen has invited me to join Psychic TV. Paula, who plays percussion, is seven months pregnant with their second child and won't be performing with the band for the foreseeable future. Besides, Gen argues, it's the right time to have a proper 'kit' drummer on board, "and you're my favourite drummer". I don't have a drumkit, I say. I lost it. But that is brushed aside. Come down to DJM studios on Monday, he says after the gig. So I do. I join the band, and Psychic TV buys me a drum kit. It's a bog-standard Premier – not as pretty as the silver Pearl Maxwin I'd carelessly misplaced, but never mind, it'll do.

So for the first half of 1985, I'm still frantically busy teaching dance at two schools – but also madly busy rehearsing, recording and playing gigs with Psychic TV. That's a whole other story, and it will be told!

Foz is also very busy with The Monochrome Set, gigging across England, Scotland and Wales, and promoting the records. He's now given up on the Hackett tweeds and reverted to a more punkish look. He has leather trousers, made by Michaelle, teamed with motorcycle boots; and a shaved head, often covered by a black airman's hat sporting a hammer-and-sickle badge. The landlady's cronies – two old ladies called Doris and Ivy who straighten up the bins after they've been emptied and make sure the porch at 44 Rosehill Road is kept neat and tidy – stare after him as he heads off down the road, guitar in hand. We thought he was a designer of some sort, they say to me. Well he is, I say – sometimes. But we pay the rent, and we are not noisy or messy, so that's all that matters really.

In early March, the band play The Escape Club in Brighton – another opportunity for an outing with Fiona and Carl. Pre-show, we go to the bar at the Metropole Hotel and stare out at the windswept sea, and the wonky old West Pier – once the posh pier, where afternoon tea dances were held, and cream teas consumed, but now closed and falling into disrepair.

+

The 'Jacob's Ladder' single does pretty well – gets radio plays, gets in to the lower reaches of the charts, and sees the band performing on various TV shows – not only on *Eastern Eye* (due to Bid's Indian heritage) but also the hip new show *The Tube*, hosted by Jools Holland, Paula Yates and Muriel Gray; plus, a few early morning kids' shows like *Saturday Superstore*, where they are introduced by Cliff Richard who pogos along nicely.

There's a second single, 'Wallflower', released – this track had been re-remixed by Ben Rogan at Power Plant studio in Willesden, where Sade was concurrently recording 'Smooth Operator'. Her producer Robin Millar had overseen 'Wallflower' as John Porter wasn't free – but the new pop-tastic mix is mostly Ben's work. 'Wallflower' – 7" and 12" versions – is released, with another lovely record sleeve designed by Foz, this time a kind of pop-art Ready Steady Go grid of twelve squares, featuring the band members juxtaposed with zebras, roses, targets, or playing cards. Ben had also mixed Foz's instrumental 'Yo Ho Ho' which appeared on the 12" 'Jacob's Ladder' single – as did 'Andiamo', which had started life in The Apaches days. You can't keep a good tune down.

The Lost Weekend album does eventually see the light of day, but it takes a frustratingly long time to come out due to record company prevarications, and the momentum seems to have been lost.

Then, in just one week in May 1985, two landmark events happen. On Sunday the 19th of May, Psychic TV curate and perform at *Thee Fabulous Feast ov Flowering Light* at Hammersmith Palais – an all-day multimedia event involving very many of our artistic associates, including Derek Jarman, Kathy Acker and The Virgin Prunes. On the 23rd, The Monochrome Set play the Electric Ballroom in Camden. Which happens to be the night that it all ends...

I'm here with my Icelandic bandmate Hilmar Örn Hilmarsson and his Reykjavik friends, including Einar Örn Benediktsson from the band Kukl, and an Icelandic poet called Johnny Triumph. Also present are Sharon D'Lugoff, drummer Dave Barbe, and filmmakers David Dawson and Akiko Hada, who work with PTV but are also Monochrome Set associates. So the clan has gathered, and no-one – least of all the rest of the band – have an inkling what Bid is about to do.

The story here is that The Monochrome Set records had done well on the indie charts, but this isn't good enough for Blanco y Negro overlords Warner Brothers, who have, they feel, invested enough in the band to demand something more than indie chart success. They want hits. They want to recoup their money. But The Monochrome Set are not Dire Straits or Simply Red, which is no bad thing in my book. It all ends in tears with Bid announcing live on stage at The Electric Ballroom that the band was splitting up, signing off with: "Rot in hell, Rob Dickins" – a jibe fired at the chairman of Warner Brothers UK.

There's a band wake afterwards at The Embassy Club – at least TMS get a good send-off, surrounded by loving friends. Although, it isn't quite the end – there are contracts to fulfil with a few more gigs here and there, including Goldsmiths College and an Oxford Summer Ball. Which feels rather odd, given that the band has decided to fold. Or that Bid has decided that he's had enough and is calling it a day, anyway.

I can understand Bid's frustration. Much lesser bands than The Monochrome Set surge ahead, building on their indie-band status into chart success with singles and album sales. TMS seem stuck at 'much admired by a select group of fans', packing out reasonably sized venues, and getting a decent amount of music press, but never going up to the next level. Bid had seen former associates like Adam Ant manage the crossover, and perhaps hoped he could too. Blanco y Negro's Mike Alway and Geoff Travis both love the band – The Monochrome Set had made records for both Mike's Cherry Red label and Geoff's Rough Trade – but parent company Warner Brothers have cast the die, making it clear that they are not going to finance a second album. *The Lost Weekend* has turned out to be a lost cause, as far as they're concerned.

It's all further complicated by Bid's recent marriage to super-fan Marion, who had pursued him relentlessly and finally nabbed her heart's desire, and is now determined that he should forge a solo career for himself. Gazing into her crystal ball – and this is not a metaphor, she really does have one, we bought them a matching pair as a wedding gift – she tells Foz that he will be very successful as a musician "but not with this band" before reiterating her belief that Bid should go it alone.

There seem to be a lot of tuneful post-punk guitar bands with a good pop sensibility who sound like they owe a debt to The Monochrome Set – and I feel that the band has never quite had the kudos it is owed. Of course, I'm biased. My life has been inextricably linked in with TMS for almost a decade. In 1976, I was co-opted by Bid and Andy into the legendary Band With No Name that eventually split into Adam and the Ants and The Monochrome Set – and I continued playing with Bid for a while when Andy absconded to join up with Adam. Andy has been the bassist in TMS since leaving The Ants, post *Dirk Wears White Sox,* in 1979; and current boyfriend Foz has been lead guitarist since the beginning of 1983 till now, mid-1985. That's almost a third of my life intertwined with the band in its various incarnations.

While Foz's commitments to The Monochrome Set ease off following Bid's dramatic announcement, mine with Psychic

The Happiest Day of Her Life - and the Most Tragic

"A JOY"

LOOK OUT FOR...

POP SEX TECHNIQUE IN MARRIAGE

NEW

THE MONOCHROME SET

Live On Stage!

This Friday Feb. 1st

University of London Union
Malet St. W.1.

It's Fun ...

... It's Fashionable

TV increase. Late summer sees an intense time of rehearsals and preparations for a big European tour. But Foz isn't totally at a loose end. Genesis invites him to come and play lead guitar on Psychic TV's cover of 'Good Vibrations', and its B-side 'Roman P' – so he's also drawn into the PTV fold. I don't know if this is with Alex Fergusson's blessing or not. Gen has a bit of a track record of pulling in other guitarists to the band. The year before I joined, he'd brought in Paul Reeson on guitar and told Alex – guitarist, songwriter and co-founder of the band – that he needed to switch to bass (although I don't hear about this until much later).

As The Monochrome Set slowly dissolves, Foz is kept busy freelancing, playing with Shock Headed Peters, alongside former Lemon Kitten Karl Blake, standing in for Dave Knight who is currently playing guitar with the other Kitten, Danielle Dax.

Hope you're keeping up here.

Shock Headed Peters are signed to Mike Alway's latest venture, él Records – goodness me, that man is everywhere all at once. Foz also does a guest appearance or two with Canadian band The Dave Howard Singers, who are often touring with Shock Headed Peters, including a very odd gig at Clouds in Preston. Dave Howard – a "This Is Not a Synthesiser" sign on the front of his AceTone organ – antagonises the sneering, suede-headed and Lacoste-clad audience by suggesting Preston could be rented out to US President Ronald Reagan as a nuclear testing ground; then offers to fight anyone in the audience who wants to take him on. Foz causes more chaos by turning everything up to full volume and blowing up the PA, and everyone eventually gets turfed off-stage by five tuxedo-clad bouncers. Suave Canadian band manager Peter Noble soothes the savage brow of the club management, gets the dough, and they all escape unscathed. Since then, Foz has dreaded seeing Preston Clouds on the tour list of any band he plays with.

He is also invited by my old friend Simon Fisher Turner – who I met during the filming of Derek Jarman's *Jubilee*, and who Foz knew through Mike Alway, his conduit to everyone and everything, it would seem – to work on Simon's first solo album, *The Bone of Desire*, playing guitar and designing the cover. Unofficially, he also has a hand in creating the soundtrack for Derek's new film *Caravaggio* (released in 1986).

Bid does indeed release a solo record this year, too. The Monochrome Set had been playing 'Reach For My Gun' and 'Love' for a while, in live sets and even on TV appearances; and Bid and Foz had done a demo of these tracks using a drum machine. Now, Bid re-records these two songs along with another called 'Sweet Chariot'. Foz does the artwork for the record sleeve, taking a psychedelic cat image by schizophrenic painter Louis Wain as inspiration for a wondrously lurid yellow-and-blue painting with a fairground font used for the lettering.

Then, there is an interesting new development when Foz acquires a Casio SK-1 keyboard, capable of sampling. Psychic TV's Fairlight cost a fortune, thousands of pounds. Carrie Booth's Yamaha DX7 cost around £1,500. But this new Casio costs Foz a mere £100. This changes everything! It's the beginning of something that will resonate down the years. Foz is no longer just a guitarist – he's learning how to create whole songs and soundscapes on his own.

This new knowledge is put to use making soundtracks to go with silent films, like FW Murnau's 1922 classic *Nosferatu: a Symphony of Horror*. Creating a soundtrack that merges with the film is a laborious business that involves feeding cables into the back of our old black-and-white portable TV. Wow, what technological miracles are now possible in our brave new world!

When invited to join Andy Warren and former Ants guitarist Johnny Bivouac in Mark Alleyne's band Mark Antony and the Centurions, Foz plays guitar but also creates backing tracks, used in their live show at the Fridge club in Brixton in late December 1985 (with Danielle Dax, as it happens). Foz samples and distorts the Glitter band's 'Rock and Roll Part 2', pairing it with a cut-up of the film *Cleopatra*, which is shown on a bank of TV monitors. The Elizabeth Taylor and Richard Burton blockbuster had long been an obsession for the Ants entourage: "She was a wide-mouthed girl..."

"The Legendary Mark Antony And The Centurions" as they billed themselves was actually – as were so many things – Andy's idea. During the last Monochrome Set tour, whenever Bid went to change guitars between songs, the leather-clad Mark would run on stage and sing whilst Andy provided accompaniment on bass. Song choices included 'We'll Meet Again' and 'Tomorrow Belongs To Me'. When TMS disbands, Andy persuades Mark to add an Antony to his name and start The Centurions. Mark designs a logo: an image of a Roman Centurion in profile, taken from a toy tambourine I'd brought back from one of my Italian trips. After a couple of gigs, it's all change again, as Foz leaves and Marco joins.

In 1986, post-Centurions, there are other adventures for Foz, further from home. In May, whilst I'm in North America, Foz heads off to Belgium with Hilmar and former PTV member David Tibet. Post PTV, Hilmar had stayed on in London, spending a lot of time at Tibet's house in Tufnell Park, mostly boozing all day, the two of them cultivating what Hilmar calls 'Byronic personae'; and having animated, if rather drunken, conversations about 1960s psychedelia, or about Aleister Crowley and the Beast's bestie, Gerald Yorke. There would be the occasional escape from this den of iniquity – which was, apparently, mostly peopled by a bunch of deadbeat drug fiends who all believed themselves to be either the reincarnation of Crowley, or a direct descendant of King Arthur who had divined the whereabouts of the lost sword Excalibur – to drink in the Sevilla Mia Drinking Club, or meet up with Catalan musician and artist Jordi Valls and sample his extensive absinthe collection.

After a few weeks of this determined debauchery comes news that Tibet has some budget from Brussels-based L.A.Y.L.A.H. Antirecords, a sub-label of Les Disques du Crépuscule run by Marc Monin – who had previously released another Psychic TV related disc, 'How to Destroy Angels', the first record by Geff Rushton (aka John Balance) and Peter Sleazy Christopherson, as Coil.

The invitation is supposedly to record a solo album, but Tibet feels quite intimidated by that idea, so drafts in Hilmar, who in turn brings in Foz. They fax through their requirements for the week in the studio (mostly a list of beers, wines and spirits they'd like provided) and head off together to Brussels.

Niki Mono, who sometimes sings with Tuxedomoon, is also on board, along with her brother Peter Paelinck, who goes by the tag Peter 77. After a couple of days staying with Niki and Peter, sightseeing and hanging out in Brussels – and drinking a fair amount of Belgian beer, I'm sure – they all head off to a recording studio in a small town nearby. The album, which they call *The Aryan Aquarians Meet Their Waterloo*, is recorded at – well yes, Waterloo. The place where the battle took place – although that historical reference now almost eclipsed by ABBA winning the Eurovision Song Contest with a tune of that name. This studio, by the way, is also where Marvin Gaye's 'Sexual

Healing' was cut in 1982, as he was living in Ostend at the time, relocating to Belgium after a serious dispute with his label Tamla Motown – and there is a whole story there, but that is told elsewhere, and not by me!

The story here is that Foz and Hilmar rather roguishly came up with the Aryan Aquarians idea as a kind of piss-take of Thee Temple ov Psychic Youth: Hilmar, following his massive falling-out with Genesis P-Orridge and his departure from Psychic TV, now being virulently anti anything and everything associated with GPO; and Foz having always been suspicious of what he saw as the cult nature of TOPY, which he felt had Nazi undertones that could be merrily parodied.

Tibet went along with it all willingly at first, but later recalled that he spent most of the time lying drinking under the mixing console whilst Hilmar and Foz made music – although his distinctive vocals most definitely feature. It's probably fair to say that the best track on it is 'My Secret Gardener' a song Foz initiated – with a nod to David Lynch's 'In Heaven', and possibly influenced by Nancy Friday's *My Secret Garden*, which is on my bookshelf – sung beautifully by Niki Mono. There's also the rousing 'Cry, Cry, Cry' ('We're the Aryan Aquarians!') and 'Bugs Bunny at Waterloo'. S&M anthem 'Dangerous' is built around the line famously used with Andy's photo on an Ants flyer: "I didn't do it I watched my body do it". 'The Aryan Aquarians Theme' is the track that is the most obviously critical of cults and where they can lead, albeit with tons of irony and humour...

Tibet later declares the LP – released as planned in 1986 by L.A.Y.L.A.H. Antirecords, then resurfacing under the auspices of Current 93 years later – as the worst record he's ever made. Although at the time, he can't have felt quite so negative about it as the music-making relationship with Hilmar and Foz continued beyond their Belgian adventure.

There's another excursion for these three in summer 1986, this time to Iceland to work with Einar and other members of Kukl – who had very recently rebranded themselves as The Sugarcubes – together with Drew and Rose McDowall, and filmmakers Akiko Hada and David Dawson. There is more to tell about this, and it will be told! Just to say here that because of delays in starting the work, and because Foz has to cut short his stay in Iceland, he doesn't get to contribute as much to the project as he'd hoped to. But he does forge a strong bond with Siggi, the Kukl/Sugarcubes drummer; and he gets on very well with Rose, so they work together on some songs, including 'Paperback Honey' and 'Crystal Days' that she later develops as a solo artist. Some of the material gets released years later by Tibet's Current 93 on an album called *Island*, although songwriting credits are a little, er, lacking.

Other than that, the friendship with Einar and co is solidified on the Icelandic trip, and there are connections made with musician Ray Shulman (of Gentle Giant fame), and engineer Mel Jefferson, that lead to Foz working with Flux of Pink Indians main-man Derek Burkett – although Derek would bristle at that title, as he always said FOPI was a collective – in a future venture called simply Flux.

Derek and Flux are very much at the core of the UK anarcho-punk movement that Psychic TV have various crossovers with, and indeed Kukl had performed with Crass and released a record or two on their label. In recent years, Crass had morphed from band to radical performance collective, making protest art that landed them in trouble, including the *Thatchergate Tapes*, a hoax recording that purported to be an accidentally overheard telephone conversation between Margaret Thatcher and Ronald Reagan. The tape was in fact edited together by Crass from real recordings. This and other wheezes got them in hot water with the Tory party, and questions were asked in Parliament. Gosh – deja vu. It's Coum Transmissions/Throbbing Gristle's "These People Are the Wreckers of Civilisation" all over again. Except that TG embraced the controversy, whereas Crass shied away. Fending off prosecutions, and feeling that they were caught up in a web of intrigue that they didn't want to contend with, the band split in 1984, with their final record release coming out in 1986.

Other people collaborating on the new Flux project (minus its Pink Indians) would include Crass associate Annie Anxiety aka Little Annie, and drummer Gordon Disneytime from The Very Things, who'd had a hit a couple of years earlier with the fabulous 'The Bushes Scream While My Daddy Prunes'. By the end of 1986, Derek has set up his new record label, One Little Indian, with Flux album *Uncarved Block*, produced by Adrian Sherwood of On-U Sound Systems fame, as its first release. He then signed up Einar and Bjork's Sugarcubes and brought them over to London to record their first album in Berry Street studio in Clerkenwell.

The following year sees Foz heading off on a late winter/ early spring tour with Derek Burkett's Flux, as they are now known – although everyone still seems to call them A Flux of Pink Indians. The music is not really his cup of tea, but he likes Derek a lot, so is happy to go along with it all. There are dates in the UK, then a substantial swathe of Europe.

Foz returns home from the tour wearing a creaky black leather coat, an enormous and cumbersome ex-military thing that was bought for him by Derek at a flea market in Amsterdam, in lieu of wages. He also got a crate of Chimay beer, which he'd acquired a taste for in Belgium the previous year. This great big heavy leather coat has replaced a shiny black PVC one that he took on a trip to Canada for Christmas 1986. It unfortunately couldn't withstand the Canadian midwinter frosts, and cracked into pieces, following a night spent on a crawl around the gay bars of Ottawa.

The Flux tour – which ended 6 March 1987, a date seared in everybody's mind as it is also the date of the Zeebrugge ferry disaster, delaying the band's journey home from Belgium – turns out to be Foz's last on-the-road experience for a couple of years.

But the music-making goes on... There is some session work for Mike Alway. There's a spell playing with Dave Barbe and Leigh Gorman post Bow Wow Wow, although that doesn't develop into anything solid. There are further guest appearances in the studio with Simon Fisher Turner, and the occasional soundtrack to work on.

Mostly, Foz is biding his time, as what he wants most of all is to find a singer to work with, rather than just making instrumental music. That will happen – but not quite yet.

THE FABULOUS FEAST
OF FLOWERING LIGHT

No more darkness and depression. We need colour!
We need a new psychedelia! We need hyperdelia!

All these monochrome people who turn up at Psychic TV gigs, dressed head-to-toe in black, with white skin that hardly ever sees the light of day. People who slavishly follow the Temple ov Psychic Youth directive. I'm fed up with all this colourless death-cult stuff, says Genesis P-Orridge, with absolutely no sense of irony, given that this dark and dirgy aesthetic was his baby, a natural progression from Throbbing Gristle, continuing into Psychic TV.

No more darkness and depression. We need colour! We need a new psychedelia! We need hyperdelia!

Let's make a show – a colourful show. Let's invite all our friends to join us. And so *Thee Fabulous Feast ov Flowering Light* is born.

A fluorescent pink poster features lots of smiley little Buddha babies outlined in gold. Hand-painted midnight blue lettering announces the line-up for the eight-hour event at Hammersmith Palais. Music from us – Psychic TV – and a whole host of other renegade sound-makers, including Irish post-punk pagans the Virgin Prunes, electronic experimenters Zahgurim, an interesting-looking new band called The Simonics, Bee's outfit The Process, and Icelandic friend Einar Örn Benediktsson with his band Kukl. There's also going to be an appearance by New York-based writer Kathy Acker, who'll be reading from her recently-published book, *Blood and Guts in High School*. There will be films by John Maybury and Derek Jarman, curated by Akiko Hada and David Dawson, with Akiko also responsible for documenting the day's events; and Derek has also designed and painted the set for a dance piece called *Mouth of the Night*, choreographed by Micha Bergese for MANTIS dance company.

The music for *Mouth of the Night* has been composed by Psychic TV and was recorded at Paradise Studios in Chiswick earlier in the year – mostly the work of the band's ferociously talented keyboard player Hilmar Örn Hilmarsson, working with producer Danny Hyde, using holographic sound techniques and a combination of frighteningly fancy synthesisers, including a rare and very expensive Fairlight, and other machinery that made me glad I was a drummer and thus didn't even need to try to understand how it all worked. I just hit things, that's my job. ("All bands should have female drummers," says Hilmar – who is sometimes a drummer, too.) Hilmar tells me later that he was unfamiliar with the Fairlight, as almost nobody had one at the time, but on day one had taken the manual from the studio, read and ingested it overnight, and returned the next day a Fairlight expert! Hilmar had first heard of Psychic TV through his friend Einar, who had given him a copy of *Force the Hand of Chance;* the pair going on to co-organise the PTV

Official — PTV H.Smith

I LIKE YOU
Just Like ARCADIA
Good STAR
Roman P
UN CLEAN
BABY'S Gone AWAY
Southern Comfort
WE Kiss
STAR LITE MINE
OU POWER

gig in Reykjavik in December 1983, a joint headline with Kukl. Hilmar's first live appearance with Psychic TV was at Heaven in London on 23 December 1984, just before I joined. He'd landed in the UK just days before the gig, having spent his time on the plane learning songs – and he has been an intrinsic part of the band since.

The Fabulous Feast is going to launch an exciting new line-up for Psychic TV with Hilmar, me, bass player Mouse, and performance art prankster Monte Cazazza 'on guitar' announced as the new members who are joining the core of Genesis P-Orridge, singer, lyricist and manifesto-writer; and Alex Fergusson, the band's lead guitarist, songwriter and co-founder. Although unannounced, Drew McDowall is a vital part of the new line-up, taking over on tapes and effects; and Drew's wife Rose McDowall (half of Strawberry Switchblade) is also on board as a backing vocalist.

Actually, it's not that new a grouping: we've been working together for quite a few months now: meeting up, rehearsing, and – post *Mouth of the Night* – recording a brand new album, provisionally called *Thee Starlit Mire*, which is incidentally the sub-title for the Hammersmith Palais event (just in case anyone was worried that everything had gone completely sunshine and flowers for PTV). We are also doing a warm-up gig with the full band at Brighton's Zap Club. Alex is placed in charge of rehearsals for the new line-up, while Monte is in charge of all things related to the Temple network and what is rather vaguely dubbed 'research'.

Throughout the early months of the year, we've been readying ourselves for the launch onto the world via the many live events being planned – Gen wants there to be a whole run of Fabulous Feasts, as well as a UK and European tour later in the year – but also for the album recording dates.

+

So, here I am – but how did I get here?

The story goes back to the late 1970s, when I used to hang out with Genesis P-Orridge at 50 Beck Road in Hackney – his home, but also the HQ for Throbbing Gristle. It was theoretically also the home of Cosey Fanni Tutti, but she rarely seemed to be there – spending a lot of her time with fellow band member Chris Carter. Throbbing Gristle were pulling apart, with new ventures on the horizon. Chris and Cosey would soon be a living together/working together unit.

Gen has started talking about a thing he's going to do with Peter Christopherson, aka Sleazy – the fourth TG member. It's called Psychic TV and is envisaged as a radical pirate TV station that will show sound-and-vision pieces made by Gen and Sleazy, along with other friends and collaborators.

Meanwhile, Gen is also trying out some ideas with guitarist Alex Fergusson, formerly of Alternative TV. They're writing songs together, and looking at ways of getting them out into the world. One of these is a synth-pop song called 'Softness' – which they want to submit for consideration as a European Song Contest entry – and I'm invited in to do a breathy spoken-word vocal, à la Jane Birkin.

We end up also creating another very poppy track called 'I Confess', which was originally planned for the B-side, but the tracks get swapped over, and 'I Confess' becomes the A-side. It's released on Industrial Records – confounding people's expectations of the label, which is better known as the home of 'industrial music for industrial people'. Although 1980 also sees the label release jazz classic 'Stormy Weather' sung by Elisabeth Welch, who had performed it with magnificent aplomb in the finale of Derek Jarman's *The Tempest*.

Yep, there are changes a-foot – we are entering the post-Industrial era.

There are other songs emerging from the pen of Gen and Alex – quite 1960s-sounding, definitely somewhere on the psychedelic spectrum, and very different to Throbbing Gristle. Let's form a band, Gen says. You've always been my favourite drummer, Max, and Alex has always been my favourite guitarist...

I decline – because somehow alarm bells are ringing. It's just a gut feeling, but I go with it.

A year goes by, TG disbands, and I learn that Gen and Alex have indeed formed a band. But surprisingly, Sleazy is in it too, and it's called Psychic TV. So the proposed two new ventures have merged into one. The intention was for Psychic TV to be a video group that does music rather than a music group which makes videos. Or at least, that's how Sleazy saw it.

On another Beck Road visit, Gen says he wants me to walk around the corner with him to the supermarket on the Broadway. He wants to show me something. So off we trot to Tesco's where Gen points out the check-out girl, who surely can't be older than 15. This is Paula, says Gen,

Next thing I know, Paula is going out with Gen, and also in the band, playing percussion.

Psychic TV make their live debut in October 1982 as a part of the *William Burroughs' Final Academy* tour, and a month later the band's debut album, *Force the Hand of Chance*, is released by Some Bizzare Records, with a very sweet single, 'Just Drifting' taken from it – a song that bears the mark of Alex and Gen's 1960s pop-inspired songwriting collaboration.

A second album, *Dreams Less Sweet*, is released in 1983. Gen gives me cassette copies of both of these – cassettes are very much the medium of the moment. C30, C60, C90 go!

Between that 1982 debut and my joining Psychic TV in early 1985, there's quite a bit of coming and going. People coming, and then going, include Geff Rushton, aka John Balance – I knew him as the sweet young editor of *Stabmental* fanzine, who had been very supportive of my former band, Rema Rema. Geff, wearing his *Stabmental* hat, had come to the recording of TG's final album, *Heathen Earth*, where he'd palled up with Sleazy. Marc Almond of Soft Cell had joined PTV as a guest singer; and David Tibet was involved too, his PTV stint concurrent with a new project which he calls Current 93, with a nod towards dear old Aleister Crowley. Composer and arranger Andrew Poppy had been brought on board to create beautiful John Barry-inspired orchestral parts for the songs. This is Gen's forte, really – finding people and persuading them to contribute their know-how to the Psychic TV project.

Somewhere along the way, Geff and Sleazy become partners in love and life, leaving Psychic TV after *Dreams Less Sweet*. Geff had already started work on a music project called Coil, and now Sleazy joins him in that venture. John Gosling then joined PTV. He also worked under the name Zos Kia, and later also collaborates with Coil. It's a very loose, incestuous musical circle – and it's hard to keep up with all the changes. The beautiful Bee (aka Paul Hampshire) is kind-of involved, although I'm not quite sure if he's an actual band member – he looks great in the photos, though. There are some people who think PTV would have had far more chance as a high-flying psychedelic pop group with Bee as lead singer! In 1984, Paul Reeson is brought in on guitar, having previously worked with PTV as a graphic designer – he created the template for those classic black, red and white live album covers.

But come the new year, 1985, Gen wants to start afresh. Paula is about to have a second baby – they already have a two-

BRIAN JONES

‡

Died For Your Sins

year-old called Caresse – and won't be part of the band for now. Gen's latest idea, that he repeats often, is to bring together all the musicians he most admires, from wherever they might be, to join him and Alex in a line-up to wow the world. So, long-time artistic collaborator Monte Cazazza is here from the USA, Hilmar from Iceland, Drew and Rose McDowall from Scotland – Glasgow, where Alex also hails from – and me and Mouse from London. An international ensemble.

After meetings and rehearsals through February, we are booked in for the album recording dates at DJM studios in Holborn from the 13th to the 20th March.

I'm not needed for the first couple of days in the studio, earmarked for working on 'Godstar', which has already had its backing track laid down. I'm not sure who has played on it, and I'm rather hoping I'll get the chance to re-record the drums – in rehearsals, I've been working on giving the track a punchier and more raw and earthy feel. But that doesn't happen, it stays as-is. The song is an homage to Rolling Stones founder and guitarist Brian Jones. His death, Gen suggests, might have been murder rather than an accident – he's been interviewing people and amassing evidence.

PSYCHIC TV
GODSTAR
A Single

photograph of Brian Jones by Gerard Malanga

'Brian Jones Died For Your Sins' say the stickers on the side of the band's amps and cabs.

We're all encouraged to come into the studio anytime, regardless of whether we are on call or not: the schedule given to us by Gen and band manager Terry McLellan warns that sulking and depressive behaviour is expressly forbidden, and that mini-cab claims are to be kept to a minimum. Monte is also not needed for the first few days, but he's here too, and we do a lot of bonding over cups of tea and digestive biscuits.

I'd first met Monte sometime in the late 1970s, at 50 Beck Road. I spent a lot of time hanging out there between 1977 and 1982, often after a booking at one of the East End pubs that employed me as an 'exotic dancer', as it was euphemistically called. "I do enjoy thee tea and pussy afternoons" Gen had said in a letter he'd sent me. Sometimes Monte was there, and sometimes he wasn't. He went back and forth between London and California.

I remember Monte's fabulous wolfish grin and famously wicked sense of humour. I'd been a bit nervous around him at first, frightened almost. His reputation preceded him, and he exuded a dangerous energy. And my God, he had a sharp tongue, pouncing on anything he saw as misinformed or untruthful. But I soon learnt that his extreme cynicism about almost everything – politics, art, music, popular culture – actually came from a deep love and concern. He's a gentle soul, despite his wild reputation and sometimes-jagged exterior.

On one of his London trips, Monte brought his then-girlfriend, Tana Emmolo, around to my home at 69 Exhibition Road. When was that? Probably around the time I made 'I Confess' – 1979 or 1980. I liked Tana – a strong, vibrant woman, a filmmaker and occasional singer. Monte was a big fan of the

'I Confess'/'Softness' record, and of course totally sure it should be chosen as a Eurovision Song Contest entry.

Meanwhile, Monte was also making records for Industrial, often with input from Tana. There's 'To Mom on Mother's Day' (1979) and 'Something For Nobody' (1980). There'd been a live show featuring Throbbing Gristle, Leather Nun, and "international recording star Monte Cazazza" at the Scala Cinema in Tottenham Street in Soho, on leap-year-day 29 February 1980. This was an awesome event featuring a malfunctioning negative ion generator that at one point exploded with a lightning flash, startling people in the front row – who of course assumed it was a deliberate effect – and recordings from this and other Monte shows in the UK had been released as an Industrial Records Cassette. The Scala event had come just after the *Heathen Earth* recording at Martello Street, and just before 'I Confess'. Busy times for the dying days of TG and Industrial. That legendary negative ion generator was, by the way, the work of one Tony Bassett who made time machines and radionics devices that he sold in Camden Market.

So I'd known Monte for years, but now that we're both in Psychic TV, and spending more and more time together, a strong friendship develops.

We talk and talk. We talk about our favourite JG Ballard novels: *High Rise* and *Crash*, but especially *Concrete Island*. We both reckon we know the exact roundabout underneath the Westway where it's set. We marvel at the fact that when Ballard wrote *Hello America* he had never been to the USA, yet manages to parody the country's culture so perfectly. Spinning off from the *Crash* conversation, Monte tells me some harrowing stories about working as a paramedic with a Californian ambulance service. We also talk about Monte's work on the Survival Research Laboratories project with Mark Pauline, creating monstrous hybrid automata made from roadkill rabbits, and enormous metal dinosaurs that rampage around warehouse spaces, terrifying audience members. We talk about other cathartic and shamanistic performance events – I tell Monte about the Bow Gamelan Ensemble, who do wild and spectacular outdoor shows in places like the old London docklands, setting off fireworks, clanging big metal bells, and smashing panes of glass to smithereens; and he tells me about this effigy-building-and-burning thing that happens on Blaker's Beach in San Francisco to mark the Summer Solstice (a year or two later it'll move to the Nevada desert and be called the Burning Man Festival). Monte also tells me all about advances in this new-fangled thing called electronic mail. The US military are finding ways to send messages between computers in far-flung places, rather than just between computers in the same building. It's going to change everything, says Monte with that famous lupine grin. Who knows where it'll all end?

Hilmar and producer Ken Thomas join us in the chat now and again, until they're anxiously called back by Gen. They've moved on now from 'Godstar' to 'Thee Starlit Mire', and although we're supposedly not needed (according to the schedule), Monte and I end up going in to improvise with percussion instruments and guitar feedback, giving the track some extra sound layers.

In subsequent days, we lay down three more tracks. 'Being Lost' has a strong 1960s vibe, seemingly influenced by the Beach Boys and Phil Spector's Wall of Sound, with a mid-tempo on-beat drum rhythm. There are lots of ascending "ah-ah-aaahs" in the backing vocals, a few "bom-bom-boms" and even a recurring "schloop-schloop". The next one, 'She Was Surprised' is a synth-pop number that will eventually include vocals by Caresse, Gen and Paula's little daughter. It will never be my favourite track, but still – it comes out OK.

But now it's time to record my absolute favourite, 'Just Like Arcadia'. I've given Arcadia a nice twisting-the-night-away double-then-single snare-beat, and Ken beefs up the drum sound very nicely, emphasising the crisp, metallic snare. And it's such a lovely tune – Alex at his best. Gen's lead vocal, given a slightly warped effect, merges very well with Rose's angelic backing vocals. Ken's production on this one is absolutely magical.

Next up, 'We Kiss' – another favourite song, one of Gen and Alex's pretty and gentle psychedelic pop numbers. I'd been to the drum shop and bought some new toys, including a couple of large good-quality Zildjian cymbals and some very nice wooden beaters, which are great for this track. 'We Kiss' has a sturdy beat but simultaneously a lovely floaty feel, the tom-tom drums and spacey cymbals working well with Hilmar's multi-layered keyboard and synth lines.

So that's it for now, as far as recording goes. Ken and Hilmar, who have become best buddies, head off to Jacob Studios in Surrey to work together on the new Laibach album. Gen goes off to Rouen to meet up with the Sordide Sentimental people. This small but perfectly formed label puts out beautifully packaged vinyl records, which have included TG's 'We Hate You (Little Girls)', Psychic TV's 'Roman P'/ 'Neurology', and Monte's 'Stairway To Hell' backed with 'Sex Is No Emergency' – featuring a great Monte collage inside, a typical mix of porn and butchery, and a beautiful photo on the back cover (by Linda Burdick) of a naked and dramatically-lit Monte.

Gen leaves Alex in charge, with a set of instructions for tasks to be completed whilst he's gone. I meet with Alex at the usual band gathering place – Battista cafe on Charing Cross Road – to go through some admin stuff, and we end up going to the Screen on the Green to see the new Terry Gilliam film, *Brazil,* a dystopian romp that film critic Pauline Kael describes as "a melancholy, joke-ridden view of the horribleness of where we are now and the worse horribleness of where we are heading". I seem to have hardly spent any time with Alex since joining the band, and it's good to do something together, although I do come out of the cinema quaking. Monty Python this ain't!

Back from Rouen, Gen asks me to help with developing visual imagery for the new direction the band is taking – branding, I suppose we could call it. I start in on some ideas, inspired by the date that the *Fabulous Feast* will take place – 19 May, on the cusp of Gemini. I was born on the 21st of May, so I'm very interested in the astrological indications. I muse on the notion of the heavenly twins, the whole self divided into two halves, masculine and feminine. I start thinking around birds as aspects of the feminine spirit: owls, swans, hawks. I think of the bird masks in *The Story of O* and sketch some hawkish women. For the masculine element, there are goats, horses, wolves and werewolves. I draw pictures of twins joined at the hip with human top halves and horse lower halves, the word 'pandrogynous' written next to the pencil sketches. But in the end, Gen goes with a kind of hermaphrodite satyr Pan playing a violin, rather than my conjoined twin centaur. The press release announces the new(ish) line-up, and the plans for the Fab Feast: "Our aim is wakefulness, our enemy is dreamless sleep."

A T-shirt image is also needed for the show merchandise. We talk through possibilities, and decide on a kind of new take on Ostara, pagan goddess, fertility symbol and herald of spring. Gen wants me to be the model. Into the infamous Beck Road Nursery we go. I strip off and kneel, posed holding a giant

"FABULOUS FEAST OF FLOWERING LIGHT"   1985
     (THE STARLIT MIRE)

PSYCHIC TV announce two special events this week. <u>First</u> they have now confirmed their new line-up. The new members are MAX- drummer (formerly of The Weekend Swingers and REMA REMA), MOUSE- Bass Guitar (formerly with Bob of BLOOD & ROSES), MONTE CAZAZZA - Guitar (formerly with Himself & FACTRIX) and HILMAR ORN HILMARSSON - Keyboards, Drummer (formerly with THEYR in Iceland). This line-up will be featured for the first time at the day long PTV organised event in May along with a full stage show. (see enclosed photo of 4 new PTV members).

<u>Second</u>: PSYCHIC TV have confirmed the special guests for their show at the HAMMERSMITH PALAIS on SUNDAY 19th MAY 1985. Tickets will be £4 in advance and £5 on the door. The event begins at 2pm.

SPECIAL GUESTS will be <u>THE VIRGIN PRUNES</u> and <u>MICHA BERGESE'S MANTIS DANCE COMPANY</u>.

It will be the first LONDON show in over a year for the VIRGIN PRUNES. Micha Bergese (who played lead role in the film "COMPANY OF WOLVES). His MANTIS Dance Company will perform exerpts from the highly acclaimed Ballet "MOUTH OF THE NIGHT" (Music by Psychic TV- Set by Derek JARMAN).

Other Artists appearing so far confirmed for this Day Long Event are:- KUKL (from ICELAND); THE SIMONICS ; THE WEEDS ; BEE THE PROCESS ; ZAGURHIM ; DEATH AND BEAUTY FOUNDATION ; THE WAKING ROOM.

There will be a mixed media reading by KATHY ACKER.

Film and video projections will be supervised by DAVID DAWSON AND ARIKO HADA. Works by JOHN MAYBURY and DEREK JARMAN will be featured. There will also be video-scratch interludes by CLAUDE BESSY'S CHURCH OF THE CATHODE RAY TUBE (of Hacienda Infamy).

If that doesn't seem to be enough, further acts will be announced. See you there, with or without flowers in your hair!

2323232323232323232323232323232323232323232323232323232323232323232323232323

psychic cross. Snap, crackle, pop and there's a Polaroid. There's no naughty business: Gen and I had vowed years ago that our relationship would remain platonic. Back in 1980, when we were making the 'I Confess'/'Softness' single we'd acknowledged our mutual attraction and appreciation of each other, and decided that we'd keep sex out of the relationship. We then said that if we were both still on this earth, we'd consummate our relationship on Gen's 70th birthday. Fast forward four decades: the now-pandrogynous Genesis Breyer P-Orridge dies in March 2020, a week or so after their 70th birthday. I'll say no more.

But right now, here we are in the Nursery, with a look in Gen's eye that suggests that he might perhaps be changing his mind about that vow. The moment passes, I get dressed, and out we go. Hilmar and Monte are standing outside the door, looking like a couple of naughty schoolboys. We couldn't help ourselves, they say – we really wanted to know what was happening. They approve of the Polaroids, and congratulate Gen on his self-restraint...

The photos are given to artist Val Denham, who is doing the design for the T-shirt, as well as performing at the Feast with their band, Death and Beauty Foundation. Val converts the photo image into a kind of cartoony Max flower maiden, all zingy dayglo pinks and greens and yellows, and voilà – we have a T-shirt. When it goes on sale, it's with the tag-line "A rebirth, a flowering of the TOPY ideal, and a looking to the future, aware of the past... Let's discipline ourselves into colours". That's quite a lot of work for one T-shirt.

April sees a few more recording and mixing dates at DJM, with a definitive version of the cathartic and earthy 'Southern Comfort' yet to be laid down, and much mixing of all the other tracks needed, which is mostly down to Ken, Hilmar, Alex and Gen. Mouse usually only comes in when she's needed;

or comes in and sits reading poetry on the sofa in the corner. Rose comes in occasionally to record her backing vocals, and it's always lovely to see her, but she isn't there a lot of the time as she has a 7-year-old child to care for. Which leaves me and Monte to continue with our tea drinking and intense conversations. Occasionally, something stronger than tea. Wine, perhaps, or a nice single-malt whisky – Monte seems somehow to have acquired access to Dick James's personal cellar. No drugs, believe it or not. Monte doesn't even smoke cigarettes, and is vehemently anti-drugs of most kinds, especially heroin – having witnessed, when working on the ambulances, babies born addicted. It'll happen here soon, he warns. London is currently awash with heroin. And addiction itself is the biggest addiction, he says, whether it's heroin, Valium, or buying a new car every year.

Besides the studio time, there are a number of interviews with the music press – including a long one with *Sounds*, and an even longer one with Gabriella Bregman for Canadian magazine *TransFM*. Then there's this strange and extremely long filmed interview for Italian TV with an old friend of Gen's called Red Ronnie which is almost Warholian in style and ambition – the camera just rolls and rolls.

Quite a lot of the footage is of Caresse: there's Caresse talking into the mic, me feeding Caresse spaghetti, and Caresse showing the dead stuffed cat on the sideboard to camera. "Be careful with Moonshine," says Gen. "We don't want any more bits broken off." Then, there's Tanith the dog – very much alive – with a long sequence of Caresse throwing a ball for Tanith to fetch.

Ronnie is also interested in the snake in the glass tank. Her name? Isabella – Bella for short. Does she bite? Put your hand in and see, says Gen mischievously. They discuss the snake's diet. She eats rabbits. I chip in to say that one of my dance students is a zoo keeper, and I'd been taken 'backstage' in the reptile house. The keepers knock the rabbits out, banging their heads with a spade out of sight of the public, before feeding them to the snakes – you can't feed dead meat to snakes, they need things to be still alive...

Once all the shenanigans with children and animals is done, there is an interview with Gen, me, Hilmar and Monte.

First the focus is on Gen, who shares his modest hopes for the new incarnation of PTV: "We're trying to set up a worldwide network," he says, "events everywhere, publications, books, films... to put pressure on the culture, and ultimately trigger a new stage of evolution for human beings."

Is Gen still interested in Charles Manson and Gary Gilmore, Ronnie wants to know.

"No! I'm interested in Brian Jones! Because he was the scapegoat, the sacrificial goat, and so am I," says Gen, telling Ronnie that the new single 'Godstar' will be out on 13 May – although as it happens, the release will be delayed – and that a video is being made to go with it. This is being directed by longterm PTV associate Akiko Hada.

"We're having a party!" I say as Monte comes into the room, smiling at Caresse dancing wildly in the middle.

"I'll sit with the girl in the party dress, then" he says as he squeezes in on the sofa, referring to my 50s frock decorated with musical notes and dancing figures. "Party, party!" chants Caresse. Monte is asked about his views on America, and why he spends so much time in the UK.

"Are you un-American?" asks Ronnie.

"Compared to most Americans," he replies.

"In what ways?" Ronnie asks.

"He has a brain!" I say.

"I have a brain," says Monte with the trademark grin, "And you're not allowed to think in America. I mean, just look at who we've got for a president. Ronald Reagan, a brainless actor."

"So, now you're in Psychic TV?"

"I'm the incorrigible part of Psychic TV."

"He's our Sid Vicious," says Gen.

"But I'm here and he's not!" Another grin from Monte.

Throughout the interview, the two sides of Monte alternate. The Trickster has a piercing look, a wide grin, and an almost-camp delivery. The Bleeding-Hearted Lover has a much softer expression and a serious tone.

The Trickster talks about how dreadful New York is. We need some population control, we should poison the Kool-Aid in the supermarkets, or drop a bomb on the city. "I'd do it," he says. "Maybe we need No New York. They don't like me, and I don't like them."

The Lover steps up when talking about the current state of the USA in general: "Reagan got elected by a massive majority, and so many young people voted for him.

The scale of the problem is so big – it's like trying to kill millions of flies with one fly-swatter." As for the bland TV reportage on the Iran-Iraq war. "We are not told the truth. They learnt their lesson from the Vietnam War. Despite having satellites that can watch everything going on, we're not told what's happening. They want people to have the least amount of access to information as possible."

As this morphs into a discussion of the Cold War and the Bomb, back comes the Trickster:

"I don't care about the Bomb. I don't care if they drop it or don't drop it. It'll all be over in a flash. I won't be here. It doesn't scare me. They just use all that to scare people and keep them in line. Fine. I'll go push the button!"

Between the talk, there's entertainment – 'Baby's Gone Away' goes on the stereo, and we all clap along and sing as Caresse dances.

"See, it *is* a party," I say.

"Which is why you're in your party dress,' says Monte. Then, to, Ronnie, "We've gone all pop."

"But you don't look like Duran Duran," says Ronnie.

"We look better! We're the real thing!" replies Monte.

"You see what you've got here?" says Gen. "You have some of the world's most incorrigible cynics doing the most pretty and positive music possible!"

"Though I don't think anyone here wants to be a big pop star..." says Hilmar, but Monte and I both say "I do, I do!"

"I'd buy some land in the desert and build a house with no neighbours," says Monte, "so I could just do what I wanted."

"I think we can be everything," I say, "Why not be everything? Be light, be dark. Sun, moon. Pop star, cult hero. Just do everything you want to. To *not* do a pop song is as much of a restriction as anything else. If you limit yourself, you're dead. You should be free to do anything."

"So you'd like to be famous and make money?" Ronnie persists.

"Music is just one of our considerations," says Hilmar, sidetracking him nicely. "In some ways, we are much more orientated towards making visual things, and having an effect on people on a psychic level."

At this point, we bring young painter Jym Daly into the conversation, which turns to the whole question of the point of painting in the modern TV and video age. Jym is working on a new interpretation of automatic painting, creating psychedelic imagery that accesses the subconscious.

"What we're trying to do is actually change the language of culture," says Gen. "Fragment the culture, shatter it, and see what happens."

Ronnie and Gen head off into a different room to do a separate short interview with a heavily pregnant Paula. Monte and I head off out on one of our drifts through the streets of Soho and Piccadilly, eventually ending up on a bus back to Wandsworth, to join Foz for dinner. We find ourselves talking about Monte's prankster past, and those infamous 'killed a cat' stories – Monte didn't kill any cats, they were already dead. He set fire to dead cats. We decide to write a song together called 'Dead Cats Don't Swing'. We don't get round to it immediately, but three different versions eventually emerge. Monte stays the night, and the next day we all head off to the British Museum to see the mummies. Which include the dead cat mummies. Which are showing no sign of swinging.

+

There is a lot going on in the PTV camp, and the energy is high, but with some odd undertones. When he brought us all together, Gen said that he saw this new incarnation of the band as his dream team of long-term friends. But when Monte, Hilmar and I start spending a lot of time together, developing an intense three-way friendship, Genesis clearly feels threatened – because (I presume) we are each, individually, his special friends, and we are not supposed to pal up and exclude him by spending time together without him. He's perhaps also feeling the weight of family responsibility on the verge of becoming a father-of-two.

We three musketeers hang out together at the watering holes of Hackney and Soho, or go back to Wandsworth to meet up with Foz and cook great big pots of paella or noodles, all washed down with gallons of red wine. Monte and Hilmar often end up staying over, as getting from our place to anywhere north of the river is nigh on impossible after 11pm.

When Hilmar and Monte represent PTV at a film event at the Zap in Brighton – for which they create a live soundtrack behind a screen to footage that includes Monte and Tana's infamous *SXXX-80* film, described by one critic as "polymorphic sexual dysfunction as home movie" – I meet them there beforehand and we head off together to take in the sights of Britain's naughtiest seaside town. I know Brighton well, and enjoy showing my dear friends the Lanes and the Pier. We buy pink peppermint rock, race each other on the Donkey Derby, and feed two-pence pieces into the penny-pusher machines. Hilmar is pleased to discover that there is a crystal shop in the Lanes – it's a pretty new thing over here, but he is seriously into his crystals, telling us that we need to place amethyst and black tourmaline next to any electronic machinery we use (like those new-fangled computers we have in the studio), to counteract the negative emissions. Or something. It all sounds rather – well, Icelandic – to us. Monte says he'd like to live in Brighton – it's a bit like San Francisco, but more trashy, which is a good thing. I dash away early to catch a train back to my parents' house in Haywards Heath, where I'm staying for the night. Hilmar and Monte stay over in Brighton, creating chaos in their digs, and nearly burning the place down after an incident involving liquid bubblegum remover, as I later learn.

Back in London, Genesis seems to be particularly unhappy with Monte 'monopolising' me as he puts it. He knows that we've been going out and about together a lot: walking the streets of Mayfair, exploring the churches around Leicester Square and Piccadilly Circus, picnicking in St James's Park.

A strange, uneasy vibe has developed between Monte and Gen. There are lots of factors, including money – or lack of, on Monte's part, as of course none of the DJM advance for the album we're making has come his way – and there are issues around control and dictatorship, as well as the complications of the entangled personal relationships within the group. Suddenly, Monte absconds back to California, a few weeks before the Fabulous Feast, avoiding any potential big clashes. This is, by coincidence or by design, on the day that Paula gives birth to the second P-Orridge daughter, Genesse – the 22nd of April.

A letter Monte sends me not long afterwards, handwritten on the back of one his collages, says "I'm really sorry we couldn't be together... what with all the stuff within and outside of PTV". So Monte has gone, and Gen – looking sternly at me – says it's probably all for the best.

There are tensions of a different sort building, too. In rehearsals or in the recording studio, Gen makes it clear that he is boss, and that he calls the shots. But Hilmar has an immense amount of musical knowledge and skill, and has formed a deep alliance with producer Ken – we can feel the edginess in Gen when he senses that he is out of his depth.

In the week before the Fabulous Feast we play a warm-up gig at the Zap – unannounced other than to TOPY subscribers or Zap Club members, as Gen is keen that all the media and public focus is on the London event. Although the advertising has been low-key, there's a good number of people in the audience; many die-hard fans who greet the new line-up enthusiastically. It's our first live outing in this new constellation, and it feels so strange without Monte, but still – we enjoy ourselves.

+

At last the big day dawns. The 19th of May 1985. *Thee Fabulous Feast ov Flowering Light*, Hammersmith Palais, 3pm till 11pm (and not a minute over, warns manager Terry – there's a Sunday evening curfew in these parts).

All the get-ins and soundchecks have to happen early as the doors will open at 2.30pm. Psychic TV are headlining, it being our show – but we decide we'll go on stage at 8.30pm, with the Virgin Prunes ending the evening. I say "we decide" but I mean Gen. The royal "we". Genesis makes all the major decisions – which has, as noted, already ruffled some feathers in the PTV camp.

And now here we are at midday, which feels ludicrous, bringing our equipment on stage at the Hammersmith Palais for our soundcheck. Someone helps me set up my drum-kit, and Mouse is nearby, fiddling with her bass and amp. Hilmar is messing around with his bank of keyboards and synths, and Drew is sorting out a stack of cassettes that are marked up with names like 'temple monks' or 'wolves' or 'bells', and making sure his various tape players are working and connecting up to Hilmar's machinery. Guitarist Alex is chatting with his usual intense nervousness to special guest keyboard player Dave Ball (from Soft Cell, longterm PTV associates), and Rose is talking to Gen about vocal mics and effects, laughing with her usual sweet enthusiasm. The band's backing singers and 'extras' are billed as Thee Angels ov Light.

Meanwhile, the MANTIS set is arriving into the space in front of the stage. It looks like a number of oversized jigsaw pieces: odd, curved shapes embellished with lusciously thick paint in rich, deep colours: blood reds, rusts, and ochres with thick black outlines – very Derek Jarman. One stand-alone piece takes the form of a giant skull. Other sections form an expressionist landscape with the suggestion of rocks and shells and humanoid shapes. Dancers, wrapped up to stay warm in woolly leg-warmers and hats, begin slowly peeling off their layers and stretching. And here's Micha himself – a handsome man with a touch of the Nureyevs about him: perhaps it's the hair falling over his forehead and the intense eyes, not to mention the sculpted dancer's body. He is not just a famous dancer and choreographer, but also an actor: many people know him as the beautifully dark and dangerous lead in Neil Jordan's 1984 adaptation of Angela Carter's *The Company of Wolves*.

Filmmakers Akiko Hada and David Dawson are twiddling with the video players, and the multiple monitors stacked up each side of the stage bring up images of entwined human and mannequin bodies, hands sliding over hands, and close-ups of disembodied mouths – this is John Maybury's *Unclean* video. Then, there's Derek Jarman's *Catalan*, made the year before in collaboration with artist and musician Jordi Valls: a surreal mini-masterpiece featuring Madonna-and-child shots in eery juxtaposition with burnt-out cars, broken bodies, burning crosses and black-hooded penitents that look disturbingly like Ku Klux Klan members. Both of these, and other videos shown, have soundtracks by PTV. They'll play for the first hour, and at intervals throughout, but will also be shown when we're onstage. Are they accompanying us, or are we accompanying them? Who knows.

Soundcheck done, set-ups completed, we head off out into the spring sunshine to get some lunch. It's odd doing daytime events. I then split off from the others to meet up with Foz, who is just arriving back from a tour with The Monochrome Set. When we come back to Hammersmith Palais, Einar's band Kukl are about to start playing.

They have an interesting lead singer – a little pixie girl who hops and skips around the stage and whoops and squeals into the mic in a wondrous way. Bjork is her name.

I'd first met Einar a few weeks earlier – he's doing Media Studies at Central London Poly, and is renting a room in Stoke Newington that has become a refuge for exiled Icelandic artists. When Hilmar came over to join Psychic TV, he asked Einar if he could sleep on his floor for a few days, and stayed a couple of months. Other regulars include the poet and would-be novelist Sjón, who I don't realise is called Sjón until many years later as he's introduced to us as Johnny Triumph, on account of the leather belt with a big chrome Triumph insignia that he wears. Now Einar's Kukl bandmates are here in London too. Surely they're not all sleeping on his floor? With Foz away on tour, leaving me with time on my hands, Hilmar had taken me to Stoke Newington to meet up with Einar and friends. We'd gone to a nice Stokie pub with bookshelves lining the walls, eaten in a restaurant called Spices, and then gone back to Einar's room for a nightcap – where Hilmar had (inevitably) fallen asleep on Einar's bed, with Bjork at his head and me at his feet, and Einar wondering where he might squeeze in.

But now, here at the Hammersmith Palais, I learn that not only are the Icelandic crew nice people who are fun to be around, Kukl are truly something special: the rhythm section a post-punk powerhouse of relentless drumming and heavy bass, with jangly guitar and psychedelic keyboards weaving through, and Einar's strident trumpet lines cutting above it all. I mean, a trumpet-playing punk, who'd have imagined? Then there's the vocals from pixie-girl Bjork, who looks about 12, but has an extraordinary vocal range and style, her voice dipping up and down and around, veering from horror movie screams to breathy prayers, like a mutant merging of Diamanda Galás and

Ari from The Slits. Einar sings on some songs too, which gives it another dimension. They go well together. It all sounds like a score to an experimental Gothic movie yet to be made. They'll go far, I think to myself – which ends up being half true.

I also manage to see Kathy Acker, who has carved a niche for herself as the new queen of transgressive American literature, exploring a cut-up and collaged approach that has echoes of Uncle Bill Burroughs. *Blood and Guts in High School* is a mash-up of dream-diaries, poetry and a candid, free-flowing prose style, exploring childhood abuse, sexual addiction, abortion and prostitution. She's reading us a section about garbage and rats and landlords burning down slum houses to get the insurance. You might think sitting on the edge of the stage reading from a book, in between sets from wild and noisy music makers, might not work too well – but it does. People are entranced and give her words their full attention.

Now it's almost time for us to go on. I go backstage to hang out with my bandmates. Gen is in a very good mood – he's happy with how it's all going. He has encouraged us all to dress as colourfully as possible, excited to be challenging people's expectations of PTV. We are the future, he says. The new Children of the Revolution. Hilmar and I have a quiet moment in a corner, voicing how much we miss Monte and how we wish he was here. With us in spirit, we agree. Drew smiles over at us. And off we go, to take our places on that big old Hammersmith Palais stage.

We start with a slightly ramshackle version of 'I Like You', which goes into a run of psychedelic pop numbers that bring Alex's chirpy songwriting to the fore. First, 'Just Like Arcadia', a song I've always loved playing. Rose's sweet vocals on this pretty little song sound almost Country and Western tonight. Which is not as off-piste as that might sound, as her band Strawberry Switchblade have done a great cover of Dolly Parton's 'Jolene'. Then comes 'Godstar' – the would-be breakthrough hit that Gen sees as the flagship song for this particular incarnation of PTV. It all goes a bit out of tune, but never mind – Gen sings it with great gusto. 'Roman P' is a cheery sounding ditty, the upbeat vibe belying the fact that it's about Roman Polanski and the murder of his pregnant wife, Sharon Tate, by Charles Manson and his Family. Time for something a bit more tribal – 'Unclean', which gives Gen an opportunity for some shamanic chanting, the vocal weaving around a relentless drumbeat and some neat synth and keyboard sounds from Hilmar. Two more pretty, poppy numbers, 'Baby's Gone Away' and 'We Kiss', are sandwiched around the orgy of howling that is 'Southern Comfort', in which Drew's wolf tapes try hard to compete with wolf man GPO's live howls. There's more noise-music with 'Thee Starlit Mire', which is the working title of the album we've recently recorded, then a celebratory rendition of 'Ov Power', an anthem to female sexuality.

Gen is pleased with our set but, looking out into the crowd as we walk offstage, says he is disappointed that so many of the audience members are still – he can hardly believe it – dressed in gloomy old black clothes. Hopefully they've all bought their Fabulous Feast T-shirts and will be decked out in glorious dayglo at the next gig.

+

But when will that next gig be? Gen is still saying that he wants to have a whole series of Fabulous Feasts, but nothing solid is materialising. The focus switches to rehearsing and recording, and doing all the PR related to the launch of the single,

'Godstar', originally planned for a May release to coincide with the Hammersmith event, with an album supposedly to follow soon after. We do a photo session for the single with Gered Mankowitz, the person who'd taken the iconic Brian Jones shot we're using for the cover of 'Godstar'. Although Paula isn't currently playing in the band, she comes along for the shoot, and Caresse runs round us wildly whilst it's happening, and gets herself included too – although when we see the contact sheet we realise that in a lot of the shots, Caresse is sitting there in a T-shirt and no knickers so that rules those out. In early June, Godstar gets remixed – but there's still no release date.

Meanwhile, life goes on.

By June, I've given up work at one of the dance schools – freeing up more time for Psychic TV, and more time for outings with friends. The Fridge re-opens in a bigger venue in Brixton, and the opening party sees a mighty gathering of the clan: guests include me and Foz, Andy, Marco, Hilmar and Einar and a posse of Icelanders, Ted and Lynn, Mark Alleyne and his girlfriend Kay.

Gabriella returns from Italy to England, arriving at Victoria on the boat-train from Dover. We take her, along with Hilmar, to the Alice in Wonderland psychedelic night at Gossips. We've also, via Hilmar, befriended former Psychic TV member David Tibet. In various combinations, we down spirits in The Spice of Life at Cambridge Circus, go dancing at the Wag Club on Wardour Street, and eat Chinese meals at the Chang Mang Mai in Lisle Street. Foz and Hilmar are very taken with the name of this restaurant. It means the Great Big Green Duck – but it could also mean The Really Small Green Duck. Apparently, the literal translation is "a green duck of extraordinary and remarkable size" – which could go either way, I suppose. This dissection of language goes on for hours – long after we've dissected and eaten the duck itself.

On one occasion we're joined here by Kathy Acker. I'd assumed she'd travelled over from New York for *Thee Fabulous Feast ov Flowering Light*, but she's living here in London at the moment, she tells us. Between Foz and Hilmar and their heated discussions on ducks, and Kathy loudly critiquing everything that moves and telling us all about her new show *Lulu Unchained*, an experimental interpretation of Berg's opera *Lulu*, which is being staged at the ICA in early July, we're attracting quite a lot of attention in this tiny restaurant. I think the staff are quite pleased when we leave.

Back at Beck Road a couple of days later, Gen tries to teach me how to manage the mail-order Temple of Psychic Youth stuff – I think Paula is finding it all too much with a toddler and a new baby in tow, and Monte has left, so another administrator is needed. I'm told all about the TOPY 'application process'. Temple initiates have to send in three samples of bodily fluids – blood, saliva and semen – but I forget to ask what female applicants need to send in place of semen. Cervical smears? Menstrual blood? I never find out as there aren't any missives from women in the mail box today. I do just one afternoon of posting out newsletters and whatever, then tell Gen that I'm happy to do press and PR stuff for Psychic TV, but don't have much interest in TOPY, and admin is not my forte. So I get off the hook, and am not sure who then does it.

Wearing my PR hat, I help to arrange press interviews, draft news releases, and nip back and forth to Walkerprint delivering artwork and collecting postcards featuring dear old Brian Jones, which are advertising the single's imminent release (soon! soon!).

In July I head off for a holiday in Italy with the Pirronis – but get summoned back early by Gen, as I'm needed for the next round of PTV rehearsals, booked in for the second half of August and first half of September. Why that means I need to be back by the end of July, I don't know – but I do as I'm told and take a flight back from Milan, leaving my luggage for Dino and Bruna to bring back in the car.

Back in Blighty, there are band meetings at Battista and visits to the drum shop across the road in Denmark Street to buy new sticks and drum skins. And being back earlier than planned means I can go with my mum to see Torvill and Dean's ice skating extravaganza at Wembley Arena in early August. I find myself thinking of JG Ballard's 'Answers to a Questionnaire', featured in *Ambit* magazine – a short story in the format of 100 answers to unseen questions, a number of which reference ice-skating in general and Torvill and Dean in particular. I must tell Monte, I think...

The letters to and from Monte come in quick succession: "So how is 'Godstar' coming along and when are all of you going to turn into big superstars so I can watch you on MTV?" he says, going on to add "No, Gen hasn't written so I don't know what is really going on; and I guess he is still mad at me or whatever. I wrote him twice but no real reply – so there's nothing I can do." But then it gets a bit darker. "I've ripped the telephone out of my wall as I didn't want to converse with a single person, and threw my instruments in the closet since I returned. And if I'm lucky I'll never have to touch them again for the rest of my life." Of course, I call – and he now has the phone plugged back in and is in a much cheerier mood. It is how things are – how he is. "How is everyone?" he says, asking that I especially send his love to "that old rascal Hilmar", then going on to joke about Caresse and Genesse forming a band. "I'll manage them. Look out Pointer Sisters, it's the P'Orridge Sisters."

Mid-August and we start rehearsing in earnest. We're no longer working at DJM – there seems to be something odd going down with them, although I'm not sure what, and Gen isn't very forthcoming – and are based back at Martello Street, the studio in Hackney which Gen has had since the TG days.

And what are we rehearsing for now? A tour! A proper full-on European tour in the autumn, being booked right now – plus, hopefully, a smaller UK tour, yet to be confirmed.

Rehearsals are intense, but the energy is good, and we're doing a lot of band bonding over meals at our new favourite restaurant, The Olive Tree on Wardour Street, which boasts 'Middle Eastern and Vegetarian Specialties'; or get-togethers at my flat in Wandsworth, or Mouse's in Nettleton Road in New Cross. We rarely meet up at Beck Road – I think Gen, Paula and kids are temporarily staying in Stamford Hill, although I don't know why.

At the end of August, we head off en masse to the October Gallery, to see a selection of films made by William Burroughs, Brion Gysin et al, which include *Towers Open Fire*, and *Bill and Tony* (the Tony in question being cinematographer Antony Balch). In early September, I go with Gen and Alex to meet someone called Steve Angel at Utopia in Chalcott Street in Camden, to cut the single. So we're finally getting there with 'Godstar'.

But as for live shows, a number of planned gigs haven't materialised. The Shaw Theatre in London had been mooted, along with other UK dates, but as it happens our only outing is to the Northern College of Music in Manchester on the 18th of September. We play well – one of our meandering, atmospheric sets – and are greeted and lauded by Tony Wilson and Martin Hannett of Factory Records, and afterwards taken to the Hacienda, with various members of A Certain Ratio in tow, to dance the night away.

This is followed by another evening at October Gallery, this time a PTV special. We're showing films – *Terminus*, *Soul*

Eater, Catalan and others – and talking about our work, but we don't play live.

Now, all the focus is on the upcoming European tour. We script the show, discuss travel plans, meet the press, pack up the gear.

A few days before our 11th October departure, I collect my new leather trousers from Michaelle. She's suggested putting in a zip that goes from the front of the waistband right round to the back. Handy for taking a pee by the side of the road when on tour, we agree.

I'm all ready for the big adventure.

EUROPE ENDLESS
(LIFE IS TIMELESS)

We arrive two hours late, and weave our way in
through the audience, carrying the gear aloft.
We manage to lose a drum somewhere along the way.

Europe, lots of it. We'd left Hackney at 3pm Friday; it's now 1pm Saturday and we've just reached the Italian border. I feel tired, but I'm sure Andrew, who's driving the van, is more tired.

First leg: London to Dover, then a ferry from Dover to Calais. It's a chilly autumn evening, and we've wrapped up well. We drink Campari and play cards, looking out over the railings at the wake of frothy sea as we wave goodbye to those famous white cliffs, leaving old Blighty behind.

Half-past France, as John Cale would have it, I'm snuggled down under a blanket in the back of the van, drinking whisky with Gen and Hilmar. Ever deeper darkness as we motor through the night. There's a stop at a service station where we see rows and rows of sleeping lorries, scuttling mice, and a sliver of waning crescent moon in a clear sky. Then, all back in the van. At one point, I poke my head out of the blanket for long enough to ask where we are. Lyons, apparently. Then, somewhere else that sounds like Cherbourg – but it can't be that, as that's back by the coast, and we are most definitely inland. Mountains are looming. We go through a tunnel underneath those mountains, and that seems endless. When we emerge, the sun is high in the sky and we are close to the Italian border. We cross over with no bother, flirting merrily with the customs officers, who hardly glance at our passports, and don't even bother to look at the ridiculously long carnet forms documenting not only every instrument and piece of equipment but also every single spare string and screw.

We stop to eat – I'm not really sure if this is breakfast or lunch, but what does it matter, it's food. The restaurant owner looks over slightly warily as we tumble out of the van and come through his door. Seven people. Some wearing leathers with studded belts and wrist bands and chunky silver jewellery. Some wearing shapeless Icelandic jumpers. Some wearing cowboy boots. Some with dyed jet-black hair. Some with heads that are partly shaved, with a bunch of rats' tails hanging down at the back. Some with nose piercings and ear piercings (and cock piercings, but at least he can't see those). Some with black astrological symbols tattooed on their muscly bare arms. Some wearing sweatshirts with seven-pointed stars or strange triple-barred crosses on them. We are Psychic TV on tour.

It's warm and sunny – October, but it's T-shirt weather here – and after eating we take photos posing with the Alps as a backdrop. Some of us head off on a short walk down the road, and – somehow, due to Alex's inbuilt radar for such things – come across an odd little stash of ripped and torn porn mags.

We designate it an artwork. An *objet trouvé* – or should I say *perso e travoto* as we're in Italy now. Gen documents it by recording details in a voice memo on his portable cassette machine, and we add an artist's signature – a psychic cross sticker placed nearby. Before we hop back in the van, we visit the cash-and-carry to buy chocolate, wine, and Campari. Well, that's what I buy anyway. The wine and chocolate is for the rest of the journey. The Campari is for later, although it doesn't survive. When we arrive at Hotel Moro, in the marvellously named Cattolica, my carrier bag drips Campari all over the bedroom floor, and the contents are hurriedly emptied out onto the balcony – a sodden mass of ripped-up porn mags, Camel fag packets, and broken glass. But I clean it all up like the good girl that I am. Rock and roll!

We have no show tonight, and once we're settled in and unpacked, we head off into Rimini. Oh, we're at the seaside, how exciting! Early evening sunshine, golden beaches, palm trees and all. We stroll along the prom, eyeing up the locals, who are (naturally) eyeing us up in return. There are a lot of boys wearing ironed jeans with immaculately clean white T-shirts and pastel coloured cashmere jumpers thrown over their shoulders. They walk with cigarettes in one hand and their other arm around girls with super-long brown legs who wear ra-ra skirts and very tight tops, hair squeaky clean and make-up immaculate. Then, there's the scooters – mostly Vespas – weaving in and around the promenaders. Everyone is talking, constantly, whilst walking, standing or riding. It's a familiar scenario – Rimini is in the Emilia-Romagna region, which also includes Bologna, Modena and Parma where I've spent many a summer with Dino and Bruna Pirroni, the last visit just three months previously.

We find a local pizzeria – no shortage of those – and toast our arrival with *chianti*.

After such a long drive you'd think I'd sleep like a baby, but no. My roommate Hilmar falls asleep early and is snoring loudly, and there are church bells sounding through the night. Then come the thunderstorms, and the buzzing flies – which I guess might be nasty bitey mosquitoes, so that thought makes me even more restless. At one point, I decamp to the room that Gen and Mouse are sharing. After a while it's clear that three's a crowd, so I head back to my own room, and manage around an hour's sleep. Next morning, I'm fine after a breakfast of bread and cheese, washed down with cappuccino...

Come Sunday evening, we're all wired up and more than ready for our first show of the tour, which is at the Aleph Club, just outside Rimini. It's a big, bright, state-of- the-art disco, and at the soundcheck I'm a bit worried that the club have made a mistake booking us – surely there are no Psychic TV fans in these parts? And if there were, would they come to this shiny dance-music hub? But come showtime, the place is packed. Turns out those immaculately dressed Rimini boys and girls like a bit of hyperdelic excess.

It's all a bit chaotic. We play for half an hour longer than we're supposed to, but nobody minds – far from it. The film projection breaks down, but it doesn't matter. At one point during the set, Gen disappears into the audience for ages and is carried aloft back to the stage, like a football hero. At the end, there is tumultuous applause, posing for photographers, interviews with the local press. Our dressing room is invaded by a posse of young men that Hilmar dubs The Rocking Vicars. They are all dressed in black cossacks with dog-collars (the clerical kind, that is, not the S&M kind), and sporting giant crucifixes, pristine copies of *The Confessions of Aleister Crowley* sticking out of their pockets. "They are so wirginal..." Hilmar says to me in a stage whisper, as they crowd round us adoringly, making me giggle. But no, we resist temptation and leave them behind as we head off back to the hotel, Hilmar and I holding court in our pink-and-yellow polka-dotted room. From here on in, whatever town or city we're in, we become the designated post-show party hosts. But really – we're hardly The Who, not even The Birthday Party. No TV sets thrown out the window, or sinks pulled off walls. A bottle of wine and a cigarette or two (occasionally something stronger), some chatting and possibly some dancing – we're more like a bunch of arty intellectual students at summer camp than a hardcore rock band on the road.

Monday morn we're off to Turin – a pretty hefty 300-mile drive westwards, right across the top of the boot of Italy. And we have a show this evening, so there's no dawdling. We stop briefly somewhere along the way to buy the usual goodies (wine, chocolate). The shop has a whole shelf of interesting looking adult comics, and I buy a few different ones. The best are the Sukia cartoons – she's a kind of Italian Vampirella.

Our get-in is at 3pm, but we're late – seems like the rush hour starts early here. But perhaps it's always this busy. The car rules in Turin. The Fabbrica Italiana Automobili Torino (FIAT for short) is based here, not to mention Maserati, Lancia and Alfa Romeo – and we've all seen that fabulous scene with the Minis in *The Italian Job*. Car, car, car trouble. We manage to get there without any fancy four-wheeled trips down ancient steps, but it's all a bit rushed from now on. The Big Club is indeed a big club, staffed by tough looking PA guys – heavy metal fans one and all. Alex impresses them by playing 'Smoke on the Water' in the soundcheck. The gig goes well, and the dressing room afterwards is full of photographers. Hilmar and I jump ship and go off to dance, joining the others later for nightcaps in the hotel bar. Gen is looking none too happy with us, and glares at Hilmar a lot, but he softens after a few whiskies.

Oct 10th   France   5th – 13th
                      Nov.   Scand.
            Svitz.   15th   Hamburg.
                       17th   Nov.

Oct 13th   Rimini
    16th   Turin
    15th   off
    16th   Gratz – Anchr
    17th   Vienna
    18th   travel
    19th   Munich ??
    20th   travel
    21st   Berlin
    22nd   off (Bochum?)
    23rd   Groeningham – holland
    24th   Leiden – or off
    25th   Utrech – holland
    26th   Appledoorn
    27th   Amsterdam – Paradiso
            –   Paris ?
    28k or 29th.

Tuesday is a day off in Turin. Hilmar and I head out on walkabout with Drew and Andrew. As these two are our designated drivers, we see them as two heads on one body, or perhaps that's one head on two bodies, and have dubbed them DREWANDREW. Andrew – sometimes also called Eden, his Temple of Psychic Youth name – doubles as roadie, and Drew is in charge of all the tech, and is really another musician in the band, manipulating tapes of found sound rather than playing a conventional instrument. We walk through streets that are trying to outdo each other in their baroque or rococo splendour, past palaces and piazzas, opera houses and gardens. As we walk, we talk – ruminating on public stranglings, the 1922 Turin Massacre (when fascists murdered a couple of dozen communists in the most gruesome of ways), and the famous face-of-Christ Shroud of Turin. We consider going off to the cathedral to see the shroud, but end up instead going to a cafe to sample the city's famous Gianduja chocolate – which is basically a kind of posh Nutella.

Hilmar and I then pay a visit to a learned doctor, a famous brain specialist no less, who we had met the night before. He is researching the cerebral behaviour of people listening to our music, and had invited us to his rather grand villa, to talk and take a dram or two.

Later in the day, there's a long interview with a journalist from *La Stampa*. We ricochet from Brian Jones' death to the art and life of Austin Spare; from the recent 'information wars' scandal about MI5 and the BBC, as reported in a whistleblower article in the *Sunday Times*, to the use of technology in our music; and from the role of random chance factors in film and music to the power and beauty of Pre-Raphaelite painting. There's then a group outing to – yes – a pizzeria, where we are recognised and treated like royalty. Well, this is all OK – London life feels a long way away. Perhaps I could stay on tour forever? I'd toured before as a cabaret dancer, but although that was fun, it was an odd existence, travelling alone and forging very short-term friendships along the way. Now, we're a group, a pack, a clan. We are family. Rock and roll!

So that's Italy done and dusted. Where next? Austria, that's where.

We're heading to Bregenz, on the shores of Lake Constance. This involves going through Switzerland, with the Alps to be navigated. This time we go up and over rather than under. The roads are steep and narrow, a succession of hair-raising hairpin bends as we climb up a lot, then down a bit, then up a whole lot more. Drew is driving and there's many a harrowing moment as the van skids around a bend, just feet from the edge of the precipice. Once again, and for all the wrong reasons, I'm thinking of *The Italian Job*. No sleeping under a rug this time. I'm sitting up, as alert as a hyperdelic bunny. Hilmar makes it worse by telling tales of a journey his friend took behind a family vehicle that disappeared over the edge whilst the children in the back of the car were still waving at them and pulling funny faces.

It's evening when we reach the Swiss-Austrian border, and pitch-dark. We've made good time – it's 7pm, so once we get through here, there's plenty of time for dinner before we continue on to Bregenz and find our hotel. This is a very different scenario to sailing into Italy in the sunshine. Instead of one little booth manned by a couple of smiley guys, there's a whole complex of huts and portacabins, and the border guards are surly looking, dressed in black and grey uniforms. They each have a gun and a large German Shepherd dog straining on a leash. It all feels a bit like a scene from a Len Deighton novel. One of them collects up all our passports and is looking through them slowly and suspiciously. Another one has opened up the back of the van and has let his dog in to sniff around – searching for drugs we presume. Well, good luck. We're really not that sort of a band, contrary to expectations. (And if we were, we wouldn't be stupid enough to smuggle stuff across borders.)

Unfortunately, Hilmar chooses this moment to remark that Hitler's father was an Austrian customs officer. And that's it. Our passports are handed over to a plain-clothes officer – that is, someone dressed almost identically to the guards, but with no gun and wearing rimless glasses and a shapeless anorak rather than a military jacket – to be run through a computer search (to find out if we are international terrorists on the run, we suppose). We are then taken out of the van one-by-one whilst the others remain inside, guarded by men, dogs and guns.

When it's my turn, I'm taken off into one of the portacabins and strip-searched. And I mean searched. Every orifice investigated. Every item of clothing meticulously run through, fibre by fibre. Then there are questions and more questions about who I am and where I'm from and what I'm doing here with these people. When I get back to the van, I quietly swap stories with the others. Mouse had her tampon taken out and dissected. Some of the boys with body piercings – Prince Alberts or nipple rings or whatever – report on the barely-concealed shock and embarrassment of the guards, who have never seen anything like it in their lives. Eventually, the guards are satisfied that despite our weirdness, we haven't done anything wrong or have anything illegal about our persons or vehicle, so we're free to go. It's now late. Will there be anywhere to get dinner? Two of the guards – the ones that originally looked at our passports and searched the van – are now all smiles and friendly suggestions. There's a Gasthof near here, they say. We're going off-duty now, so we'll take you there. So we get an escort to the inn, our van led off by armed guards on massive motorbikes.

When we get there, we don't get a free meal (we were hoping for recompense), but gratis pitchers of beer are sent over to our table. All's well that ends well.

The next morning, we get to see where we are. We discover that Bregenz is a very pretty place. It was once part of the Hapsburg dynasty, and then briefly under Bavarian rule. Despite being bombed by the allies in 1945, it still has its castle and old town walls, and there are Gothic churches on every corner. Lake Constance is enormous, the place where Austria, Germany and Switzerland meet. I wonder where the borders are on the water, and who guards them. There are plenty of little boats out there, and the occasional larger tourist boat goes by. There's a big famous music festival here, with an enormous outdoor stage set on the water, but that takes place in the summer months, and we're here in the autumn, playing the Opal club.

This is all very different to Italy. A smaller venue, more low-key. Fewer adoring fans and no press or photographers – although there are at least two people here who are academics writing dissertations about Psychic TV. The show is good, but far less manic than the Italian ones. There's a lot of post-show conversation with the learned professors. Hilmar gives as good as he gets on Freudian analysis, Gestalt therapy, and the work of Austrian psychoanalyst Wilhelm Reich – and specifically his experiments with 'orgone energy' – but we do manage to get a bit of dancing in too.

From Bregenz, we head off to Vienna. That's 420 miles through the Austrian Tyrol, in one day. Whose idea was that? Of course, we don't make the soundcheck...

The Arena is a massive great place – an old slaughterhouse reached by negotiating a complex network of motorway intersections stretching through industrial wastelands on the outskirts of the city. We arrive two hours late, when the support act are on, and weave our way in through the audience, carrying the gear aloft. We manage to lose a drum somewhere along the way. As soon as the support have finished, we set up and play. When the gig is done, it feels a little odd – as if we haven't properly arrived and are yet to play. But no, all done and dusted, and we are scooped up and taken off to eat at a cafe that I think is called the Beatrix. Or perhaps that's the name of the person looking after us. Who knows. It's got to the point in the tour when everything is a bit blurry. But nothing a good long walk won't fix.

Later that evening, Drew and I head off from the hotel into the old town. I'd been to Vienna before, but for New Year's Eve when it was snowy and sparkly and full of fairy lights and fireworks and merriment, chattering people heading out to masked balls or *Die Fledermaus* concerts as the bells rang out. Now, close to midnight in the third week of October, it is much quieter – deadly quiet, footsteps echoing on cobbled streets, with figures emerging from shadowy arches to make us start. Ah, old Vienna. Cue Ultravox song. Or perhaps the Harry Lime theme from *The Third Man*.

We head down Wolfgangstrasse and eventually make our way to St Stephen's Cathedral, a magnificent Gothic beauty of a building. We walk through the night, taking in the Heldenplatz (Heroes Square) with its massive great statues of warmongering men mounted on monstrous looking horses, and we hang out for a while in an empty sentry box close to the Hofburg Palace. As dawn breaks, the city is invaded by roadsweepers clearing away the fallen leaves. We catch the wrong tram, but eventually get back to the hotel.

Next stop, Munich in Germany. After a smooth drive and an uneventful border crossing, we get to the Alabamahalle. We're on another industrial estate, but here there's a large stage and a decent PA. We're part of a festival, and compadres Test Department are playing before us this evening. And boy, are they good. I'd seen them before in London, but here on this big stage with this fantastic great PA system, egged on by a massive crowd of cheering 'industrial' fans, they really soar up to the heavens and down to hell with the sound of clanking metal and fierce drum beats. Perhaps there's something in the air, because we too play like there's no tomorrow. Rock and roll!

Post-show, we hang out with the Test Department clan, who include a girl called Psychedelic Lucy who's wearing a fabulous bright pink wig. I get chatting to the lovely Angus Farquhar, who trades me some Yugoslavian cigarettes for one of my Sukia vampire-porn mags. Then, Angus and the gang all pile into their tour bus – an ancient coach fitted with bunk beds and crammed full of scrapyard metal – and they roll off and on to their next gig, waving and whistling as they go.

We stay overnight in Munich, then set off early for the 360-mile journey to Berlin. To get there, we need to cross into the DDR (Deutsche Demokratische Republik – East Germany to you and me) as West Berlin is an 'exclave' of West Germany, surrounded by a wall that keeps it separate to East Germany. A wall that protects the virtuous East from the decadent and fascist West; or an Iron Wall that secures the West from the Communist threat – depending on your point of view. So, an island of Western Europe in Eastern Europe.

Getting through the border takes forever. No strip searches, but endless enquiries about the van insurance, carnet forms, itineraries, and other legalities. Yawn. Once through, we find ourselves travelling down a strange corridor – a motorway with really high wire fencing on either side separating us from the forests and fields beyond. When we need to make a pit-stop, we find that what's on offer is the Intertransit shop, staffed by formidable old women who look us over with frank curiosity, hardly speak, and definitely don't smile. We have to show our passports to buy anything – which seems odd as you can't get on to the Intertransit road without showing your passport, and it is most definitely hemmed in by those fences. We buy snacks and drinks in strange old-fashioned packaging, looking like stuff from the 1950s that has sat there waiting for us for the past 30 years.

Eventually we get to Berlin, and after more boring border kerfuffles, cross through Checkpoint Bravo back into the West, and find Hotel Econtel on Soemeringstrasse. Hilmar and I are in the corner room on the fourth floor, with good views out over the river and the city. We take showers, mix up some rum cocktails, and listen to Klaus Wunderlich on the radio. Hilmar falls asleep – as he is wont to do, at any hour of the day or night – and I head off to eat out with Gen and Drew. We three then head back to Gen's room, where Gen too nods off. Seems like an early night is calling, so Drew and I give up on any thoughts of partying. Rock and roll? Not tonight, Josephine.

The next morning, I sleep in and miss breakfast. There's a plan for everyone to go to Checkpoint Charlie, the only place Westerners can cross by foot into East Berlin, which we'd be allowed to visit for a few hours. But actually, I don't feel like a group outing – I need some time by myself, so I head off alone to the zoo. I use up almost a whole film on my Kodak Brownie camera photographing the zebras and the beautiful white wolves, who I commune with for a long time.

The zoo is right next to – indeed a part of, and surrounded by – the famous Tiergarten, which I'd misheard as 'tea garden' but apparently it means 'animal garden'. Which all makes sense – not only because it contains the zoo, but also because there is an abundance of wildlife here. Corvids galore: I don't know what's a crow and what's a rook, some might even be ravens, but whatever they are, there's a lot of them. And squirrels – red ones! I'm not sure if I've seen red squirrels before, although childhood favourite Tufty the Squirrel is red, as is Squirrel Nutkin who I hated, so I presume England used to have lots of them. The Tiergarten is mostly empty of people, which is just what I need – I've hit the point in the tour where I just need to be in the company of squirrels and birds rather than the human beings I'm in a band with. There are a few folks out and about: dog walkers, cyclists on squeaky bikes and a few people who look like philosophy students, wrapped up in duffle coats, sitting on the weary looking wooden benches, drinking tea from flasks (see, it is a tea garden, too!). And there are statues – lots of them. A golden angel on a column. Men fighting beasts. Beasts fighting beasts. There's a river, a lake and a stagnant pond covered in algae. There are trees – stubby pines and towering sycamores. My feet crunch through the top layer of autumn leaves to sink down into an older mulch of leaves fallen in earlier autumns. Ah, that's better. Nothing like a city park to revive the spirits. I'm ready to face my friends again.

An hour or two later, we gather up at the hotel lobby and drive over to The Loft, which is part of a venue called the Metropol, a Studio-54 style nightclub set in a classical-looking columned building in Nollendorfplatz, at the heart of the gay area of the city. It's an area still full of Weimar era cafes; and Nollendorfstrasse, where Christopher Isherwood lived in the 1930s, is just around the corner. As is the building that once housed the Eldorado, the real-life cabaret venue where Jean Ross, inspiration for Isherwood's Sally Bowles, performed.

Sadly we've no time to dawdle around drinking Cafe Creme and eating Bienenstich cake – there's a soundcheck to do, and a new tom-tom drum to buy to replace the one we somehow lost in Vienna.

Everyone seems to have found a new burst of energy, and yes – it's a good show. One of the best of the tour. The place is heaving and the audience all seem to be hardcore fans. The dressing room afterwards is mobbed. And would you believe it, here are the Rocking Vicars, who have followed us across Europe from Rimini to Berlin!

Mouse, perhaps inspired by Gen's former lover and Throbbing Gristle bandmate Cosey Fanni Tutti, decides to dangle a used tampon from a light fitting in the dressing room. I feel a bit uncomfortable with this, which is perhaps a bit hypocritical, being one of the team who put on the notorious *Prostitution* exhibition at the ICA. But then, the used tampons were in glass cases. And that was pre-AIDS. Maybe that's why I feel weird – things are different now. Or maybe I prudishly just feel worried someone will think it was me. I'm a rebel on the surface but a law abider at heart, with a desperate need to please.

The next morning, after a hearty breakfast, we leave Berlin (more red tape, naturally, to get out) and drive westwards to Bochum, with the promoter on board, too – so we behave politely, although Alex is in a mischievous teasing mood. Our journey takes us right through Germany, bypassing Potsdam, Hanover and Munster. I'm sure they are all very nice places, but we don't get to find out. We do, though, get some picture-postcard views as we get closer to Bochum, rolling up and down gentle hills. Pretty rivers, and lots of greenery. Extremely green greenery. Verdant, that's the word. It just means 'green' but it sounds fancier. There are lakes too – but having come from Lake Constance, it's hard to be overly impressed. I'm still

far more of a city girl, when it comes down to it. But this is all very picturesque. Bochum itself is a university town, and traditionally also a mining town and industrial hub. It's not the most attractive of places on first view – bombed heavily in World War Two so that's maybe old Blighty's fault.

We go straight to the venue – the Zeche club, a rather odd red-brick building that looks unimposing from the outside, but turns out to be a big and well-equipped music venue and disco. It all goes well enough: we do the soundcheck, play, eat in the onsite restaurant. But it feels a bit low-key after the highs of the previous two shows. And Bochum? We don't really get much of a sense of it. No doubt it has hidden treasures and pleasures, but we're on a flying visit so we don't really get to discover them. We check in to our hotel after 1am – a bland businessman's hotel with plain white walls and digital clock-radios, and bathrooms that smell of TCP. I sleep soundly, regardless. Better than I had in Berlin, where the adrenalin seemed to be racing day and night. We get up promptly, pack up, and drive away.

So that's Germany done. Next stop: the Netherlands. We're playing El Paradiso in Amsterdam – but not until Sunday. We first have a week of playing smaller towns – we are going to be based at the Hotel Mikado in Amsterdam for the week and do day trips out to the other places. Amsterdam is a mere two-and-a-half hour drive from Bochum – a doddle compared to some of our van journeys – and we are on a day off, so when we arrive, the day is ours. Hotel Mikado is – yes! – on a canal. One of those tall thin buildings that goes right up to the water.

Hilmar, Drew and I dump our bags and head on out to explore. The Venice of the North is indeed delightful: skinny gabled houses, cobbled paths, criss-crossing canals with pretty stone bridges, scores of cyclists – all present and correct. We decide to try out one or other of the renowned coffeeshops, which are famous not so much for the coffee but as a place that marijuana could be smoked openly. Not that I am particularly into weed, but when in – well, not Rome. When in Amsterdam…

There's one in the Red Light district that is apparently famous for being full of statues of world deities, which appeals to Hilmar, so we head there. We've got used to dodging the bicycles, but are suddenly surprised to find trams bearing down on us. We survive the chaos, and now here we are. This area in Amsterdam Centrum is sometimes called De Wallen as apparently the canal walkways here used to be walled up. It feels like a film set: girls sitting in windows, which are indeed lit with red lightbulbs, plying their trade. Neon lights advertising strip clubs and peepshows. Theatres with 'adult shows' – live sex on stage, apparently. There seem to be coffeeshops on every corner here, and we don't find the one we were looking for – partly because we've forgotten what it was called – but the one we do go into seems pretty typical: painted wooden furniture, a mash-up of greens and blues; Van Gogh prints on the walls; and the fug of dope from the smokers. OK, been there, done that. It's not really our scene. We head back, early. An odd kind of lethargy has set in.

Over the week, we play shows in Leiden, Utrecht and Apeldoorn. The first two are just 20 miles away, so easy peasy. Apeldoorn is around 60 miles away, and there is talk of getting a hotel there, but in the end we come back to the Mikado. It's all fine, but it feels a bit different, this day-tripping thing. And over the week, the group expands as other people join us at the hotel. Paula and the little ones, three-year-old Caresse and baby Genesse, arrive. Hilmar immediately teaches Caresse to say "Rock and roll!" with her fist in the air, a cry taken up by everyone, our silly private joke now losing its irony. Foz, and Mouse's boyfriend Geoff, arrive too. Our producer, Ken

HOTEL
MIKADO

AMSTEL 107-111
1018 EM AMSTERDAM
Telefoon 020 - 237068

BANK: AMRO BANK,
AMSTERDAM,
REK.NR. 43.61.80.464

HOTEL-NOTA   05359   Datum: ....

ONTBIJT EN SERVICE INCLUSIEF
FRUHSTUCK UND BEDIENUNG EINBEG.
BREAKFAST AND SERVICE INCL.
PETIT DEJEUNER ET SERVICE Y COMP.

Kamer	Prijs per nacht	Aankomst	Vertrek
Zimmer	Preis pro Nacht	Ankunft	Abfahrt
Room	Price per night	Arrival	Departure
Chambre	Prix per nuit	Arrivee	Depart

....   *Tel   28x35*   *9.80*

.... nacht(en)-Nächt(e)-night(s)-nuit(s)

à fl. ....   Totaal fl. *9.80*

Deposit bet./bezahlt/paid/paye fl. ....

fl. ....

.... sleutel(s)   % Tourist tax fl. ....
.... Schlüssel
.... key(s)   fl. ....
.... la clef   à fl. .... deposit fl. *9.80*

Totaal fl. *9.80*

DRIJ V.D. WATER TEL. 010 - 15 81 11

Thomas, is here – actually, he's been with us for quite a while, having flown over to join us early in the tour. Some other friends and associates are here too, including Tom Vague, who is writing about us for *International Times* (*IT*).

Which is all very nice, but the dynamic has shifted away from the Seven Samurai on the road together, a tight-knit band of brothers and sisters, to a more regular kind of 'playing a gig' thing. Plus, Gen's moods are really getting to be an issue. He seems to be finding his family's arrival difficult, amongst other things. He and Hilmar seem to be at odds a lot of the time.

Our Paradiso show on Sunday night has a suitably full-on finale feel. We dress in our most colourful psychedelic finery and give it all we've got. Tom notes in his *IT* article, 'Hyperdelia in the Starlit Mire', that there is "not a skull or a combat jacket in sight" and that he is the only one backstage "dressed in an industrial grey mac". We play with great gusto, and the show is recorded by VPRO Radio; the place chock-a-block with liggers, journalists, photographers and music biz types, along with a pretty solid crew of Psychic TV fans, some of whom have travelled over from London or Paris, as our dates there didn't materialise.

But despite the upbeat feel and the positive audience response, there's something about it all that I don't like. Too many hippies? Too many drugs? It all feels so dark and murky, literally and metaphorically. Backstage, we are grilled by numerous people at the same time, all speaking at once, and it all feels very intense.

Afterwards, I write to Monte to tell him about the tour, and he writes back to say he too hated the Paradiso – so an interesting similar response from my blood brother... Regardless, he says: "I'm so jealous I didn't get to go on tour with you... I bet it was a blast!"

On Monday morning, we head off home. Our friends and family have gone back by plane or boat and it is once again just us – Psychic TV on the road. The journey home is much shorter. Just Belgium to get through...

But would you know it, we are once again stopped and strip-searched at the border. It somehow rounds the trip off nicely, and we are far more nonchalant this time round, laughing rather insolently at the border guards. We have no gig to get to, and nothing much to lose, I suppose – so we call their bluff, behaving uncooperatively. Do what you will, we say – we have the time. They grow bored with us pretty quickly and send us on our way.

Our trip reverses itself out. Road, ferry, sea, cliffs, road, home. It's been a mere 18 days but it has felt like a lifetime. A bubble of intense experiences and shifting relationships.

Europe endless. Life is timeless. Real life and postcard views. Elegance and decadence. Endless.

But then it ends.

We reach my home in Wandsworth, and Hilmar and I get out of the van. We say our goodbyes to the others. We don't know it, but our days are numbered as members of Psychic TV. We are both sacked a few weeks later, deemed to be disruptive and subversive elements – although Hilmar apparently had already decided to leave, fed up of a situation in which he was being treated as an unpaid jobbing musician, rather than as the formidable creative force that he was, integral to the band's new musical direction.

I write to Monte and tell all. "It just makes me sad," he replies. "It was a great line-up. Gen just does not seem to know what he wants. I'm glad you had a good tour, though... And I wish I could have been there, because I know I would have had a great time with you and Hilmar. So he's left as well? Chrissakes.

But sounds like you two burned a blazing trail, and you know how much I love arson."

Hilmar never forgives Genesis. He and his girlfriend Gunna Sigga, who's visiting from Iceland, come to dinner a few days later, and Hilmar rants about Gen's selfishness and arrogance. He has no talent for anything other than self-promotion, says Hilmar. He uses people around him: people who are the real artists. He steals all the money owed to the musicians – Hilmar hasn't been paid a penny for any of his work, and when he raises that with Gen and the nasty manager Terry, he's warned that if he kicks up a fuss he'll be reported to the authorities for working illegally in the UK.

And that's it. It is broken, and it can't be fixed. There can be no forgiveness. Gen tries to re-establish contact over the years, but Hilmar refuses to engage. Even when Gen dies 35 years later, Hilmar is unrepentant. I email to tell him that Gen has 'dropped their body' and that this body has been cremated. Hilmar had already heard the news through the Reykjavik grapevine. "It is a shame that there is no grave to piss or dance on," he says.

As for me – despite my outward confidence, I often find it hard to be clear about my feelings, and to stand up for myself. I feel immensely wounded, and the scars from that wound stay with me for many years – but just a week or two after I'm chucked out of PTV, Gen invites me out to meet him at Battista, our old band haunt on Charing Cross Road.

Why do I go? It's obviously just an opportunity for Gen to try to vindicate his actions. He suggests that Hilmar is the real problem, not me; that I am under his (magickal, of the dark kind) spell, and would be better off extracting myself from his influence. In fact, he's done it for me. He doesn't quite say "it's for your own good" but it's implied. So, first Monte and now

Hilmar. I am a weak-willed maiden who needs protecting from people who might lead me astray, it would seem. To be honest, this is all starting to sound a bit Dennis Wheatley. Mysterious balderdash, my friend.

What is clear is that to be a member of Psychic TV, you must be an acolyte, a disciple – not someone self-determined with a mind of your own. PTV, even if it hadn't started that way, had soon become what Sleazy later called "a cult of personality" – and the personality it all circled around was that of Genesis P-Orridge. I think I always knew this, and that this is why I shied away from joining the fledgeling band with Gen and Alex that emerged after we made the 'I Confess' single in 1980. Alarm bells rang then, but a few years down the line I'd forgotten or buried those reservations. Why had I not looked more closely into how and why Sleazy and Balance and Tibet had left the fold? Why had I fallen for Gen's "this incarnation of Psychic TV is the band I'd always dreamt of" line?

Of course it ended in tears – and tears. Ripped and torn. Inevitable, with the wonderful gift of hindsight. Of this fabulous 1985 line-up, this dream team, everyone dropped off, or were dropped, one by one. Monte ran away early to avoid a meltdown, and always said afterwards, in numerous letters to me over the years, that his relationship with Gen would never be the same. Hilmar would never communicate with Genesis ever again. Drew and Rose would walk away pretty soon afterwards. Mouse – clearly under Gen's spell, but having to play second fiddle to Paula – would hang around for a while, but not long later would also be gone. And dear, loyal Alex – the co-founder of PTV, and the principle songwriter? In the coming year, Gen would sign a Psychic TV management and record deal in which only he was named, not Alex. So Alex would have no choice but to leave his own band. Which leaves Gen and Paula. From then on, it's their baby – until the day, many years later, when Paula would wake up from under the spell and walk away, too.

The album that the dream team recorded for DJM in Spring 1985 eventually gets released, in 1988, as *Allegory and Self* – although what's put out was never intended to be the final mix. It features a rather lovely Austin Spare drawing on the cover – which is ironic, I feel, as it was Hilmar who introduced Genesis to Austin Spare's work.

The wounds scab over. I park my anger and resentment, although it never completely disappears. Gen and I remain friends, despite everything, but I always hold back a bit. There will never be the love and trust, and the ease that we had in each other's company, before I joined Psychic TV. The bond is broken. Being lost we fall apart.

TEN YEARS AFTER

Maybe everybody wants London
to be the London they inherit when they come of age.

no clause 28

BY GEORGE

ZIGZAG

MONTHLY **MUSIC** MATTERS £1.25 JANUARY 86

THE CLASS OF 76 - TEN YEARS ON

BILLY IDOL · · · THE WINNER

THE DAMNED · SHANE · SIOUXSIE

FEARGAL · ALEXEI SAYLE · VERMORELS

B A C K IN TO THE FUTURE

It's 1986 – ten years after – and everyone is falling over themselves, and each other, to mark the 10th anniversary of punk. The Sex Pistols may have played that famous first gig at St Martin's School of Art in 1975, but 1976 has been officially sanctioned as year zero – the year of the 100 Club Punk Festival, the Pistols EMI signing, the release of 'Anarchy in the UK', and the Bill Grundy tea-time TV debacle. Plus, gigs and records by many other first-wave punks, including The Clash, The Damned and Buzzcocks.

ZigZag editor Mick Mercer asks if I'll write an article – so I do, for their 'Class of 76' special. *The Face* runs a piece by Jon Savage (who will go on to write *England's Dreaming*, seen by many as the definitive account of UK punk). The recently relaunched *International Times* ignores it all and runs an article about Stonehenge and psychedelic drugs.

There are exhibitions, too. At Hamilton's Gallery in Mayfair there's a Jamie Reid retrospective, which I go to with Foz and Andy. Yep, the safety pin through the Queen's nose, the collages of ripped up union flags and blackmail lettering, the Anarchy tour buses to Nowhere posters, the *Never Mind the Bollocks* record sleeve – all of that. Of course, we know that this happens to all art movements, but it feels all wrong – a kind of Situationist nightmare, seeing these things that by rights should self-destruct after a short time preserved and framed in a Bond Street gallery.

I'd lost touch with Jamie Reid. We'd had a very brief flirtation a few years earlier, after going to a party that, I think, was for Vivienne Westwood's birthday. It was a party, anyway, in an East End flat (so not her own flat, as she still lived in Clapham as far as I knew). He took a rather fuzzy photo of me in my grey and gold World's End shirt (worn as a dress) and sent it on to me. We met up for a drink a few times, then had a weekend in Brighton that wasn't quite a dirty weekend – I think we were both easing in or out of relationships at that point, and it wasn't quite the right time to start something.

We had some great chats and a few stolen kisses, and there was this rather odd thing that happened in a pub right next to London Road station: I went to the Ladies and when I came back, Jamie was rubbing his jaw. Some geezer had walked up to him and socked him in the face for no reason either of us could think of, then walked out of the bar. Did they recognise him, or know me, or perhaps just liked hitting random people in pubs? We'll never know. The punk rock life, eh?

Anyway – back to where we were. Ten years after.

Not just music paper and magazine articles. Not just exhibitions. There are films too. The most high-profile is *Sid and Nancy* directed by Alex Cox, which will premiere at the

Cannes Film Festival later in 1986. There's the hope that this could work out well – after all, Cox's first feature was *Repo Man*, starring the brilliant Harry Dean Stanton, which cleverly combines an homage to the LA hardcore punk scene with a bizarre sci-fi plot about aliens. Maybe he'll do something similar with *Sid and Nancy* – freely mix fact and fiction, make the story into something surreal. I could imagine their story re-worked as a kind of Cronenberg horror tale, with weird slimy things coming up through the plughole in the Chelsea Hotel bathroom. Or zombies: Nancy re-imagined as a zombie would be great. But no, when it comes out we find that it's a regular kind of bio-pic, with the cast of characters silly cartoon versions of the real people. John Lydon is predictably scathing. They claim they consulted me, but they didn't talk to me until after the film was shot, he says. They had Joe Strummer from The Clash as an advisor, says John, and what the fuck does he know about any of it?

+

So what does 1986 feel like? There's a feeling in the air not of revolution but of gradual shift and definition. The ideas that germinated in 1975 and exploded onto the world in 1976 have been working their way through the system, crystallising into styles and expressions which are losing their common thread. Things run not in ten-year cycles, as the music business believes, but in spirals of no fixed length which circle outward and away from the origin. The marvellously multi-faceted musician Jim Thirlwell (of Foetus fame) talks about the punk "big bang" – with everything exploding out from that Bill Grundy swearing-on-TV moment, creating a multitude of different galaxies. It's the perfect analogy.

A few months back, in late '85, I'd written an article for the Canadian magazine *TransFM* – and this has now become a regular writing job. I'd been helping Andy write a 'Letter from London' column, which he did under the name John Bull, but we then decided it'd be better if I just took it on, as writing was more my thing than his. But what to call myself? Obvious, says Andy. Jane Bull. So I write and dispatch my first column.

In that first article, I note that people don't have lives anymore, they have lifestyles. I despair at the looting and plundering of the counter-culture that has gone on in recent years: Sunsilk Hairspray's use of a Debbie Harry lookalike was probably the first example, way back in the late 1970s, but since then it has really escalated. The punk aesthetic is now everywhere, with a spiky-haired girl on the can of Sparkle Furniture Polish, and a rubberwear spread in the *Sunday Times* magazine.

This Alice in Rubberland journey from underground to overground is one of the oddest aspects of the new anything goes 'we are all punks now' mainstream. Jordan once shocked commuters on the Shoreham to London commuter train as she made her way in to work at Malcolm and Vivienne's SEX emporium dressed head-to-toe in latex, and Adam and The Ants caused consternation with their songs about rubber fetishists illustrated with filched Sweet Gwendoline graphics. But now there are not only rubberwear fashion spreads in the Sunday supplements, there are fetish clubs galore – Skin Two aka Maitresse and Der Putsch being two of the first –there's even a Rubber People boat trip down the Thames. Is this a good thing, indicative of a more tolerant society, or just another form of exploitation, capitalism cashing in?

+

London, my London, is changing so quickly it is hard to keep up. Is this what being 30 feels like?

I remember when I first started going to the jazz clubs of Covent Garden in the mid 1970s, a wide-eyed 19-year-old soaking it all up. The walk down Charing Cross Road looking for number 84, browsing the weird Russian political pamphlets in Collets, then nipping into Watkins in Cecil Court to pore over the books about Atlantis. The wild gardens filled with poppies and cornflowers, hidden behind corrugated iron fences near the old Covent Garden Market. The weird brown rice and lentil stuff on offer at the Food For Thought vegetarian cafe on Neal Street. The Actors Church, which had a special service for Punch and Judy professors and puppets once a year. It was all so brilliant, so exciting, so absolutely not the suburbs.

But to the old jazzers and beatniks at the Seven Dials club in Covent Garden, London in the 1970s was done for, all washed up. Oh, if you'd only seen it in the 1950s and 1960s, they moan! It's a pity you never got to Better Books to hear Ginsberg read his poetry and Kenneth Anger show his films. Shame you never went to the original Ronnie Scott's on Gerrard Street to hear Ben Webster play. Charing Cross Road and Tottenham Court Road have been decimated by new building works, they say, and Soho is a shadow of its former self...

Maybe everybody wants London to be the London they inherit when they come of age.

So now I've become one of the grumblers: it's not like it used to be. Soho is filling up with new cocktail joints and cappuccino bars – "put a brick through the window of anywhere selling cappuccino" advises JG Ballard, as Monte Cazazza reminds me when I write to him telling him how London is going from bad to worse. Well, it can't be as bad as Berkeley and San Francisco, Monte says. The Yuppies are everywhere, and you can't move for hip new coffee shops – "I'm the last person in our neighbourhood who isn't either a drunken transient or a businessman bar owner. It sucks."

I do like a nice cappuccino, but I know what Ballard means. There are far too many new cafes, muscling in on the traditional favourites like the Stockpot, which sells a good, cheap Spag Bol; the pretty little Maison Bertaux cake shop, where ladies of a certain age dress in their best frocks to take tea and exchange saucy snippets about their days as Windmill dancers; and the legendary Bar Italia cafe, whose staff could show these young upstarts a thing or two about operating a Gaggia machine.

No one actually lives in central London anymore – well, nobody other than a few people lucky enough to have hung on to their council flats despite the Tory sell-off of social housing; and those old guys and gals living in the flats above the Soho shops that they refuse to move out of, despite pressure from property developers, resolutely walking their little dogs and buying their daily newspapers from that place on Old Compton Street that sells papers from all over the world. They get their fruit and veg from Berwick Street Market, but who knows how long that's going to hold out with supermarkets opening up all over the place. A lot of the smaller independent record companies, clothes shops and art galleries have decided that the rent hikes are not viable, and have moved out to the hinterlands of Hackney, or Camden, or even – God forbid – Wandsworth.

Even dear old Fleet Street is changing. The monstrous Rupert Murdoch has led an exodus to the unglamorous Docklands, a brown-ground wasteland of bomb-sites and abandoned warehouses. Here, Murdoch is setting up a new sort of printing method using computers that'll see the traditional linotype printing processes abandoned. Margaret Thatcher has made it another *cause celebre*. She is still fully embedded as our ruler, fortified by her victory over the striking coal miners, and intent on wielding more and more power over all the unions and indeed all of the workers who don't tow her line.

Whilst the world of print media is in turmoil, things have also gone a bit wobbly in the broadcasting world, but for very different reasons – although those reasons are also linked to the right-wing ethos pervading everything these days.

We're all still reeling from the *Observer* newspaper's revelations of connections between the BBC and MI5 – or some of us are, anyway. I mean, really, this surprises people? Jon Savage had written just a few months before, in *ZG* magazine – that the only war that is real now is the Information War. In April, there is another big media furore when a certain Winston Churchill Junior introduces an amendment to the Obscene Publications Act that will, he hopes, see censorship extended from stage and screen to TV. The battleground for this one focuses around Channel Four's planned broadcasting of Derek Jarman's *Jubilee* and *Sebastiane*. Derek's new film *Caravaggio* has hit the cinemas, and he's getting a lot of attention, so people are now interested in his earlier work.

Derek will never be mainstream, but he is now approved arthouse, part of the British Film Institute's roster of supported film-makers, so things are shifting for him. But he remains a controversial figure: openly gay, outspoken on the Torys' appalling Clause 28, which forbids schools from 'promoting homosexuality' even by mentioning that it exists, and ultra-critical of the government's failure to address the AIDS pandemic – instead of doing anything sensible like provide free condoms for all, or give out any genuinely helpful information or practical support, they're pouring resources into the scaremongering Don't Die of Ignorance campaign, with its sci-fi style public information film (directed by Nic Roeg, who'd given us *Performance* and *The Man Who Fell to Earth!*). This features explosions, tolling bells and a giant black monolith with the letters AIDS carved on its side, bolstering up the doom-and-gloom narrative. Derek has recently been diagnosed as HIV-positive – and is, I'm pretty sure, the first public figure this side of the pond to announce his status publicly. He is exactly the sort of person that the dreadful Mary Whitehouse of The National Council for Christian Standards wants to see silenced. She has also sunk her teeth into *Gay News*, which she wants prosecuted for obscenity. Burn again Christians, we call Whitehouse and her cronies.

But censorship takes many forms, and sometimes it manifests as left-wing political protest. At the Tate Gallery's *Forty Years of Modern Art* exhibition, the Allen Jones sculpture *The Chair AJI* – one of his infamous 'bondage girls as furniture' pieces – is attacked, on International Women's Day, by paint-stripper-wielding feminists. I'm a feminist, but I like Allen Jones' work. I see it as a commentary on objectification, rather than objectification of the female body. And besides, the sculptures look good. I'd have one of those chair or table girls in my home, for sure. Allen Jones defends himself by saying that he considers himself to be a feminist – and I believe him.

This moment seems to sum up how confusing everything has become. The old 'them and us' divides don't seem to be holding, and massive cracks are opening up in the counter-culture. Maybe it was always thus, and I'm only now really seeing and understanding it. Actually, when I come to think of it, it was always clear that being a right-on artist didn't mean that you couldn't also be a misogynist (well hello, Pablo Picasso, who, as Jonathan Richman told us, would "pick up girls and

Q ♥

Q ♠

never be called an asshole"); or that being a hippy and main-man of the alternative scene didn't mean you couldn't also be a hard-nosed capitalist (greetings, Richard Branson). And I'd had personal experience of how bigoted and sectarian some members of the gay community could be towards others: the radical feminist lesbians who had no time for drag queens; the butch mustachio'd clones who were wary of women and hated anything or anybody camp; the general derision of the notion of bisexuality, or the idea that sexuality and sexual identity could be something that shifted and changed throughout a lifetime.

Now, things are hotting up into real battles to the death. The bizarre New Puritan pairing of Mary Whitehouse's 'Christian family values' advocates and the feminist anti-porn campaigners is a worrying one. Both groups want to tell women what they can and can't do with their bodies. I have numerous friends and associates who work in the sex industries. Some, like Cosey Fanni Tutti and Annie Sprinkle, incorporate this work into their art-making. In Cosey's case, her porn work, her art work, and the music she made with Throbbing Gristle and beyond were all part of the same package. American porn star turned performance artist Annie Sprinkle describes herself as 'a conceptual artist hooker' citing the Dada and Fluxus artists as influences. Other artists use sex work to finance their art-making, freeing them up from the burden of relying on arts funding. Both choices are fine by me. I'm no longer working as a glamour model or exotic dancer, but I retain a 'sex-positive feminist' view that people should be free to do whatever they want with their own bodies. Oh bondage, up yours, as Poly Styrene so eloquently said.

I'd recently read *The Handmaid's Tale* by Canadian writer Margaret Atwood, about a dystopian near-future America in which women are kept shrouded and shackled and used as baby-making machines. She was nominated for the Booker Prize in 1986, but didn't win, and in interviews says that everything in her novel has happened somewhere, at some point in human history, and she is only extrapolating trends that are currently happening in the United States. The red warning light is on.

In other news, the long-mooted abolition of The Greater London Council has happened, Maggie having taken her axe to another enemy; and now former GLC leader Ken Livingstone, known affectionately or otherwise as Red Ken, has gone back to his South London bedsit to look after his newts. Later in the year, there'll be the infamous Big Bang decommissioning of the London Stock Exchange, opening it up to 'foreign investment', a nice euphemism for the army of oligarchs and gangsters that move in and wreck the country.

Thatcherism has many different manifestations, but one seems to be a new-found hedonism linked to a re-working of the spirit of anarchy to somehow mean "I can do anything I want, regardless of anyone else's needs". This will get worse. By the 1990s it'll be a fatal disease – but for now, 1986, it's a nasty virus taking hold wherever it can.

Capitalism is encroaching on everything, even on time itself. Once, when you dialled 1-2-3 to hear the talking clock, you heard a plummy but reassuring lady tell you the time in minutes and seconds. Now you get an arsey male voice telling you that "the time according to Accurist is..."

+

Ten years is quite a while, I suppose. And there's something about marking a decade. Punk all of a sudden feels like – well, like something historic. Something to be chewed over and analysed: What did it all mean? What is its legacy? Will it happen again?

Everyone has been obsessed with finding the next Sex Pistols, still not understanding that the Pistols were the Ad Reinhardts of the rock and roll world. When, in 1962, Reinhardt unveiled his 'Abstract Painting no. 5' – a white canvas painted black – that was it. There wasn't anything outrageous left to do. Not that there was no longer any point in painting (there was), or that painting was no longer an interesting medium. Painting lives on. But 'Abstract Painting no. 5' was a rubicon moment. Painting as a shock medium was done. Ditto rock music and punk. Yes, there could be good and interesting things happen subsequently, but a line had been crossed.

And if you're looking for the Next Big Thing, just know that when these big cultural shifts occur, they break out in unexpected places, not where you're looking. You'll know the future has arrived when you can't put a name to it... Revolution is a continuous process, not one point in time.

Look beyond rock and roll if you want to find the next punk, we could have said to all those eager *NME* journalists back in the late 1970s. Malcolm McLaren, who always seems to be ahead of the game when it comes to spotting (and exploiting) fresh cultural trends, gave up on rock and roll post-Bow Wow Wow and embraced hip hop. His 1983 *Duck Rock* album had a track called 'Double Dutch', the accompanying video featuring footage of girl skipping teams from Brooklyn – reminding me of my brief time in New York in late 1982 when I was bowled over by the groups of b-boys and girls showing off their breakdancing and skipping skills on the Fifth Avenue junction with Central Park.

By 1986, hip hop has well and truly broken out of the Bronx and conquered the world. The old-school hip hop heroes

Sugarhill Gang, Grandmaster Flash and Afrika Bambaataa are still revered, but they've now been joined by the Likes of Run DMC (who have two massive hits in 1986 with 'Walk This Way' and 'It's Tricky'), the first ladies of hip hop Salt-N-Pepa, and frat boy party animals The Beastie Boys. And that's just the stuff that's hit the headlines – I know there's lots going on that I know nothing about. So, there have been big cultural events since punk – with hip hop being one of the biggest, shifting the energy away from White Britain to Black America.

Meanwhile, back in Blighty, there's been the whole electro-dance synth-pop thing, from the relaunched Human League to Soft Cell, to Orchestral Manoeuvres in the Dark, Blancmange, and The Eurythmics. Frank Tovey's Fad Gadget are at the quirky lo-fi end of the spectrum, supplemented by some outrageous live performances. Trevor Horn and Paul Morley mastermind the success of both Frankie Goes to Hollywood and The Art of Noise, the label-leaders of the duo's ZTT label, which prides itself on "promoting fractured, provocative takes on synth-pop". Horn uses a Fairlight (which we'd also used in Psychic TV) to make sampling and cut-and-paste techniques a mainstay on commercial pop songs.

Both the American hip hop community and the British synth-popsters owe a lot to the European electronic explosion led by Kraftwerk, who managed to inspire everyone from the Essex disco boys to the Chicago house music maestros.

But there are other things going on. Whilst The Human League headed off into pop stardom, Sheffield contemporaries Cabaret Voltaire are still flying the flag for electronic experimentation, although minus Chris Watson who is following a path as a solo sound artist. Meanwhile, bass player extraordinaire Jah Wobble and his post-PiL band Invaders of the Heart are creating an interesting mash-up of a million and one influences from what some are calling 'world music'. Wobble has recently been collaborating with Can members Holger Czukay and Jaki Liebezeit, which is an exciting development.

Meanwhile, up in Scotland, former Psychic TV bandmate Rose McDowall is doing very well for herself with her group Strawberry Switchblade, a two-woman outfit, formed by Rose and Jill Bryson, making perfectly lovely psychedelic pop. Rose had formerly been in a band called The Poems with husband Drew (who was also part of the mid-1980s PTV line-up). Rose and Jill formed Strawberry Switchblade a few years back with two other girls, but after a while they mutated into a duo, having a surprise pop hit with 'Since Yesterday'. They're part of a Glasgow scene of whimsical popsters that includes The Pastels and The Vaselines. Very much my cup of tea! Glasgow would seem to be a hive of musical industry, mid-1980s – *Psychocandy*, the debut studio album by Jesus and Mary Chain, was released in November 1985 on Blanco y Negro Records (yep, another Mike Alway signing!), capturing my heart and that of much of the post-punk world with its wonderful mix of Phil Spector-ish pop tunes and feedback-drenched guitars.

Down south, the anarcho-punk scene, spearheaded by Crass and Flux of Pink Indians, and championed by fanzine *Kill Your Pet Puppy*, is also thriving, with various crossovers with Psychic TV and Test Department, and a lot of activity going down in New Cross. My Icelandic friends Kukl are tied in to this clan, and when they realign and change their name to The Sugarcubes, it is Derek Burkett from Flux who signs them to his new label, One Little Indian.

As Reykjavik starts to attract attention, another city that feels vital to the mid 1980s music scene is Berlin, which has had a pull on the post-punk world ever since David Bowie, Brian Eno and Iggy Pop used it as their base to create a series of extraordinary albums, mostly at the now-legendary Hansa Studios, right by the wall that divides East and West. Native bands gaining international reputations include Xmal Deutschland, Malaria, and Einstürzende Neubauten.

Einstürzende Neubauten in particular have made a mark here in the UK. They have a pouty-pretty Gothic boy singer called Blixa Bargeld, who also sometimes played guitar with The Birthday Party, which morphed into Nick Cave and the Bad Seeds. Neubauten, as they get called – it's the easier part of their name to pronounce – make a lot of noise. They have drills and a concrete mixer on stage, use broken supermarket trolleys and random lumps of metal as percussion instruments, and love the sound of breaking glass – and they do cover versions of Jane Birkin and Lee Hazlewood songs, so what's not to like? Malaria are an all-female band who are fans of Rema Rema and have some common ground with us in the sounds they make, so of course I like them too. Rema Rema singer Gary Asquith had recently formed a new outfit called Renegade Soundwave, and he'll end up spending a fair amount of time in Berlin, collaborating with the Malaria girls.

Another band flying the flag for noisy musical experimentation are Laibach, from Slovenia, who are modelling an aesthetic that blends Soviet-inspired military iconography with Eastern European folklore. Their second album *Nova Akropolia* has just been released on Cherry Red, and PTV bandmate Hilmar and our producer Ken Thomas have had a hand in making the record, so Foz and I both have connections there, and we get in to their Bloomsbury Theatre gig on the guest list, taking Andy and Gabriella along with us.

The band look great, standing stern in their military uniforms, adorned with chunky black crosses, used repeatedly as a branding tool in the same way Psychic TV use the three-barred psychic cross (aka the TV aerial). The stage is dressed with incongruous objects like bells and antlers. Their sound is loud and percussive – lots of banged metal things, reminding me of Test Department. But there's also fierce shouting and chanting, political speeches cut up and worked into the soundscape, and some Psychic TV-style wolf howls and other wild animal noises. Sometimes they are symphonic – ultra-slow and moody, like a soundtrack to a Tarkovsky film. Then come the big crashing organ sounds, and it all goes a bit Dr Phibes. Although they are a very different kettle of fish to PTV, there is crossover, reinforced by the shared production input of Ken Thomas.

Soviet iconography, by the way, seems to be everywhere at the moment – be it big brash T-shirt designs in Hyper Hyper, which has replaced Kensington Market as the place to shop, or little metal pin badges – red stars, or hammers and sickles, or red black and chrome pictures of space rockets saying CCCP, which it takes me a while to learn is USSR in Russian. There's a fair few images of first dog in space Laika, too.

My old band label 4AD put out a lot of things that I also like a lot. And as they have now moved down the road from me in Wandsworth, I occasionally pop in to be given a handful of new releases. My former Rema Rema bandmates Mick Allen and Mark Cox are now in Wolfgang Press – described as 'avant-dance groovers'. They have a single out called 'I Am the Crime', and Mark is also working on 4AD founder Ivo Watts-Russell's project This Mortal Coil, which uses artists from the label recording in new combinations. Oddly, Mark had ended up playing on a cover of a Rema Rema song, 'Fond Affections', which was on the 1984 album *It'll End in Tears*. The vocals on this are courtesy of a very lovely Scottish singer called Cinder, who like countrywoman Rose McDowall, has the voice of an angel.

One of my favourite 4AD tracks, recently acquired from the Alma Road office, is the 12-inch single 'L'esclave Endormi' by Dutch singer Richenel, licensed to the label by Belgian company Megadisc. The original recording was switched to the B-side while a much more ethereal and spacey remix was used as the A-side. Ivo subsequently invited Richenel to sing on This Mortal Coil's *Filigree & Shadow* album, which includes a fabulous cover of Tim Buckley's 'I Must Have Been Blind'.

Belgium is another European destination that seems to be having a bit of a moment. We all know it as the land of Jacques Brel and Plastic Bertrand (not to mention the Singing Nun who had a hit with 'Dominique') but there's more. Apart from Megadisc, there's Les Disques du Crépuscule, a Brussels label which Foz has a connection to, having joined Hilmar and Tibet to record the Aryan Aquarians' record with Niki Mono from Tuxedomoon. Crépuscule's roster of other artists includes Michael Nyman, Harold Budd, Cabaret Voltaire, Josef K, 23 Skidoo, Erik Satie, and Ludus – not a bad mix. They see themselves as more than a record label, running esoteric events and happenings. In 1984 they'd opened Interferences, a chic brasserie cosmopolite that they describe as "a sort of Haçienda in downtown Brussels, but with a better wine list".

They also have Wim Mertens on the label, at first under the alias of Soft Verdict, but by 1984 Mertens is using his own name, and has released *Maximizing the Audience* – one of a growing number of releases that could be called contemporary composition, another direction music in the 1980s has gone, with established composers like Michael Nyman, Philip Glass and Steve Reich together with young bloods like Laurie Anderson and Meredith Monk sitting somewhere within the triangle points of pop, classical composition technique, and avant-garde experimentation.

I'm keen to know more about these unclassifiable artists. Laurie Anderson I've been aware of for quite a while, having bought *Big Science* when it came out a few years earlier, and more recently the live album *Home of the Brave*. I'd also encountered her through her work with John Giorno and William Burroughs, and her collaboration with performer Spalding Gray on his film *Swimming to Cambodia*. And she's a pop star, with a number two hit record, 'O Superman', which hit the airwaves in 1981! Meredith Monk is a more recent discovery – after seeing a documentary about her while in Canada, I'm now on catch-up to learn as much as I can. I saw Steve Reich at London's Dominion Theatre in January 1986, excited to see works like 'Clapping Music' and 'New York Counterpoint' performed live; and had seen some of the programme of Reich music films screened at the ICA in the week before the show.

All things considered then, music in 1986 is in a pretty good place. It's just not quite gone where some people thought it might go. Punk hasn't killed rock and roll, but it has changed it. The massive great budgets for bands to record albums – with the even more extraordinary budgets for album cover design, and ludicrous use of resources to create them (pink pigs flying over London, statues dragged up Everest *et al*), are both now a thing of the past. It's amusing to think that much of this excess was the work of the Hipgnosis design studio which Peter Sleazy Christopherson worked for, whilst simultaneously playing in Throbbing Gristle, who were at the forefront of the drive for DIY music-making. Oh, irony of ironies. And Sleazy is now, after forming then leaving Psychic TV, part of one of Britain's

most interesting new musical ventures, Coil – the band formed by Geff Rushton (aka John Balance) that Sleazy joined in 1983. They started out in a rather low-key way. In Summer 1983, they'd played live at the Magenta Club, accompanying films by Derek Jarman and others, but, other than doing a few overseas festivals, have since focused on recording, with three excellent and very different records released over three years: the *How to Destroy Angels* EP in 1984, *Scatology* in 1985, and *Horse Rotorvator* in 1986.

The rise of independent labels pioneered by punk and industrial has, by 1986, permeated all genres, and that DIY ethos has been picked up enthusiastically by young artists, with the past decade seeing a massive increase in entrepreneurial music projects. There are small labels, vibrant independent shops, and live music venues a-plenty across the land.

There is still, inevitably, exploitation of artists by the major record labels, who often seem to sign someone up only to try to change them into something else; or sign them up then drop them speedily if they don't have the big hits hoped for immediately. Gone are the days of longterm nurturing. Foz and I have both experienced this personally, he with The Monochrome Set's conflict with Warner Brothers resulting in the band's demise, and me with Psychic TV's fall out with DJM, leaving *Thee Starlit Mire* album ditched – although in PTV's case it was a bit more complicated...

But there is hope, and that hope lies in the success of alternative labels like 4AD, who come with a strong vision and a morally sound approach to their artists; in the adventurous attitude of companies like Disques du Créspecule, who are breaking down barriers between pop, rock, contemporary classical, and experimental sound-making; and in brand new independents like One Little Indian, who are putting their trust in an odd-bod Icelandic band featuring a trumpet-playing punk and a wondrously wild and witchy girl singer with a three-octave range.

Ten years after, things are – all things considered – OK. It's a brave new musical world.

BABY LOVE

The bride wore a white Vivienne Westwood pirate shirt,
white stockings with blue garters,
and red patent leather stiletto boots.

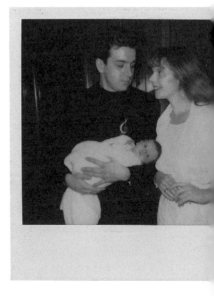

21st May 1985. It's my birthday, and we're in The Olive Tree restaurant in Soho's Wardour Street. 'We' are me and Foz, Genesis and Paula, their three-year-old daughter Caresse, and brand-new baby Genesse, who is currently in Gen's arms. Foz is in deep conversation with Gen, I'm sat next to Paula. Just as we start talking, little Genesse starts to mewl and head-butt and is handed over to Paula, who lifts her shirt and places the baby on to her breast – all done with nonchalant ease, hardly a beat in the conversation skipped. I glance around the restaurant, slightly nervous that someone might be looking over disapprovingly. I've never seen anyone breastfeed a baby before – I have no sisters, know very few people with babies, and I certainly didn't realise that such things could be done in public. But here's Paula, this smiling Madonna with braids, totally oblivious to anyone else's issues around her body and her baby's needs. Throughout the meal, Genesse is put to the breast many times. Can she really be that hungry? They need to nurse whenever they want to, to satisfy their need to suckle as well as their need for food, explains Paula. I just follow the baby's lead, she says.

Paula is much younger than me – 22 years to my 30 – but seems very self-assured in her maternal role and has had many life experiences that seem almost worryingly grown-up. Gen had shown me a video of Caresse's birth – a home birth, but with the baby 'breech', which is kind of the wrong way round, coming out bottom- rather than head-first, something that would normally ring alarm bells and get people scurrying off to hospital. But Paula had an independent midwife, I'm told – an NHS midwife would have certainly insisted on a move to a maternity unit – and they made the choice to stay put, the baby eventually arriving safe and sound after a long labour. This video is the first time I've seen a filmed birth that isn't someone lying on their back on a hospital delivery bed whilst attached to various monitoring machines. For much of the time, Paula is on all-fours, gently rocking, the midwife and Genesis giving calm encouragement.

I offer to hold Genesse while Paula eats her hummus and pitta bread. I'm shown how to carry her on my arm, with the elbow crooked so that her head is held safely, but with enough slack for the baby to feel she is being supported, not suffocated. I'd worked part-time as a nanny, years ago, but I've never held a baby this tiny. She's just weeks old, so, so small – those little fingers with their weeny fingernails! Those miniature shell-like ears!

Until this point in my life, I'd been sure that I didn't have a maternal bone in my body. I'd decided way back that I wouldn't have children, although very happy to spend time with other

25/12/85
Max.

Week 34
(July 6th '86)

— August 20th '86 —

03'09'86

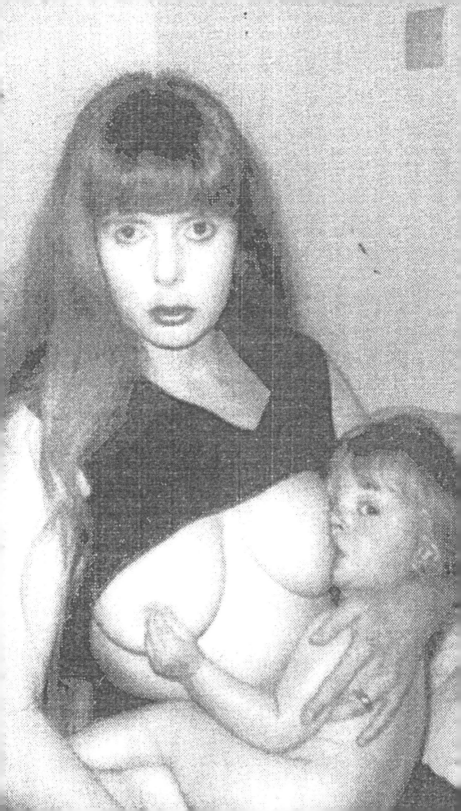

people's. I'd recently been spending a fair amount of time with Caresse, taking her to the park or playing with her at home, so that Paula could focus on Genesse, and Gen could get on with the Psychic TV and TOPY admin. Now, with little Genesse in my arms, warm and milky-breathed and totally trusting, there's a new sensation. I could do this, I find myself thinking. I really could. Gen looks over. He can read my mind. "Not yet, though," he says. "We have a few years of work with Psychic TV to do first, then it'll be time enough." He talks enthusiastically about the current line-up and starts in on all the hopes and plans for albums, and live shows, and tours to places near and far. And when that's done, well...

As it happens, the 'years' with Psychic TV get curtailed. In the end it is just one year. By November 1985, I've left. Been sacked, as it happens, but I would have left anyway, I'm pretty sure – although I was a bit peeved that it happened just before the band went to Japan, somewhere I'd always wanted to go. But Paula was on board for that one, and I realised with a sudden burst of annoyance that with Paula back in the band on percussion, I wasn't needed. All that stuff about the dream team, and me being Gen's favourite ever drummer! I'd been maternity cover, basically.

So, well, if I can't go to Japan, I'll have a baby. This is not 100% planned, but it's not *not* planned either. I'm more than two months pregnant by the time I make it to the doctor's, muttering about missed periods and having had flu recently, so it might be that. I've had a bit of a stomach upset, too, and wine and coffee both make me feel sick. The brusque lady doctor looks exasperated when I suggest a pregnancy test. She places one hand on my belly for a few seconds, and announces that my womb has grown and hardened into a small tight ball. I don't need to take a test – I'm clearly about 10-weeks pregnant.

I look so shocked that she assumes it's because I don't want to be pregnant, and starts in with a "right then, we need to move quickly to get you a termination within the next few weeks". I jolt out of my shock and tell her, almost outraged at her stupidity, that of course I don't want a termination. Now it's her turn to look surprised. Go home and think about it and talk to your boyfriend, she says, and come back in a few days. Unmarried, living in a small rented flat with a musician boyfriend – she's clearly not impressed. I go home and tell Foz, who is a bit shell-shocked, but says he's not really that surprised. When I met him, he'd told me he wanted six children, so is quite happy to start with this one.

Back to the doctor's to confirm that I'm going ahead. I mention that I'd like a home birth, and the doctor snorts and says firmly that this isn't possible for a first birth. I don't know where to start with a counter-argument – if we're using the NHS rather than an independent midwife, we have to do what they tell us, I suppose. I'm booked in for a trip to meet the midwives – as a compromise on the home birth thing, I'm put on a community midwife programme, sent to a tea party, and reassured that this small group of midwives that I'm assigned to will be jointly responsible for my antenatal care, and one of the team will be with me for the birth, which will take place in a hospital room made to look as much like home as possible. Of course, that depends on what your home looks like. Mine has William Burroughs and Anna Kavan on the bookshelves, a recent edition of *RE/Search* magazine on the coffee table, and Derek Jarman film posters on the walls. The 'home birth in the hospital' room is painted sickly yellow and has cheap reproductions of Van Gogh's sunflower paintings on the walls and a vase of artificial pink peonies on the table.

So, midwives met, hospital visited. Now it's April, and I have a 20-week scan arranged, before heading off on a six-week trip to North America. On the scan day there's all sorts of shenanigans about not getting a clear enough picture of the baby's head, so I'm stuck drinking gallons of water and getting re-scanned until they're happy with the results. I'm not too fussed about seeing scans, but I can't just up and leave as I'm relying on them giving me a letter to say that everything is normal and fine and that I'm safe to fly. I've been warned that in the States I'll struggle to find domestic flights that will accept a pregnant woman without a doctor's letter. I eventually escape, with my letter stating that I'm fit to fly. My due date of 19 August is confirmed, and I'm advised that I ideally need to plan my long-haul flight home to be before the 30-week date, 23rd June.

Almost time to go! I have a ticket to San Francisco, so I can visit dear friend and Psychic TV co-conspirator Monte Cazazza. Then, I'll head to Canada. I'll be going to Ottawa to stay with Gabriella Bregman, the Italian-Canadian DJ, broadcaster and journalist I'd first met through Andy and who is now a firm friend. She has visited England many times, and sometime in 1985 she'd interviewed Psychic TV for the radio station's linked arts magazine, *TransFM* – I'm their London correspondent, writing a monthly column on music, art and whatever else takes my fancy. Hopefully, I'll get some time in Montreal and Toronto, too. I'll next head over to New York, to stay with Monochrome Set associate Sharon D'Lugoff, whose dad Art runs the legendary Village Gate jazz club. I book my return flight from New York to arrive back home at the end of May, well before that cut-off date in June.

As it happens, the first leg of the journey to San Francisco gets scrapped. I speak to Monte – we usually communicate by writing letters, but manage the occasional transatlantic phone call – and he's in one of his reclusive phases, heading off for some time alone in the Nevada desert. So now's not a good time to visit. There's other stuff hinted at too, but I don't want to go there, and neither does he – neither of us are 'deconstructing our feelings' kind of people. Would I like to come anyway, and he'll make sure I'm OK, will put me in touch with people? No, that's no good. I want to see San Francisco as I've never been to the West Coast, but mostly I want to see him. Another time we say. There isn't another time – we don't see each other again, although the letters to and fro continue for a number of years. The pregnancy has been mentioned briefly – Monte ends the conversation by wishing me luck and saying he thinks I should have a girl: "You'd have a really wild daughter," he says. Well yes, but whoever she or he is, it's done and dusted now, I think but don't say – so just laugh and agree.

So it's a slightly shorter trip, and straight to Canada I go, to Ottawa via Toronto on Dutch airline KLM, with a quick change-over at Amsterdam – last visited as the final date of the Psychic TV tour, at the Paradiso in October 1985. Now, the visit is a mere few hours in an airport lounge. When I arrive in Ottawa, I'm met by Gabriella and a tall smiley German-Canadian called Norbert who has a car, which gets us to Gabriella's apartment.

The next day, I'm drawn straight into the city's heartland. "Ottawa's quite nice really. A bit like Milton Keynes," Andy had said, a little ominously, before I'd left England. Despite being a capital city – chosen, I presume, as a compromise to appease the Toronto-Montreal rivalry, a bit like Brasilia being Brazil's capital rather than Rio or São Paolo – it's not a large place.

CKCU, the radio station based at Carleton University, is the hub around which all of Ottawa's artistic life circles. Gabriella works for CKCU when she's not running the Lightning Bakery in the trendy Glebe area. I meet Gabi's close friend Lorenz Eppinger, another German-Canadian who runs a record label called Amok. Bands on his roster include Dissidenten, an ethno-beat outfit weaving together rhythms from Africa and Southern Europe; Canadian-Swiss electro-funk quartet Look People; and Ultima Thule, who (like PTV) work with both film and music, creating synthesiser-driven works accompanied by montaged short films.

Then, there's John Tobin, editor of *TransFM*, CKCU's aligned magazine, which punches way above its weight, with a roster of local, national and international contributors. It scoops interviews with leading bands and counterculture figures (like experimental performance-maker Robert Lepage, who goes on to conquer the theatre world; and, of course, Psychic TV!) and has a nose for new developments in art, film, performance and music, with correspondents feeding in from all over the place – Montreal, Toronto, New York, Berlin, Rome, London... John congratulates me on my Jane Bull 'Letter from London' column, and teaches me how to use a computer. The first thing I do is draw a cat with a mouse.

Over the coming days, I meet many of the city's other artistic movers and shakers. The Glebe seems to be where most of them hang out, in bakeries, bars, bookshops or record stores. At Cafe Vienna, I'm introduced to Gabi and John's friend Peter Gould, an artist and illustrator who creates collages and vividly coloured cartoons for various hip small-press publications. Together, we head to S.A.W. video gallery on Sparks Street, which promotes innovative moving image work by Ultima Thule and others, also producing a video series called Paper Tiger Television, which aims to "talk back to the media". Nearby, there's Shake Records, who stock a wonderfully eclectic mix of vinyl goodies. I meet the radio station's DJs, including Steve

Kirkland whose Monday night show *British Airwaves* focuses on the best from Blighty. He is very interested in hearing about all the various bands I've been in or have connections to – from The Ants and The Monochrome Set to Rema Rema, Bow Wow Wow, Throbbing Gristle and Psychic TV. Gabriella herself presents a show called *Euronova*, which goes out on Thursday evenings and plays all sorts of aural delights from mainland Europe. Current faves include 'Fred vom Jupiter' by Andreas Dorau, Die Zwei's 'Einsamkeit Hat Viele Namen', Hermann Kopp's 'Paul Getty's Ohr', and Die Form's 'Prefazione di Pompei'. German-heavy, with a dash of Italian, you'll notice. That's our Gabi!

The month passes in a whirl of radio broadcasts, cafe conversations, and meals out. I do guest slots on both Steve and Gabi's radio shows. I pal up with John's boyfriend Ian, a very camp young creature who takes on the role of Ottawa tour guide, taking me to the mainstream monuments and museums, but enhancing the experience with his tongue-in-cheek observations. So when we go to see the Inuit artefacts at the Snow Goose Gallery, he takes me to the gift shop, saying loudly, "Oh look: you can buy toy baby seals made out of real sealskin. I think you should, Baby Pierre would love one..." Ian and John, who dub themselves The Gay Uncles, are sure my baby is a boy. John has named the baby Otis, and Pierre is Ian's choice. Ian also introduces me to the less-well-publicised tourist attractions of the nation's capital, such as Myers Hill Park, which I'm told is the place to be at sunset, especially for those keen to experience a close encounter with a Canadian Mountie.

So plenty of fun is had. The only slightly weird thing hanging over my Canada visit is this odd news that slowly leaks out about a massive disaster involving a nuclear reactor in a place in the Soviet Union called Chernobyl. Apparently, it

happened the day before I flew out of Heathrow, although the world only learns about it via Swedish TV a few days later, and it takes weeks before the scale of the disaster is understood. As the news unfolds, I find myself wondering whether I'm safer from drifting clouds of radioactive material here in Canada than I would be at home in England. And worrying that I might give birth to a two-headed baby...

But there is plenty to distract me from dark thoughts. There are live shows that include jazz legend Dave Brubeck in collaboration with choreographer Murray Louis at the mainstream National Arts Centre, and Jonathan Richman's Modern Lovers at Barrymore's, a beautiful old music-hall venue.

And yes, there are trips to Toronto and Montreal.

Lorenz takes me on one of his business trips to Toronto – and is infinitely patient when I demand yet another 'restroom' stop along the motorway. I learn to love McDonalds, who are always willing to let me into their loos without purchasing anything. Once we arrive in downtown Toronto, Lorenz heads off for his meetings whilst I head up the CNN Tower – the tallest edifice in the world – which has a scary outside glass lift. OK baby mine, here we go again – another adventure. There's lunch in a Milanese-style *tavola calda* restaurant, the type with a chrome bar that people stand to eat at; a visit to the Eaton Centre, the 'world's largest shopping complex', a mall boasting 300 shops, 17 cinemas and hundreds of (model) flying geese; and an afternoon coffee with Lorenz at somewhere called the Queen Mother Cafe – I kid you not.

And there are two full weekend trips to Montreal, the first with Lorenz and Gabi.

I like Toronto well enough, but Montreal wins my heart. I love that it has a European soul set in a North American body. There's a touch of Paris about it – and of course it is French speaking. Try talking to your Quebecois taxi driver in English and he'll pretend he doesn't understand you. Speak in French and he'll quite likely clock your accent and reply in English. It's an interesting game.

Montreal is hilly, the streets are cobbled, and there are plenty of lovely squares and luscious trees. It has artist-occupied lofts and warehouses a-plenty, and a hot-line of artistic exchange with both New York and Boston. Here, you'll find the best of the old and new worlds. There are the streamlined chrome and vinyl diners that are typical of North America, where you go for a hearty brunch of eggs over-easy and home fries, with great service – when people here say "Have a nice day!" they mean it. But there are also wonky cafes with scratchy wooden floors, standard lamps and bulging leather armchairs, where Beatnik girls play Django Reinhardt or Serge Gainsbourg discs on tiny old-fashioned record players, and silently serve you coffee in tiny cups with little *madeleine* cakes on the side.

I like Montreal so much that I decide to go back again the following weekend. I have an invitation to stay with someone called Will (who I met in Ottawa – via CKCU, of course) and his partner Sylvie, and together we scour the record shops and second-hand bookshops, including the wonderful Tabou Records and Russell's Book Nook, and visit as many cafes as we can fit in. I especially love the Cafe Méliès, attached to Le Cinema Parallele on Boulevard St Laurent, which has great bagels and a brilliant independent film programme. What's not to like? I go with Sylvie to see *Four American Composers*, a Peter Greenaway documentary that looks at the work of (yes) four New York-based musicians: John Cage, Philip Glass, Robert Ashley and Meredith Monk. I'm excited to learn more about Meredith Monk, who is not only an extraordinary vocalist and someone who experiments with the possibilities offered by the human voice as instrument, but also a dancer, choreographer, and film-maker. Renaissance woman or what!

Back in Ottawa, there are more radio shows and outings, and a birthday party – mine. Gabriella hosts, and all my new Canadian friends come. There is cake a-plenty, as you'd expect from someone who runs a bakery when she's not being an ace radio DJ and music journalist. Lightning Bakery's blueberry and triple-sec cheesecake is, I decide, the very best birthday cake ever.

+

By the time it comes to flying to New York, after a month in Canada, I'm looking most definitely pregnant, and my doctor's letter is scrutinised sternly at the ticket office. I hadn't pre-booked a flight – just turning up at Ottawa airport to buy a ticket, a bit like getting on a bus, which is the norm here. The Pilgrim Airlines plane is a teeny tiny thing, with around 20 seats. One pilot and one air hostess, and five or six passengers. That's it. There's a curtain dividing the pilot's cabin from the passenger seats, but this is pulled back for the whole flight so that he and the air hostess can chat away whilst we stare through his curved-glass window at the blue sky and scurrying clouds. He turns his head to speak to her quite often, which makes me nervous, but I suppose it's OK. I mean, these things more or less fly themselves, yes? When we come in to land at LaGuardia, it's a bit of a fairground ride. The plane tips right over to the left as it circles in, then tips right over to the right before straightening up. My baby gets very excited and joins in. I'm expecting a loop-the-loop but luckily for both of us that doesn't happen.

I take the subway, then take my time walking through Greenwich Village, past kids shooting baskets on caged-in courts, people of every denomination having loud conversations on street corners, and stalls selling every kind of street food imaginable. Smells mingle: chilli oil and garlic and seared meat and frying falafels and cinnamon and toasting flatbreads and hot dogs and popping corn. Ah yes, Bleeker Street – I remember. I'm meeting Sharon D'Lugoff at the Village Gate. She gets me a cold drink, and sorts out some comps for tonight's show, called *Beehive* – an homage to girl bands like the Supremes and the Shirelles, it would seem. From there, we walk together to her home.

Sharon's apartment is in a run-down old building on Elizabeth Street, on the edge of Little Italy, running parallel with the Bowery. Her building is just a few doors away from the house that film director Martin Scorsese was raised in, and it doesn't take much to see where *Mean Streets* came from – just look out of the window and you're there. There are groups of men sat around card tables, sipping beer straight from the bottle, women shaking rugs out of windows, grandmothers sitting on the sidewalk in wrecked old armchairs, kids playing a kind of makeshift baseball, and tiny tots in those strange little circular baby-walkers, scooting themselves up and down the street, seemingly unattended – perhaps the whole street is collectively looking out for them. There are dogs and cats and old mattresses and heaps of cardboard. Most houses have those *West Side Story* metal fire escapes. Young men in vests sit smoking, and young women with recently-washed hair sit out to comb it dry.

To get into Sharon's building, you first have to battle with a sticky, rusted old front door lock, then negotiate your way through a dank and gloomy hallway which has a wire fence along the end of it – to keep the dogs belonging to the mad bad basement man in check, apparently. Then you go through another locked metal door and up lots of rickety stairs. It's late May and really hot, so all the windows in the apartment are open – and it is very loud, the chatter and laughs and shouts of people on the streets below mingling with the sounds of fighting couples coming from other open windows. All punctuated by the rat-a-tat gunshots from Alphabet City, which I foolishly think are fireworks until Sharon tells me otherwise. Then, there's the noise from the apartment above: lots of small children running up and down and banging toys on bare floorboards, and lots of shouting in Spanish. This might be borderline Little Italy, but the street is also populated by people from Puerto Rico and South America, along with a healthy number of Jewish residents of Eastern European heritage.

There are good times with Sharon – picnicking in Central Park, eating clams in white wine with spaghetti at Vincent's Clam Bar in Little Italy, or hanging out at the Village Gate – but there's also lots of time alone. Although I'm never actually alone as there's this small human being on board, kicking and wriggling inside me.

I – we – continue the exploration of tall towers with a trip to the World Trade Center. For no particular reason, just to see how far up the Twin Towers we'll be able to go. After some random trips up and down in the North Tower, the one with the broadcast mast on its top, sometimes sharing an elevator with media types heading to their offices on floor 44 or 77 or wherever, I find out from somebody that there's an official indoor observation deck in the South Tower, on the 107th floor. Wow, 107 floors! And that's not even the top! This has to be done. Looking out over Manhattan through the floor-to-ceiling glass panes, it oddly doesn't feel like being up a tower – more like being in an airplane as everything below is so small, plus there's an odd sensation that we're moving. I think about the walk that acrobat Philippe Petit had made a few years back on a high-wire line fixed between the towers at roughly the height we were now at – 1,300 feet. Even thinking about it makes me feel giddy as a goat.

Then there's the art galleries. The Museum of Modern Art for the old familiars: Jasper Johns, Robert Rauschenberg, Claes

Oldenburg, Roy Lichtenstein. Boys, boys, boys – as ever. There are women in here – there are the subjects of the 'Naked/Nude' exhibition that's just opened, for example. Only four or five of the 50 or so artists showing work are female, but most of the models are – surprise, surprise. But I'm not the only woman noticing this. I learn that there's this great new counter-culture art thing happening in New York called the Guerrilla Girls. A bunch of anonymous female artists dress up in gorilla suits and invade openings, or make big posters to hang outside art galleries. One reads: 'Do Women Need to Be Naked to Get into the Met Museum?' Another, 'The Advantages Of Being A Woman Artist' ironically lists those advantages: Working without the pressure of success. Not having to be in shows with men. Knowing your career might pick up after you're eighty. Being reassured that whatever kind of art you make it will be labelled feminine...

I also discover an exhibition by someone called Nan Goldin, who takes photos of her friends and associates, many of whom, like Cookie Mueller and Lydia Lunch, are stalwarts of the New York underground scene. She is one of a number of artists drawing attention to the escalating number of AIDS deaths, and to the ACT-UP movement that is taking radical measures to protest them, and the lack of research into a cure. Nan has also made a film called *The Ballad of Sexual Dependency* that focuses in on the small, intimate details of her friends' lives: sex, drugs, rock and roll – the lot. Some people are calling her the new Andy Warhol. Talking of whom, he's recently been collaborating with a hip young artist called Jean-Michel Basquiat, who has risen to great heights over the past few years, since he first appeared in the video for Blondie's 'Rapture' and made his first ever painting sale to Debbie Harry for $200. He'd been part of the Whitney Biennial in 1983, their youngest ever artist, at just 22 years of age, and now had solos all over the shop, as well as his much-touted collaboration with Warhol – although rumour had it they were no longer talking.

On other days, I forgo the galleries and stay closer to Elizabeth Street, wandering up and down the Bowery – past CBGBs, looking out for Bill Burroughs' gaff, known as 'The Bunker'; chatting to the street dwellers who all wish me luck with the baby. Maybe I'm being naive, but I never feel unsafe – there's always a sense of the guardian angel coming along for the ride. Talking of angels, there's a day when there's some sort of summer festival going on in and around Mott Street. There's a gorgeous church nearby with an extraordinary name – the Most Precious Blood church – and from here comes a group of people carrying a very kitsch Madonna on a platform, bedecked with a ridiculous amount of yellow and white flowers. They process through the streets, a big crowd gathering and following on. An old lady comes up to me, and places her hand on my belly, which is a bit of a surprise. She's working her rosary with the other hand, and reassures me that my baby is healthy and that I will have a safe delivery. "It's a girl," she says, with absolute confidence. What am I going to call her? Francesca, I'm about to say, as that's the girl's name we favour mostly, but find myself saying Gabriella instead. In honour of my friend, I add. A beautiful name for a beautiful baby, says the woman. An angel's name. She will be an angel, watched over by angels. She presses the rosary beads into my hand, and I put them over my head, which she's pleased to see. I offer her some money for the beads, but she doesn't want any. A gift from the angels, she says. Suddenly, out of the blue, I remember something dearly beloved Andy Warren had come up with a few years back. He'd suggested we start a 'predict the sex of your baby' service. His very logical reasoning was that if you offered a 100% refund if you got it wrong, you'd be right around 50% of the time, and therefore still quids-in.

Eventually, it's time to leave New York. At the airport, the KLM airline folks read and re-read my doctor's letter, checking the dates. At the six-month mark, women often look their most pregnant, and I'm very obviously blossoming. I'm wearing a billowing yellow-with-black-squiggles Vivienne Westwood pirate shirt, which probably makes me look even bigger. Great maternity outfits, though, these World's End shirts. While the airline staff deliberate, I find myself musing on the fact that if my baby is born on the plane, they'll have Dutch nationality. But all is fine, I'm cleared to fly, a straightforward journey, no mile-high births, and now here I am at Heathrow's brand-new Terminal 4. Foz is waiting for me at Arrivals, and I can see him do a double take. I've clearly changed a lot! Whilst I've been in North America, Foz has been having his own adventures – in Belgium, making *The Aryan Aquarians Meet Their Waterloo* – and he'd only got back a day or so before.

Back in Blighty, there are preparations to make. There is maternity benefit to organise (apparently my PAYE stint at Arthur Murray's dance school has earned me some kudos), plus additional Social Security payments. A cheque arrives with a batch of milk tokens. There are cradles and nappies and muslin squares to buy. I'm planning on breastfeeding, but my mum and dad (who are buying all this baby stuff for us) insist on getting a set of bottles and a steriliser "just in case". The breastfeeding advocates say it's better not to introduce bottles into the equation – it just confuses the baby – but who knows? I know nothing. Genesis and Paula come over to give us two great big bin-bags of baby clothes – babygros and matinee jackets and teeny weeny little socks and mittens, mostly in white or pink, as they have two girls. They didn't decide to dress their girls in pink, but almost everybody who gave them stuff chose pink. Well, good job my baby's a girl, then.

In the weeks after returning home, I'm running around a lot. There are outings to the Polar Bear off Leicester Square with Hilmar and Tibet, lunches at the Olive Tree on Wardour Street with Drew, trips to the Big (or is that Little?) Green Duck in China Town with Foz and Hilmar and Drew and Rose, visits to Michaele and Debden in Camden, degree shows at Camberwell School of Art to see paintings by Foz's friend Thomasina. I go to see a lot of films, too – I've always loved afternoons inside a dark cinema. There's old classics like Cocteau's *La Belle et La Bête*; and new releases like *My Beautiful Launderette* and *Letter to Brezhnev* – both good, but my favourite is Wim Wenders' *Paris, Texas*. How much is the film's narrative and the haunting soundtrack by Ry Cooder, and how much the pregnancy hormones, I can't say – but I weep from start to finish, then stay to watch it again. I'm also reading a lot. I've discovered that Geoff, my old boss at the Village Bookshop – a fabulously esoteric shop in Regent Street, of all places, where I'd worked in 1975 – has opened another interesting alternative bookshop in Covent Garden, called Horace C Blossom. Here, I find some great vintage paperbacks like William Burroughs' *Junky*, and Ira Levin's *Rosemary's Baby* – perhaps an odd choice for a pregnant woman, but still.

Despite me leaving Psychic TV in difficult circumstances, things have thawed between me and Genesis over the course of the pregnancy. Foz and I get invited to a special Psychic TV Godstar party in a basement bar on Cromwell Road, near my old home at 69 Exhibition Road. The party is on the third of July, to mark the day that Brian Jones died. 'Godstar', the record PTV made to commemorate Brian Jones, was recorded in late

1984/early 1985 at DJM studios, just before I joined, but was eventually released later in 1985 on Temple Records, not DJM.

As for *Thee Starlit Mire* album, made in Spring 1985 in the same studio, who knows when that will see the light of day. There is a long, convoluted story from Gen about fallings-out with the manager (the dreaded and dreadful Terry) and clashes with DJM, and about taking back control and doing things the way he's always done things, retaining power not handing it over. He's talking non-stop, eyes growing ever-larger, and I'm a bit too pregnancy-brained to take it all in – and in any case, I have had to distance myself emotionally from him and from Psychic TV for the sake of my own health and sanity. So I just say "mmmm" a lot, and let it all wash over me, moving on to chat to Alex, who's his usual chirpy down-to-earth self.

It's the final six weeks of the pregnancy now, and I've finally slowed down and am mostly just enjoying the summer sunshine, walking daily on Wandsworth Common which is just a stone's throw from our flat on Rosehill Road. Gabriella makes it over for a visit from Canada – she's here for two months, splitting her time between us and Andy in the UK, and her family in Italy.

I'm cooking a lot these days, and enjoying the novelty of being an at-home person. We regularly have people over for dinner, like proper grown-ups. Gen and Paula and the children plus Tanith the dog come over from Hackney or Stamford Hill or wherever they are now. Drew and Rose and their little daughter Keri, who live in Muswell Hill, also come round, as do Hilmar and his partner Gunna Sigga and various other Icelanders, all the way from Little Reykjavik aka Stoke Newington. Everyone these days seems to be living on the edges of London, it's not just us.

+

Hilmar and Foz have recently been to Belgium together, and Hilmar now moots a new plan. He's returning to Iceland, and he'd like Foz to come over to Reykjavik to do some recording. He's also inviting David Tibet, filmmakers David Dawson and Akiko Hada, and Drew and Rose. This lot will join Hilmar and Einar and possibly other former Kukl musicians – and no doubt poet Johnny Triumph will be around too. There's also an

Icelandic artist and writer called Ragna Sigurðardóttir invited into the group. She's destined to become Hilmar's wife, but we don't know this yet, and even he doesn't know this yet – right now, they are just good friends.

Together they'll all make stuff: possibly an album, or a film, or both. It's an open book. Bjork, co-singer with Einar in Kukl, had just given birth to her first child a month earlier, so she's unlikely to be involved; and my baby is due in just over a month's time, meaning I can no longer travel, so I won't be going. But is it OK for Foz to go away? He really wants to be around for the birth – and I really want him to be there. Hilmar is reassuring. He uses his psychic powers to deduce that the baby will be slightly early – 13th August rather than the 19th – but Foz will be home by then. Besides, it will be easy to get a flight back if need be.

So off Foz goes, wearing his summer clothes – because it's July, right? But July in Iceland, especially when camping near the glaciers of Snæfellsnes Peninsula in the west of the island, can be very cold, so he and other foolish foreigners have to be kitted out by the Icelanders in emergency jumpers and woolly hats.

It is apparently something of a fraught trip, for numerous reasons. There are delays getting into the studio – hence the camping excursion, where Foz and Rose spend a lot of time loitering outside other people's tents pretending to be elves. Then, David Dawson suddenly ups and leaves on a mysterious calling that Hilmar later finds out is a film shoot in California with Genesis and Paula for Psychic TV's 'Good Vibrations' single – so Hilmar is not very happy about that, and neither is Akiko. When they do eventually get into the studio, Tibet and producer/engineer Mel Jefferson don't see eye-to-eye, and there's a big fight.

On the upside, Foz is getting on very well with Mel and with Kukl drummer Sigi (Sigtryggur Baldursson) and gets some good tracks started in on. He also plays on some songs that Tibet is laying down with Rose on vocals. Foz and Einar have lots of chats about Kukl's new direction. They – or some of the constellation of people who were in Kukl, at any rate – have recently regrouped under a new name. Apparently Kukl (which means 'witch' in Icelandic) was too difficult a name for English people, and the group wanted to move in a different direction. "What do English people like?" Einar had asked Foz, a month or two earlier. "Sugar" Foz had replied. Which may or may not be why they ended up being called The Sugarcubes.

Meanwhile back at home base: a week or so later, I start getting contractions. But it's OK, I know what this is – they are called Braxton-Hicks contractions, and they are normal in the last month or so of pregnancy. Nothing to worry about – it doesn't mean you are in labour, just that your body is practising for the big moment. Or at least, say the textbooks, you're not in labour unless they continue at regular intervals for a number of hours, and each contraction is more than three minutes long. Er, right. I phone St George's Hospital maternity unit. They ask lots of questions, then tell me to come in. The contractions continue, unabated. I'm monitored for a couple of hours, and then the nurse calls the doctor, and the doctor tells me that I'm in labour. I need to stay put here, in the hospital maternity unit. Where's my birth partner? In Reykjavik, that's where. No, not even in Reykjavik. Up a glacier, somewhere in Iceland. Well, there's a dilemma. I make a long-distance phone call. I speak to someone – I think it's Hilmar's partner Gunna Sigga but I'm a bit phased by all this, so I'm not 100% sure who I'm speaking to – and there's no time for small talk. Just time to deliver the message that the baby is on its way. Eventually, I get a message relayed back that Hilmar is on the case, his mission to get Foz back in time. But it turns out that there are no commercial flights in the next 24 hours, so there is (I learn later) a lot of panicked running around the desolate outbacks of Keflavik airport – which, although being redeveloped, is currently still an American military airport consisting of little more than a couple of runways and a few huts, far from a proper commercial airport – trying to find out if anything is possible. Are there cargo planes? Military planes? I've no idea how he gets back to Britain, but by the time Foz arrives in London three days later, I've left hospital.

After a night at St George's, the contractions had subsided, and on his mid-morning ward visit, the doctor revised his opinion. I'm not in labour after all. False alarm. Or practice run, if you prefer. I'm discharged to Foz's mum's flat in Churchill Gardens, so she can keep an eye on me till Foz returns. I binge-watch TV and VHS movies. I enjoy *Troll* and *Alien*. One features small imps running riot and wrecking the house; and in the other, a live creature grows inside a person, then bursts out in a horrific explosion of blood and gore. Both seem like good primers for birth and motherhood.

+

11th August. The baby is due in a week's time, 19th August, and Foz's birthday is on the 20th – so I suggest that we go shopping to get him a present, just in case I'm otherwise engaged on his actual birthday.

It's hot. Very, very hot. We take a bus from Wandsworth to Beaufort Bridge, near the bottom end of the King's Road. I'm exhausted in this heat, and stupidly heavy. The baby has 'dropped' so I'm not as sticky-outy but still merrily gaining

weight, and the baby has 'engaged' as the medics say: which means stuck head-down, with their little head bouncing against my bladder, so I feel like I have a melon stuffed inside me, and I constantly need to pee. Nice. I lean against a lamp-post and breathe. We look in Beaufort Market, then on to Johnson's where we find a psychedelic orange cotton shirt with a midnight blue geometric pattern. That'll do nicely! We head home, but forget to buy anything to make dinner with. Never mind, there's some kidney beans and rice, a few onions and chilli peppers, and a bit of bacon. I make a kind of poor man's chilli con carne, washed down with some cans of Budweiser beer. I'm just tidying up after dinner when – whoosh! What's this? Have I wet myself?

No, no – of course – my waters have broken. When I'd heard this expression before, I had no idea that it meant that actual cascades of water would come out of you. I call the hospital. Come on in, they say. We don't drive, so are told to call 999 and ask for an ambulance. How exciting! I'm wearing another one of those Viv Westwood pirate shirts – this one is white with red squiggles. I'm feeling a bit exposed, so grab my Fiorucci red PVC raincoat as the ambulance draws up, and quickly add a pair of flip-flops, which look a bit loopy with the white ankle socks, but never mind. I remember that you're allowed to bring your own duvet, so I ask Foz to grab the red and white polka-dot one, plus a pillow. It's only as we step into the ambulance that I realise I'm still clutching my can of Budweiser. So I'm a bit of a dishevelled mess, and the paramedics look a little startled, but still – at least I'm nicely colour-co-ordinated in red and white, right down to the can of beer. I'm sure they've seen worse.

11pm. We're shown in to our 'home birth in the hospital' suite. Yep, we've got the yellow Van Gogh sunflowers room. Hey ho. And I don't have a midwife that I know – so much for that scheme. Although my waters have broken, I'm not in 'active labour' – but that changes soon enough. As we pass midnight, contractions have started to come at regular intervals. Midwives, nurses, doctors and student doctors come and go. It's a bit like Clapham Junction, this room. Monitoring machines get wheeled in and wheeled out again. I refuse to stay still long enough to be strapped up to one, preferring to pace around. When someone insists that I lie down for a while to have electrodes stuck to my belly, I throw up all over them, and leap up, ripping the wires off.

By 4am there comes a point of no return. I seem to be on the ceiling looking down at myself, and I can hear a strange animal howling in the room. With a temporary switch back into lucidity, I realise that the howling creature is me.

Tuesday 12th August, 1986. The birthday. It's odd how important dates like those of births and deaths suddenly come into your life, with no pre-knowledge that this would be the day. Now, it seems as if there couldn't have been any other possibility for baby Gabriel – the Glorious Twelfth of August it is, was and always will be. Oh and yes – Gabriel not Gabriella – Monte and the 'angel' lady in Little Italy were both wrong, the Gay Uncles were right: we have a baby boy, albeit one that will be dressed in P-Orridge pink baby clothes and raised by his feminist mother in as gender-neutral a way as she can manage.

7am. Foz is sent home and I'm moved from delivery room to ward. Unfortunate timing as the ward is kicking in to life. Would I like breakfast? Tea? Any painkillers? A newspaper? I say yes to the breakfast and tea, and once that's done, settle down to doze, which is a bit difficult not only because of all the clatter, but because I keep startling awake confused by the fact that I can't feel the baby in my belly. Which would be because he's not in there, he's next to me in a funny little see-through plastic crib. This feels far too odd, so I pick him up and take him into the bed with me, but get told off for that by a nurse. Then, a big bossy matron comes over. I see you want to breastfeed, she says, looking at her notes. Has he fed yet? Er, no, I've tried but... Goodness me, she says. It's 9am. He's four hours old. He'll be thirsty. And ignoring my worried looks, picks up my precious little baby and feeds him a bottle of sugared water, which he guzzles down. There, she says. That's better.

So of course there's no way he'll latch on after that. I spend all day in this place, and the baby doesn't once feed, despite constant attempts. I'm told I can't go home until I've either established breastfeeding or given him formula. Foz comes back after lunch, bearing a bunch of tiger lilies and some tasty treats (bananas! cream!); and the three proud new grandparents, my parents and Foz's mum Kathleen, visit that evening. They all leave, and I suffer a whole night of restless sleep and no feeding. I hold out against the formula, but reluctantly let them give him a bit of water. Early the next morning, I do the bravest thing I've ever done: I lie and say that the baby is feeding. The nurses duly note down two feeds, at 6am and 9am, and the doctor says I can go. I've called Foz, and he's here. We take a taxi home, baby in my arms, wrapped in his blue-for-boys hospital blanket, and still wearing his 'Baby Prior' armband. I'm terrified that my baby is going to starve to death, but I remember the emergency bottles and formula in the cupboard.

They're not needed. Within an hour or two of arriving home, sat on my own bed, surrounded by my own cushions, with Radio 3 playing quietly in the background, baby Gabriel latches on with a fierce grip that takes me by surprise. He does it again an hour or so later, and again, and again, staring up at me with enormous blue eyes. It's as if he's suddenly woken up and realised that he is part of this physical, visceral, animal world.

In that first week or so, time becomes something other than its usual measured thing. Some days float by, lost in a fuzz of feeding and nappy-changing. Other days are full of activity. There are lots of visitors: Andy Warren is the first, coming round on the day I come out of hospital. In fact, he's sitting on the wall outside our flat as our taxi pulls up. Then, there are grandparents and uncles and aunts, and dear Dino and Bruna Pirroni, who turn up with a lovely old-fashioned Silver Cross pram – a Rolls Royce of the baby carriage world that you could imagine Mary Poppins wheeling around. Which is not the most practical of things as we live in a basement, but still, it looks great. Foz's mum Kathleen brings a Moses basket with pretty white *broderie anglaise* trimmings that she's run up on her sewing machine. The P-Orridges bring over a Snugli baby sling, more clothes and blankets, and various other bits of baby paraphernalia. Tom Vague comes round and looks bemused. Nick Wesolowski from The Monochrome Set, who's a photographer when he's not being a drummer, comes and takes some wonderful black-and-white naked-mother-and-baby photos. (Fast forward 12 years, and a self-conscious pre-teen Gabriel shouts "Take that photo down!")

Ten days after the birth there's some post-natal complications, a trip back to hospital, and an emergency operation. Handing baby Gabriel over to Foz as I'm wheeled into the operating theatre, I'm told that I have to put my parents down as the baby's next of kin, as I'm not married to his father. When I come round from the anaesthetic, I ask Foz to go down to Wandsworth Registry Office and get a special licence for a marriage to be held as soon as possible. It's hardly the most romantic of proposals, I know.

Early September: Gabriella has been to Italy and come back again. She and Andy end up being our witnesses at the hastily arranged wedding at Wandsworth Registry Office. No one else is invited – no parents or friends, just us four. Five, including the baby, who is placed on a red velvet cushion on the registrar's table, in lieu of rings, which we don't have yet. The bride wore (yes!) a white Vivienne Westwood pirate shirt, white stockings with blue garters, and red patent leather stiletto boots. The wedding cake is a Wall's Viennetta, and in the evening we all go to Pizza Express at Clapham Junction, then on to a party at Nick Wesolowski's house in South Kensington. Gabriel is put under the table in his moses basket, and we don't tell anybody that we've just got married.

John Tobin's boyfriend Ian, one of the Gay Uncles – because every baby needs a gay uncle or two, don't they? – is also here from Canada, and he's more than happy to spend

Montreal
XMAS 86

time with me and Gabriel looking at the ducks on Wandsworth Common or the peacocks in Holland Park.

There's also a visit to London Zoo with Gabi and Ian. The sloths are a big draw: baby Gabriel spends a lot of time communing with them. But the big cats are his favourite, the lions and the tigers. Hardly surprising, I suppose, he being a lion-tiger – a Leo born in the Year of the Tiger. The others have gone off to see some other animals. We stay with the lions. Gabriel stares and stares, and they stare back from behind their wired fence. One lion comes right up to the fence. There is no distance at all between us, and I suddenly feel panicked – maybe it'll find a way to rip through the fence and eat my baby!

I feel so fiercely protective it almost hurts. I'm ready to fight off tigers and lions. I clutch my baby tightly and move away – backing slowly off whilst never losing eye contact with the big beast that has come so very close to us. I keep going, back further and further till it feels like a safe distance, and I sit down on a bench. The lion has lost interest in us. Little Gabriel is now head-butting me and mewling. I remember baby Genesse and how astonished I was at how much she needed to nurse, and how insistent she was on getting her needs met. Now I know first-hand just how it all works. The fierceness of baby love.

BETTER AN OLD DEMON
THAN A NEW GOD

The performers emerge from nowhere, naked, breaking eggs
over heads, beating on barrels, splashing anyone who gets in
their way with red and blue paint fired from guns.

"Do anything but don't come in my mouth" bellows John Giorno to a quietly appreciative audience at the ICA, this chilly winter's eve in early 1986. For anyone brought up on Gerard Manley Hopkins and Robert Browning, this kind of poetry must be a bit of a shock. Don't get me wrong – I like those old masters too. But Giorno is something else, a charismatic New Yorker who has spent the past couple of decades not only publishing books and delivering these wild and wonderful live shows – his voice weaving in and around a freeform jazz soundscape – but also making LPs, videos, TV broadcasts, and radio shows.

There's also the legendary chocolate bar poems, the silk-screen poem prints, the T-shirt poems, the window-curtain poems, with content as well as form setting out to challenge convention: the poems have titles like 'Cancer in My Left

Ball' and 'Eating Human Meat', down-to-earth assaults on complacency.

But he remains elusive to those of us here in Blighty: the only Giorno Poetry Systems recording I'd ever managed to track down is the *Raspberry and Pornographic Poem* LP – found, unsurprisingly, in Rough Trade – who are rumoured to be seeking re-releases of the old material currently unavailable over here.

Giorno achieved a fame of sorts as the guy in Andy Warhol's *Sleep* – which I'd seen at a retrospective at the Hayward Gallery back in 1976. Warhol had said that everybody seemed to be up all the time, so maybe sleep would soon become obsolete, and he'd better make a film of someone sleeping pretty quickly. Warhol's then-lover, John Giorno, was the perfect candidate. "I was always asleep when Andy phoned," says Giorno when I talk to him backstage at the ICA in an informal interview for *ZigZag* magazine. "He'd just bought a new Bolex 16mm camera, and he filmed me for hours on end in three-minute takes."

Then, there's the Dial-a-Poem project – what's that?

"That was in 1968," he says. "We set up about 15 lines, first in New York, then other cities. We used tapes that we changed every day... I've always been interested in new forms of communication." One of the poems at the end of the phone line was the infamous 'Suicide Sutra', which invites listeners into an immersive experience, locating their body within space and the space within the body. A multi-tracked and reverberating voice kicks in: "You can't remember who you are... You can't remember where you are... You are in jail, you are locked in this space, it is dark and smelly and completely depressing... They are twisting your head off... You are closed inside a burning house and your heart is crying... There is a gun in your hand..."

Do *not* dial up if you are suicidal or on medication. Especially do not dial up if you have access to a firearm. Other poets you might hear at the end of the line included Allen Ginsberg, Patti Smith, John Cage and Laurie Anderson.

John Giorno had also worked with Patti Smith when they appeared together at the NOVA Convention, and his poem 'Last Night I Gambled With My Anger And Lost' is featured on *You're a Hook*, an LP celebrating 15 years of Dial-a-Poem, which was produced by Patti Smith Band stalwart Lenny Kaye. Other collaborations include 'You're The Guy I Want To Share My Money With' made with Bill Burroughs and Laurie Anderson – when I meet him, Giorno has been friends with Burroughs for 25 years, and cracks a smile when Burroughs' name – and my connection to him via Genesis P-Orridge and Industrial Records – is mentioned.

This current tour, taking in Chelsea Old Town Hall, the Zap in Brighton, and the ICA – possibly some other places too – has been organised by another old friend of Giorno's, British entrepreneur and performance artist Roger Ely, who was also (with David Dawson and Genesis P-Orridge) responsible for the *Final Academy* tour in 1982. Sadly I never got to this seminal event, just hearing about it all from Gen a couple of years later. A four-day bonanza at the Ritzy in Brixton circled around the writings of William Burroughs, and featured Burroughs himself together with Psychic TV, Brion Gysin and John Giorno. The *Final Academy* roll-call, which then spun out in a reduced form to other venues, including The Hacienda in Manchester, also included 23 Skidoo and Cabaret Voltaire, together with performance artists Jeff Nuttall, Ian Hinchcliffe, and Bow Gamelan's Anne Bean – who literally ate her own words, pushing the paper she'd read from into her mouth at the climax of her spot.

BOW GAMELAN ENSEMBLE

with BOB COBBING
An ICA Commission

'The most stunning cross-media group of this decade'
City Limits

In C and Air
5-16 AUGUST

ICA NOW BOOKING TICKETS £4.90 + ICA DAY PASS 60p
THE MALL SW1 01-930 3647

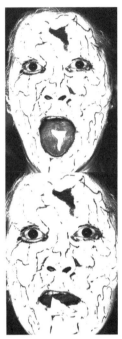

The Rites of Spring

Pearl Sallis spins the lilies

Exhibits by Richard Ward

Performances by Yvette—the Conqueror plus the Neo-Naturists
Yvette—crowns Miss Flora—Goddess of Flowers
(Budding Floras phone for details)
Thursday 15th May 1986. 9–2 am £3.00

Giorno's appearance at the Chelsea Old Town Hall is with Robert Anton Wilson, the lord of Discordianism and guerrilla ontology, who taught us, after Alfred Korzybski, that "The Map is Not the Territory" – the model of reality is not reality itself. This is a phrase (and a concept) that I take a shine to immediately, and eventually steal as a name for a performance piece I make.

Where Robert Anton Wilson sings the praises of Discordia, the goddess of strife and discord, Giorno yells out "Better an Old Demon than a New God", which happens to be the title of a compilation album he made in 1984, with appearances from William Burroughs (inevitably), Lydia Lunch, David Johansen, Meredith Monk, Richard Hell and (once again) Psychic TV. Holy Moly, that's one hell of a line-up! This was followed in 1985 by *A Diamond Hidden in the Mouth of a Corpse*, with contributors including Diamanda Galás and Sonic Youth, and cover art by Keith Haring who certainly qualifies as a New God.

Other Old Demons still going strong in the 1980s include West Coast poet Lawrence Ferlinghetti, who founded City Lights bookshop in San Francisco, and *enfant terrible* Charles Bukowski, a beat poet who is also the author of semi-autobiographical novels *Post Office, Factotum* and *The Women*. He had a regular column called 'Notes of a Dirty Old Man' in the LA underground newspaper *Open City*, which led to the FBI keeping a file on him.

My now long-distant friend Monte Cazazza bundles up Bukowski publications and other things bought from City Lights and posts them off to me at regular intervals. Sometimes they take months to arrive, but that's OK. It's always a pleasant surprise to get a letter from Monte, and a few books is an added bonus. One parcel contains a copy of the Nancy Friday book on female sexual fantasy, *My Secret Garden* – a "hidden place where women are free to express the sexual dreams they have never dared to confide before". In another comes the much-coveted copy of Bukowski's short stories, a black and white portrait of the writer set in a bright yellow cover bearing the legend *The Most Beautiful Woman in Town and Other Stories*. In recent times, Bukowski has become one of my favourite writers – something that bemuses some of my female friends, but hey, I think he's a feminist.

I do find myself increasingly drawn to these Old Demons, ignoring most of the New Gods flagged up as the Next Big Thing – although it occurs to me that it isn't a generational divide: we are drawn to the people who share our obsessions and aesthetics, regardless of age. It feels perfectly logical to note, for example, the many and various connecting threads between William Burroughs, John Giorno, Andy Warhol, Patti Smith, Genesis P-Orridge, Monte Cazazza, and Lydia Lunch – a bunch of people who range in age from 25 to 72.

Old Demon Robert Anton Wilson's ideas – and particularly his take on the cult of the Illuminati, a Bavarian secret society a bit like the freemasons, which spawned a million and one conspiracy theories – are very much of the moment, his free-form thinking and writing style suiting the paranoid postmodern vibe of the mid-1980s. The whole conspiracy theory thing is both honoured and usurped in *The Illuminatus! Trilogy*, three novels written by Robert Anton Wilson with Robert Shea. This satirical sci-fi epic is a breathtaking trek through conspiracy theory lore. They were first published in the 1970s, but were pretty obscure until the three books came out as an omnibus edition in 1984, winning the prestigious Prometheus progressive sci-fi award – and by 1986 *The Illuminatus! Trilogy* has become a kind of counter-culture bible for many of the post-punk generation. Most notably, *Vague* magazine editor Tom Vague, who is probably the key source of information for many young punks now spreading their wings to explore alternative takes on reality. Foz and I are both keen fans of Robert Anton Wilson, but Foz is almost a disciple, buying up every book he can get hold of by or about him.

+

These days, I'm far more likely to be found at a performance art event than at a regular gig. The mid-1980s has seen a growth of work presented outside of gallery or theatre spaces: in warehouses, outdoors, or in other public or private spaces.

There was, for example, the August 1985 County Hall takeover by Urban Sax, a French ensemble of 65 saxophonists who arrive on-site by truck or helicopter, or by abseiling over the rooftops – each dressed in a shiny silver suit. Small children gasp and cry out, "Look, live robots!" Afterwards, Foz and I cross over the Hungerford Bridge and are amused by the lone saxophonist (who has no connection to Urban Sax whatsoever, as far as we know) playing the *Pink Panther* theme over and over again.

Mid-1980s, the ICA seems to be picking up again as a cultural centre ready to stick its neck out, having hung low in the late 1970s after the debacle/monumental cultural highlight (delete whichever, depending on your viewpoint) that was the *Prostitution* exhibition.

In the second half of 1985 there's a run of good stuff at the ICA. We have Micha Bergese's Mantis Dance Company once again performing *Mouth of the Night*, with music by Psychic TV – as featured at *Thee Fabulous Feast ov Flowering Light* in May. This is at least my third time seeing the show, and I never tire of it, not least because of Hilmar Örn Hilmarsson's brilliant work

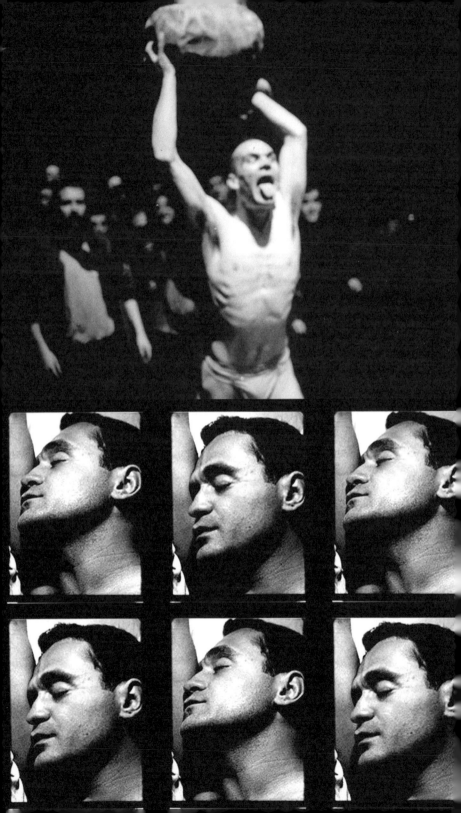

on the soundtrack, and Derek Jarman's wonderful set designs. Then, there's Gaby Agis' *Shouting Out Loud*, also a dance piece, but in this case an all-woman troupe, with a score by The Raincoats. There's also Kathy Acker's reworking of the Berg opera, *Lulu*, the ever-popular myth of the fallen woman, which is called *Lulu Unchained* – a show that is flawed, but interesting – always better than one that's unflawed but uninteresting.

One of the most exciting things programmed by the ICA at the end of 1985 – although the actual performance space is not at The Mall, but a long way off, reached on a specially licensed bus – is Catalan company La Fura dels Baus' UK debut, *Accions*, which I go to see with Psychic TV comrade Drew McDowall.

The bus, dubbed The Docklands Clipper, takes us to a warehouse somewhere on the Isle of Dogs, in the desolate wasteland of the Docklands. Squinting into the darkness as we enter the space, we realise that there is no stage, no separation between the audience and the performers, who emerge from nowhere, naked, breaking eggs over heads, beating on barrels, splashing themselves and the sawdust-strewn floor and anyone who gets in their way with red and blue paint fired from guns, wheeling preposterous hybrid metal carts into the fast-scattering audience members, setting off fireworks, and climbing walls like unleashed lunatics. As a grand finale, they dismantle a car.

Drew and I agree that it's wonderful seeing something so raw and wild – a show in which experimental music, a mix of live and pre-recorded, provides the soundtrack for such extraordinarily visceral physical action – anarchic multi-discipline performance that challenges conceptions of what 'theatre' could be. Bring it on! This, I reckon, is the future. Out with music gigs and in with multi-media happenings. This is what I want to be doing, making immersive shows in warehouses! It'll take a while, an ambition put on hold by a decade or two of childrearing – but I do get there eventually... For now, I'm pleased to play the role of audience member, which is, after all, a vital part of the live performance equation.

I'm moving – for a while anyway – from maker and doer to witness and commentator. I'm writing about the things I see for various small-scale publications, but I'm also absorbing and learning from both the Old Demons and the New Gods and Goddesses, noting the directions that art, music and performance are taking, seeing where I might one day fit in.

La Fura are, for sure, amongst the best of the New Gods. Their extraordinary, life-changing show is part of a cross-London festival called *Homage to Barcelona*, marking the tenth anniversary of Franco's death, and celebrating the decade in which Spain 'throws off the shackles of fascism', ultimately joining the European Economic Community (EEC) on 1 January 1986. Elsewhere in the season of art events of all sorts is an exhibition dedicated to architect Gaudi which is at the Hayward Gallery – in many ways the exact opposite of La Fura's presentation, being all slides and wordy explanations of the art rather than the thing itself. I suppose, being about architecture, it was hard to do anything else, but perhaps the Docklands Clipper could have been repurposed as a Magic Bus to take us all on a trip to see the Sagrada Familia church in Barcelona...

Winter '85/'86 sees other interesting new visual arts events and exhibitions. A comprehensive Kurt Schwitters retrospective at the Tate reminds us that he was not only a brilliant collagist but also a performance poet and a creator of immersive environments, forging his own version of Dada called *Merz*, which "reorganised refuse material into aesthetic shape" and was thus a precursor of punk. Eduardo Paolozzi does a takeover at the Museum of Mankind in *Lost Magic Kingdoms*, curating a Cabinet of Curiosities display of fetishistic and totemic objects from across the globe. Les Levine's *Blame God* poster series, shown at the ICA, causes controversy. Once again, it's that tricky old question of blasphemy. And on the very last day of the year, 31 December 1985, Polish-American artist Krzysztof Wodiczko makes the streets of London his canvas, in *City Projections*. He was commissioned to project onto Nelson's Column in Trafalgar Square, and decided on an image of a missile wrapped in barbed wire, as a commentary on war. But he then realised South Africa House was also in the Square, and switched the camera around to project a swastika onto the building's portico, as a protest against SA's apartheid regime. Of course, he didn't have permission to do this, and knew that the projection would be short-lived: the work remained in place for just a couple of hours, with Wodiczko removing the slide just as the police approached... By pure chance, I get to see it as I head to the ICA, just around the corner from Trafalgar Square.

Clearly, the 'live without dead time/demand the impossible' punk energy has – with a few honourable exceptions – shifted away from rock and roll and into other artforms.

'Theatre' for example is ceasing to mean a well-written play delivered by actors. I mean, it can be that, and on the mainstream stages in England that's mostly what occurs, but across the world there are a growing number of anarchic, multidiscipline collectives who have sprung up in the last few years – many with punk connections, such as Derevo in Russia, who are making a maverick and mostly word-free theatre that blends Butoh dance with a carnivalesque visual aesthetic, creating dream-like scenarios in which grotesque clowns battle to a soundtrack of distorted fairground music.

Talking of clowns: in Montreal, in May 1986, I get to see a brand new contemporary circus company called Cirque du Soleil. Their show, presented in a great big stripy blue-and-yellow tent, features no animals, just lithe acrobats dressed in leopardskin and whimsical mimes in striped jumpers carrying umbrellas.

Circus is most definitely where it's at in the late 1980s. More than one young punk has given up on the music scene and run off to join the circus. Tony D, for example, the creator and editor of the legendary punk fanzine *Ripped and Torn*, has taken up juggling and can be found busking at the burgeoning new street theatre and circus festival circuit in Europe.

And there's a new force to be reckoned with in old Blighty when French trailblazers Archaos – founded by Pierrot and Martine Bidon a couple of years earlier – comes to the Southbank for the first ever Festival of New Circus, described in the press as "the anti-circus circus" (*The Irish Times*) or "a devils' carnival" (the *Daily Mail*). Plus ça change – good to know we can always rely on the *Mail* to be outraged – or pseudo-outraged – on behalf of Middle England.

The Archaos team had made their first show in 1986, and it was described thus: "Their mascot at this time was a cockerel, and chickens (and feathers) featured as part of the first show, which opened with Pierrot ascending a wire to the top of the tent muttering self-deprecating obscenities; and which also featured Lolo the Clown with his dog Dracula performing on horseback. The style of the show swung between old-school poetic and a new punk image..."

By 1988, when I get to see them for the first time, the Archaos show has expanded to include Mad Max motorbikes roaring around the space in place of the horses, juggled chainsaws, a rip-roaring cloudswing act delivered by a death-defying punkette, and a chef-turned-clown dressed in a bloodied apron with pork chops dangling from his body.

Wow, this is something else altogether. Punk rock or what? The company are resolutely punk in attitude, for sure: "Everything we say, we do; everything we want, we find; everything is important, but we don't give a damn," they say in the advance publicity. With a clever Malcolm McLaren-ish news feed from their PR company, Mark Borkowski – who'd spread the word that their dangerous chainsaw-juggling act had been banned, which may or may not be true – stories migrate from the arts pages to the front pages, and people flock in their thousands to see this phenomenon for themselves.

Archaos come back the next year, and after great success at the Edinburgh Fringe do extended runs in London at Highbury Fields in the north of the city, and Clapham Common in the south. Their form of new/old circus (Pierrot Bidon always claimed that in both their attitude and in the risk-taking of their acts, they were closer to the circus tradition than most so-called 'traditional' circuses) inspired many of Britain's burgeoning young circus performers, and by the end of the decade, London has its very own Circus Space, a centre for training and experimentation.

Dance is also moving in new directions – with inspiration streaming in from multiple sources simultaneously. From Montreal come Edouard Lock's troupe La La La Human Steps, with a show called *Human Sex* – a kind of postmodern musical, a high-energy gender-challenging montage of acrobatics and dance duets that has more in common with all-in wrestling than ballet, bodies hurtling themselves at each other with breakneck speed through a laser-lit space.

From Germany – Wuppertal, to be precise – comes Pina Bausch, an Expressionist dancer who had trained with Kurt

Jooss, then later with José Limón. In the 1970s, she became director of Tanztheater Wuppertal, then made a film with Fellini in 1982 called *And the Ship Goes*. For Pina, distinctions between 'serious' and 'popular' music (still a thing in the contemporary dance world) were of no significance. All music was afforded the same value, and she freely chose what she wanted from any genre for her choreography – German folk tunes, Latin American rumbas, pop classics. Anything goes. Her show *Kontakthof* is set in a dancehall, and uses the mores and conventions of ballroom dancing as its raw material. Well, that certainly appeals to me, given my recent foray into that world. When it arrives at Sadler's Wells in London in 1982, it shakes up the dance world.

If anything *Viktor*, brought over later in the decade (and the first of her works that I get to see live) causes even more of a stir. The set is a 20-foot high bank of earth. An enormous ensemble of around 30 performers enact a tragi-comic exploration of life, death and everything in between. The stage is dotted with tables laid with white linen cloths and laden with food. There are weddings and burials (and amalgams of the two). Dancers smoke on stage, carry each other around as if transporting lifeless shop mannequins, dangle from aerial straps whilst wearing evening gowns, and act out games of power as they turn each other into human fountains spitting into buckets. Oh yes, oh yes! I'm in awe. It's a show that launches a thousand 'new dance' companies – including one that I join a few years later. We are all so taken with her! This is the dance work we want to make! What we all love about her is her no-limits approach to what can be placed on a stage. There seems to be no physical action, gesture, inanimate object, noise, or piece of music that is considered a no-go.

Everything is potential raw material from which she creates art. It is as much moving sculpture as it is dance.

And more on human sculptures: there are some great installation-cum-performance works being created by a group of women called the Neo-Naturists. At the core of this group are Wilma Johnson and the sisters Christine and Jennifer Binnie. They sometimes paint in a regular kind of way – you know, with paint on paper, using brushes – but are more often to be found making prints using their naked body parts (something also done by 'sex positive' American porn star turned performance artist Annie Sprinkle). Or, they paint each other's bodies in fabulous swirls of colour, then sit in the James Birch Gallery window facing on to the King's Road. Sometimes they incorporate mud or leaves. They occasionally do a fuller show at an indoor venue like the ICA, with extra performers, often including a young man called Grayson Perry. James Birch, by the way, is the first person to give Grayson a solo exhibition.

Through Foz's artist friend Thomasina I'd got to meet Wilma Johnson – we three had lunch at Melati's, a Malaysian restaurant in Great Windmill Street, just a few doors away from the legendary Windmill Theatre. We talked life drawing and figurative painting, and about the parallels between what Wilma and the Neo-Naturists do (creating living sculptures in shop windows), and the work of the Windmill showgirls who, because of laws on nudity in public, were once obliged to stand stock-still like live mannequins, with perhaps the only movement on stage coming from the gentle fluttering of the feather fans.

A few months after that, with a very young baby Gabriel in his trusty Snugli baby sling, Foz and I go to see Wilma's paintings at an exhibition called *Monolith* at Conway Hall. Gabriel is very taken with one featuring a fulsome female figure depicted in electric blue, staring longingly at the big blue breasts directly in his eye-line. So we almost buy that one, but in the end go with *II Lobsters and a Dog*, which is one of a series depicting new interpretations of Tarot cards – in this case, her take on *La Lune*. Wilma's version (as the name suggests) has just one hound, not two as is often the case – a friendly looking yellow dog stood by a tree, with a sliver of waxing crescent moon above. There are no towers, and where traditionally there might be one crustacean emerging from the murky depths, Wilma gives us two big sturdy red lobsters sat in a calm blue background. Interesting! The painting is set in a hand-carved wooden frame etched with naked female forms and flower-heads. It becomes our wedding present to ourselves, and the first of many original pieces by artist friends that we buy over the years.

Life nowadays is, naturally, all about accommodating the needs of our new arrival, but luckily he's very much an out-and-about baby. We take him to gigs – he likes Sarah Jane Morris's band The Happy End, but is not too keen on WAN. He's very fond of parks, particularly ones with exotic birds. And he likes art galleries. We regularly get the 77 bus to the Tate on Milbank – practically door-to-door, St Ann's Hill to Vauxhall Cross – for a dash around the collection. He likes both of the Blakes – William and Peter. An outing that combines parks, birds and art is perfect. So we might, for example, hop off the train at Victoria and walk to St James's Park to say hello to the pelicans; then head to the ICA to see the *Berliners* exhibition. London is a playground, and we play.

These are busy times. I'm still dancing – or teaching dancing, anyway. And yes, I'm writing little bits here and there, filing my regular column for *TransFM*, doing an occasional piece for *ZigZag* or *Vague* or other small-scale art or music magazines. Oh, and I do a lengthy interview (with baby Gabriel in tow) with Jon Savage, for a book he's writing about punk, called *England's Dreaming*. I'm keeping my hand in, just about.

I want to do more – but I just can't. I'm totally exhausted: working three evenings a week teaching dance is killing me; and working on Saturdays, given that Foz is working full-time Monday to Friday, seems stupid. So I pull back, re-assess, do less work and accept that I'll be the principle baby-carer for a while. This, surprisingly, feels like the right call. It means we now have our Saturdays free to wander down Portobello Road, take a trip to the funfair at Battersea Park, or go to Holland Park to see the peacocks. We may well head over to the ICA or Photographer's Gallery to see what's on, then meet up with Gen and Paula, or perhaps Drew and Rose, at the Olive Tree.

There's a future to come in which all the things I've been seeing and writing about and absorbing – from John Giorno and Robert Anton Wilson to La Fura dels Baus; from Pina Bausch to New Circus and the Neo-Naturists – will inspire and feed my own performance work.

I know that there will be new ventures, one day, and I'll be making and doing. Maybe not playing drums, but – something. It has yet to reveal itself, but something is germinating. Something that'll bring together sounds and visions, words and music.

For now, I'm happy to be the witness, not the protagonist. I don't know yet which direction I'll move off in – I just know that when the time is right, I'll be ready.

BRIGHTON ROCK/S

Gosh, it all feels so grown-up. We're married with a baby.
We have a flat with a mortgage. We own furniture.
Who'd have thought it?

It's December 1988, and it's bitterly cold. I thought Brighton was supposed to be warmer than London – what's this about? Turns out that whatever temperature it is on paper, there's always this wind coming from the sea making it feel colder. I'm walking down North Street from the Clocktower, towards the sea, pushing a buggy with Gabriel (now two years old) sat on a sheepskin and wrapped up in woolly jumpers and mittens, a crocheted shawl tucked over his knees.

North Street is one of the main drags, with Hanningtons department store taking up most of it. Like a lot of buildings in Brighton, Hanningtons is painted turquoise. There are Christmas lights strung across the street – but pretty pathetic ones, low-wattage old-school Santas and reindeer. Regent Street this ain't. Oh God, my London, my London. What have I done? What am I doing here?

I keep heading down the hill, then turn right along the Old Steine. The Royal Pavilion, that strange dome-topped folly built for the Prince Regent, before he became King George IV, is on my left. Now I'm at the Palace Pier, and we head off along the wooden boardwalk, the foamy sea raging below. The Pier is almost deserted. There's just an old geezer feeding the gulls, and the die-hard gamblers playing the slot machines in the Palace of Fun. Gabriel fancies a bit of a gamble too: we exchange a pound for a mountain of two-pence pieces which he feeds into the penny-pusher machine, winning nothing – not that he minds, it's the action of putting the pennies in the slot and seeing them drop that he likes. He also likes the big claw that reaches down to pick up sweets and toys. I have to buy him a small cuddly teddy to make up for the disappointment of not catching one with the claw. He's also very interested in the shop that has stripy sticks of rock, and those neon pink false teeth, also made out of boiled sugar. Rock false teeth to break your real teeth on! I manage to steer him away from these – stuck in a buggy, he has no choice.

I'm on my own with Gabriel for much of the time these days. I know nobody here in this blustery seaside town, absolutely nobody. Foz is now commuting to London daily, heading off from my parents' house in Haywards Heath with his push-bike to take the 8:20 train to London Bridge, then cycling down the Old Kent Road to the Mobile Merchandising art studios, where he's a graphic designer – a job he'd got through friend Mark Alleyne, he of Mark Antony and the Centurions – working on commercial projects for Disney and Warner Brothers. Yep, Mickey Mouse and Bugs Bunny are paying the new mortgage. He's often not home till 8 or 9pm.

+

We'd somehow made it out of London and bought a flat, despite everything.

With Gabriel's arrival, life had inevitably turned topsy-turvy. Our one-bedroomed basement in Wandsworth wasn't ideal, but we feel it'll do for now. You can't stay here, says my mother. It's not suitable. Oh for goodness sake! People live in tents. Caves. We'll be fine. We have a roof over our heads and running water.

Our landlady isn't very happy. No children or pets, she says. Well, we can hardly send him back. We dig in our heels, as I really can't face trying to move with a tiny baby in tow. A few months later, she's back with a different line, one that's all motherly concern. It's just that this is no place for a baby, she says, peering in at the bedroom with its sidecar arrangement – a metal cot, given to us by Gen and Paula, with one side taken off, pushed up next to our double bed. He needs his own room, she says. I make vaguely agreeing noises and say we're looking. We're not. But as our baby becomes a toddler, and the small flat fills with toys and clothes and buggies and baby-walkers, I am starting to feel that it *is* a bit crowded here. I start wondering if we could convert the bedroom into a nursery and have a fold-up futon for me and Foz in the living room – but there's hardly room for that with all this annoying landlady furniture squashed into the flat. Maybe she'd be willing to take away the furniture. But no, of course she isn't – she wants us out, and starts making that known more loudly. Of course, she can't legally evict us, she knows that, but it's starting to feel uncomfortable being there and knowing we're not wanted.

We start looking, but there's nowhere to be had. With baby in buggy, I traipse across South London looking at flats to rent or buy – I do still have the 69 Exhibition Road pay-off, and perhaps that'd be enough for a deposit...

Nothing. We're on a Wandsworth Council waiting list, but that's very unlikely to come to anything. Then, I'm told about a scheme for Wandsworth residents to buy ex-council flats, which our newly-elected Tory council, following the lead of prime minister Margaret Thatcher, are cheerily marketing in a bid to replace social housing with property ownership. I look at some places in Battersea and Tooting. They're horrible. We carry on scouring the property pages in the Evening News. The breaking point comes when I go to see a flat advertised as two-bedroomed in Forest Hill. It's one bedroom and one windowless cupboard, in Catford. To get there, I have to walk from Catford Bridge railway station through a God-forsaken estate for what feels like forever, pushing the buggy across a soulless landscape littered with broken glass. No, just no.

The following weekend, we're staying with my parents in Haywards Heath – they'd moved out of South London just as soon as I'd finished school, and this is where they moved to. We take the train in to Brighton, as we often do when we're down in Sussex – there's not much to do in depressingly dull Haywards Heath. We're heading down to the Palace Pier, and pass an estate agent. Foz stays outside with the baby whilst I go in. I don't suppose, I say, cap in hand with Uriah Heep humility, I don't suppose you have anything at all for under £50,000? With our £10,000 cash – thus, a 20% deposit – that's the most we could afford. We have no idea if we'd get a mortgage, but Foz now has a regular PAYE job, so perhaps. Why certainly, says the estate agent, opening a drawer and pulling out sheafs of paper. Two-bedroomed flats in central Brighton or Hove; even whole houses slightly further out in East Brighton or West Hove. This is so, so much cheaper than London! I go outside to Foz. Look, I say, look at all these.

We're both – well, all three of us – London born and bred. We love London. Is this really what we want, to move to Brighton? Could we? Should we? We take a small detour, to the King and Queen pub just around the corner – they have a courtyard with big cages full of budgies, so Gabriel's happy.

It doesn't take long to decide. In some ways, we don't feel we have much choice. The option of staying in London has been taken away from us by the ludicrous inflation in house prices, affecting both sales and rentals, that has been happening over the five years since I left Exhibition Road. And now I realise that this is not going to stop, it's going to go on and on and on, who knows for how long. If we don't do something soon, we might not be able to afford anywhere, not even in Brighton. Decision made. We're on the move.

There are all sorts of set-backs before we finally have our own front door key. The friendly woman who was selling us her enormous, lovely, clean and sunny flat in Hove – someone who'd welcomed us into her life, fed us dinner, and agreed prices for fixtures and fittings – suddenly changed her mind, leaving us starting over. Panicked by gazumping and ever-rising prices, we end up buying a smaller and grubbier maisonette at the tattier end of Montpelier Road, Brighton. The house is 140 years old – late Regency – and has clearly not been done up in years. The annual maintenance cost is very low, which we think is a good thing, not realising that this means that eventually things will fall apart badly and we'll be handed a big bill. It's a block up from the sea, on the corner of Sillwood Street, in what our building society surveyor describes as "the cosmopolitan area of Brighton". There's a gay bar called The Oriental a few doors down that has drag acts on every Sunday, and an Irish pub on the opposite corner called The Lion and Lobster that hosts bawdy evenings of live fiddle music. The Montpelier

Road/Sillwood Street crossroads is a favourite cruising area, and up the hill is an old-school nightclub called Blue Moon or something of that sort, frequented by boozy businessmen who stagger out with bare-legged white-stiletto-heeled girls young enough to be their daughters dangling from their arms. No shortage of evening entertainment here, then... who needs TV when you can look out of the window?

But we've not actually moved in to Montpelier Road yet. We're temporarily staying with my parents in horrible Haywards Heath while we decorate the new flat. I say 'decorate' but it's a complete mess, so my dad's builder friend Colin is doing the dirty work – ripping out disgusting old carpets, re-plastering the ancient walls and putting in kitchen units. Some days I take Gabriel with me in to Brighton, where we visit the flat to see how it's coming along, eating egg and chips in the local greasy spoon, Belchers (we don't yet have gas in the flat, so can't cook), and pottering around town. We sometimes go to the library on Church Street, which is rather grand, being one of the buildings that form part of the Brighton Pavilion estate. The library and museum share a space, one on each side of the grand tiled corridors with doors painted a glossy green; and within the museum is the art gallery, where there's an uncurated mish-mash of stuff – a Dali 'lips' sofa, some Chinese pottery, some 19th century landscape paintings. Hmmm... Not the V&A, then. There is, though, a stuffed goat, which Gabriel is intrigued by, and in the foyer a giant porcelain cat that eats money – more pennies needed.

We're doing all this just to get used to being in Brighton, to try to feel that we belong here, but it is all rather lonely and draining. On other days, my dad looks after Gabriel (which Gabriel likes as it involves watching *Thomas the Tank Engine* videos, tormenting Siouxsie the cat, and eating lots of

biscuits) while I go into Brighton on my own, to do some actual decorating. If it's the weekend, Foz joins me. He does a tasteful blue rag-wash thing on the living room walls. I paint the upstairs room, which we have dubbed 'the playroom', a tasteless purple.

I like the days when I'm in the flat by myself. Empty houses have a special feel to them – one of expectation. By Christmas, Colin has finished the proper building work, and we've erased the ghosts of previous tenants (it was a student let for years), and now have every room painted a different colour with cork tiles on the downstairs floors and a rough hessian carpet on the stairs and upstairs rooms. There's gas central heating and a cooker now too. We are so not the sort of people who do up houses – this transformation is miraculous, albeit brought about because my dad put in the money, and his mate Colin the work force to get the difficult stuff done.

Alone, I walk around, looking at what's going to be my new home. Downstairs, there's a tiny, square entrance hall; a yellow-walled bathroom with wooden cladding that makes it feel like a boat; and a living room with a large walk-in cupboard to one side and a corridor leading to a small kitchen from the other side, all painted sky blue. At the bay window to the front of the house there are real lace curtains with an intricate pattern featuring exotic birds and seahorses, made to measure from the little lace shop on the pier. A steep staircase goes up from the hall to the upstairs floor, which is a loft conversion. There's a sweet little alcove half way up, with just enough room for a bookcase and a two-year-old child. We paint the walls and ceiling of the stairway and alcove a warm womb-like red. Upstairs, there are two rooms, open doorways facing each other. One has our brand-new double bed – the first piece of new furniture either of us has ever bought – and a window that leads out on to a flat roof. The other, the 'playroom', is Gabriel's space. I've painted enormous psychedelic pink, yellow and turquoise flowers over the purple walls, and we've bought a roll-up double futon instead of a child's bed.

We decide it's time to take the plunge and move in to our flat, despite having no furniture other than the beds, and a well-worn red velvet Chesterfield sofa that my parents have handed on.

A few days after Christmas, Foz and I are strolling with Gabriel through the North Laine – the area of Brighton near the station that has cheap second-hand clothes and book shops, and numerous indoor and outdoor bric-a-brac markets. Our favourite is a ramshackle old building called the Jubilee Market, with stalls selling tatty old *Beano* comics, those tiny plastic toys you get free in cereal boxes, and broken reel-to-reel tape recorders. There's also a cafe where you can get a mug of tea and a fried egg on white bread sandwich, and not much else. But if you are after something fancier, there are some recently opened cappuccino bars and vegetarian restaurants in the same street, sitting side-by-side with the hardware shops and off-licences. Give it another ten years and the North Laine will be hipster central, a riot of small boutiques and tapas bars, but not yet – it's currently just aspiring, testing the water, the old and the new eyeing each other up warily.

We're somewhere near the big wholefood shop Infinity when we bump into someone we know – which is a surprise as we didn't think we knew anybody here. It's The Monochrome Set's former tour manager and driver Dave Harper.

Ah yes, we remember now. The gossip was that Dave had run off with studio engineer Ben Rogan's wife and baby, and landed in Brighton. We knew nothing about the woman in the story. Ben Rogan's little son is with Dave. He's called Conrad and he has just turned three, six months older than Gabriel.

They look shyly at each other then bond over a small metal car that Conrad kindly lets Gabriel hold. Turns out that the faceless and nameless woman is called Nicky and she is now married to Dave and pregnant with their child. Would we like to meet Nicky? Have dinner together? Why yes – we would. How about tonight? Why not! Dave mentions a place called Dig in the Ribs on Preston Street, round the corner from our new flat.

The evening's a success. Gabriel and Conrad get on very well and amuse themselves for the whole meal. Nicky and I get on too – she's heavily pregnant but we don't talk babies and births, we talk art and artists: Derek Jarman's latest film *The Last of England*, and his move to a cottage near Dungeness; Carolee Schneemann and Cindy Sherman's use of their own bodies as canvases; Nick Cave and The Bad Seeds' appearance in Wim Wenders' *Wings of Desire*.

Foz and Harper (as he now likes to be called) talk Monochrome Set on the road – the usual terrible tales of touring life: rickety vans with broken doors, piss-horrible dressing rooms, fights with promoters over money, getting lost driving the wrong way up one-way streets on the way out of Preston or Middlesborough.

So now we have some Brighton friends.

Some time later, our London friend Mike Gilbert drives our stuff down in his van. There's no furniture, but lots of books, paintings, and records. There's my vintage magazine collection and my notebooks, Foz's guitars and amps, and Gabriel's toys – including his much-loved giant papier maché duck and his very own baby Casio keyboard which is pre-set to play a synth-pop take on Leopold Mozart's *Toy Symphony*. Andy Warren has come along to help with the move. Or maybe Andy just fancied a trip to the seaside. It's a mild and sunny day, and after we unload the van we go down on to the beach. We stop for a cup of tea at the outdoor cafe by the bandstand, and Gabriel runs off towards the sea. Mike and Andy look worried. He'll stop, I say confidently. He doesn't. Foz tears after him, leather trousers and motorcycle boots getting soaked as he intercepts him and scoops him up before a wave hits him. Well, that's the Brighton baptism for them both.

Over the next few months we scour the secondhand shops and find antique wooden pigeonholes and an oak table and four chairs. We use the last of our money to buy a large and rather expensive wool rug for the living room, an Aztec-looking mirror in the shape of a sun, and a porcelain lamp-base hand-painted in a Picasso-ish style, which we get from one of the artisan shops under the seafront arches. Gosh, it all feels so grown-up. We're married with a baby. We have a flat with a mortgage. We own furniture. Who'd have thought it?

Foz is out for at least 12 hours on weekdays, commuting to London. And working in a branding and graphic design studio often means drinks after work that everyone is expected to go to, or late nights to meet a deadline. Harper is also out a lot, because that's how it is if you're working in the music biz. I spend a lot of time with Nicky. After her baby is born, a little girl they name Freya, I collect Conrad from his nursery school, which is just around the corner from Gabriel's playgroup, and take them both to nearby St Anne's Well Gardens – a park that has everything: swings, a stream, squirrels, a pond with frogs, a cafe that sells ice cream. After a while, we head back to Nicky's flat to while away the day not talking about nappies or night feeds, but instead about art, music, politics, whatever. As Nina Simone put it: "We never talked about men or clothes. It was always Marx, Lenin, revolution – real girls' talk."

The playgroup we go to is in the St Mary Magdalen's church hall right next to the park. I say 'we' because Gabriel doesn't want to be left, and the staff are happy to have me there, helping to entertain not only Gabriel but the other little ones too. Of course, most of the mothers just drop off and run – but there's another person here whose little boy, Fred, doesn't want to be left. Her name is Rachel, and she has red hair and a cheeky smile, and is dressed in a vintage cotton dress, with stripy socks and a hand-knitted cardigan. At first we just play with the children, side by side, but Fred and Gabriel have buddied up and forgotten we are there, so that gives us a chance to talk, and I learn that Fred's dad is Captain Sensible from The Damned, who I knew vaguely back in the day. I tell her about Foz being in The Monochrome Set, and me playing drums in Rema Rema and Psychic TV. Turns out she's a musician too – her band was called Dolly Mixture, and apart from playing and recording their own tunes they accompanied Cap (as she calls him, which makes me smile) on his hit tune 'Happy Talk'. So now I have another friend.

Rachel and I are both pregnant with our second babies. Except this isn't Rachel's second, it's her third. Between Fred and this new baby, there was a little girl called Bunty who died in infancy. Ah yes, I remember hearing the news, on children's Saturday morning TV of all places, and it sparking media discussions about cot death. There was that and the other Brighton story of the Babes in the Woods murders – two little girls found dead in Wild Park in October 1986 – both of these stories etching themselves onto my mind as an emotionally vulnerable new mother.

A local man, Russell Bishop, was charged with the Babes in the Woods murders, and acquitted. It'll take another 30 years before he's re-tried, convicted and put behind bars. Since moving to Brighton, I've never once been to Wild Park – with the murder unsolved, people say that the ghosts of those poor wee nine-year-old girls are hovering in the trees.

But there are plenty of other parks – and the beach! As we move into spring, and then summer, Brighton really comes into its own. Days are spent with Nicky, or Rachel, or both of them. We picnic. In Queen's Park, the kids feed their sandwich crusts to the ducks. On Brunswick Beach, the seagulls steal their chips. There are circus shows in the parks, and live music down on the seafront.

Foz is out of the picture on weekdays, but at weekends we're out and about, *en famille*. We go to Stanmer Woods – part of an enormous country park gifted to the people of Brighton by some Lord or other – where Gabriel can run wild, with no worries about traffic, and gawp at the cows. The seafront is five minutes away from our flat, so we're there a lot. We paddle in the sea close to the West Pier – the classier of the Brighton piers, once famed for its fabulous ballrooms and tea houses, but now closed, and the home to a million and one starlings. There's a West Pier tour, but we can't do that with Gabriel – he's not allowed as he's too little. Instead, we get coffees and ice creams at The Meeting Place, a beachfront cafe on the border of Brighton and Hove, next to the 'angel' peace statue, and stare out at the wrecked old Pier. The surly man who runs the cafe never once acknowledges that he's seen us before – even though I'm on the seafront almost daily, come sun, wind or rain, and sometimes I'm his only customer. We tend to stay on the Hove Promenade side of the divide, as this is a big open space with no arcades or other distractions. I'd quickly learnt that heading the other way to 'between the piers' can be a costly business, as it involves passing a million and one candy floss stands, carousels and mechanical kiddy-car rides. We leave all that to the days when grandparents are visiting, as they are happy to cough up the dosh to entertain and spoil their grandchild, and they love the kiss-me-quick brashness of it all – which admittedly I do too, but I'd be totally broke if I did it too often.

Brighton is also good for big outdoor music and arts events, we discover. A group called Same Sky are responsible for making many of these happen. In July 1989, a day or two before my baby is due, Foz, Gabriel and I go on what turns out to be our last outing before three become four. It's a night-time event at Hove Lagoon, a hefty walk westwards along the seafront. The lagoon is the site for a brilliant collaboration between musicians, dancers and visual artists – the water lit up beautifully, with music that merges live percussion with pre-recorded ambient electronics. It's very hot, and I'm very tired – this is my second summer baby, and both times the last weeks of pregnancy have been staggered through during a heatwave. Oh well, at least in Brighton it's OK to go out in your nightdress, which is what I do, using Gabriel's push-chair to rest on every 100 yards or so.

Less than 48 hours later, our second son is born – at home, on the playroom futon. Home birth was far more normalised in Brighton than in London, and my new doctor was not only tolerant but actually encouraging. Milo comes into the world as early morning sunshine streams into the room and a seagull lands on the windowsill. I think Milo sees the seagull before he clocks me, which is possibly why he grows up to be a circus aerialist. As Milo arrives, Gabriel and his appointed companion Grace come into the room. Noticing the white flakes of vernix, Gabriel asks why the baby has snow on his head – inevitably leading to him being called Snowy. This transmutes nicely into Milo, via Milou aka Snowy, the little white dog in the Tin Tin stories – although there's a blip along the way when we decide on Marlon as his name, and send out birth announcement cards saying so, then have to backtrack. *The naming of kids is a difficult matter.* We get threatening letters from the registrar of births, deaths and marriages when we get to the six-week deadline without having named our child...

And so begins the next phase. Having two tiny children to look after turns out to be the toughest thing I've ever done. I'd given up my London work as a dance teacher and choreographer when six months pregnant, including two nights a week teaching for the Inner London Education Authority in Battersea and Clapham, an occasional Saturday at the Gwenethe Walshe School of Dance, and – this one the hardest to let go of – a lucrative job as a freelance on-call choreographer to the National Theatre Studio, handed over to my former dance colleague at Arthur Murray's, Glenn. It was just all too much.

So now I'm an at-home mother-of-two, with a commuting husband. And it's all so, so difficult. I thought having one baby was hard, but it wasn't. It was a doddle compared to this. There is not a single minute of the day that's mine – it's all taken up by these two small human beings who have diametrically opposed needs. One wants me to stay home on the sofa feeding him non-stop, and one wants me to take him out all day to the park or the beach. It takes a long time to learn how to even get by; to get through a day without falling over with exhaustion or killing somebody. Whose idea was this? Who said that if you have one child, you might as well have two? Ha! Two isn't twice the work, it's about ten times the work. It's almost not humanly possible, all on your own. Or at least, I struggle to work out what needs to be done and how to do it.

Gabriel was the ultimate portable baby: he loved going out in his baby-carrier, happily bouncing along, faced outwards, as we zipped up and down escalators on the Tube, on our way out to explore art galleries or zoos or shops or parks or – well, anything really. It was all an adventure. He'd happily sleep in a Moses basket under tables at restaurants or parties. And we travelled further afield, often a long way. We flew to Canada when he was just four months old. The three of us went for Christmas and New Year, a winter wonderland of snowy streets and houses and trees decorated with glorious displays of flashing lights. The Snugli carrier really came into its own, but we did also borrow a sledge, and Gabriel rode along like a young prince, wrapped in sheepskin and accompanied by the sound of sleigh-bells. On Christmas morning we went on an outing into the wilds, to see the enormous icicles hanging from the trees, and to toboggan down the slopes.

We took a ferry to France when Gabriel was one, and went to Italy twice in the following year. He and I flew to Rome to spend time with his godmother and namesake Gabriella, whose family run an ice-cream parlour (and how good is that, a godmother who comes with her own ice cream parlour?); and for Gabriel's second birthday, we'd travelled right across Europe with Gabriel's other godparents, Dino and Bruna Pirroni, to stay with my adopted Italian family in Pellegrino Parmense.

But Milo is a very different baby. He won't feed in front of other people – so that makes going out difficult. When the Pirronis come down to meet the new arrival, we go out to Pizza Express, and for the first time ever I find myself in the Ladies' loo trying to nurse a howling baby who won't latch on. He also doesn't like me talking to anybody (other than Gabriel, who I think he sees as a kind of extension of me) when I'm feeding him. He doesn't like bright lights or loud music. Foz and I have played out our whole relationship in restaurants, wine bars and cafes, and are natural-born travellers. Gabriel was very happy to join in with that life – but Milo makes it clear that it's not what he wants. Plus, two parents and two children means one each – one nursing the baby (or trying to), one chasing up and down and in and out of the tables with a toddler. Going out to eat or drink becomes pointless. And, as we are now living on one income, there's less spare money.

On those endlessly long weekdays, home alone with two needy little ones, I arrange for people – my mother, say – to come and take Gabriel out, so I can focus on Milo, and it backfires. Gabriel won't leave my side. He's like a jealous lover who won't leave me alone with his rival in love. Oh well, says my mum, we'll all go out and get a bit of lunch. So I end up dragging myself and baby Milo out with Gabriel and her, making the whole thing pointless as the idea was to give me a rest.

The only time I do get to stay home and rest is if Foz's mum, the wonderful Nana Kath, comes down from London. She's a mother of six and foster mother of God knows how many others. She's been looking after Gabriel since I started teaching two evenings a week, when he was just six weeks old. Then, she'd pick him up like a kitten and put him face-down on her big belly, jiggling him in time to the theme tune to *Eastenders*, telling me to go out the door right now and not to worry. "Your baby will be grand," she'd say in her broad Dublin accent. And she'd looked after him when I'd done week-long stints at the National Theatre, taking him to the family fruit and veg stall in Tatchbrook Street. How will you manage, I'd asked. "Listen now," she'd said, "I'm used to working on that stall with one in the pram, one in the push-chair, and three or four running around me. Your one will be no bother at all." And of course, he's fine. When I go to collect him at the end of the day, he's happily sitting in his buggy to the side of the stall with a bag of fresh peas, podding them and throwing them at the pigeons. Now, Kathleen comes down and takes both of them away for a blissful hour or two. Once, she comes back with the story that whilst waiting for the lights to change at the crossing outside Waitrose, Gabriel had said, "Push the pram into the road, Nana! Push him away! Get rid of him" – a story she retells gleefully at every family gathering until the day of her death, 23 years later.

Eventually, I shift into some sort of routine. I mean, I've never been a 'routine' kind of mother, but Milo is teaching me that some babies thrive on routine, and Gabriel is now three years old and for the first time ever needs a regular bedtime as he's given up daytime napping. Often I put both of them to bed together and end up falling asleep with them on our big bed, which is where Foz finds us all, curled up together like a basket full of puppies, when he gets back from London. If I'm awake later than 9pm, it's a rare occurrence.

It's a different life now. A life circling around the needs of little ones. Nicky and Rachel are lifelines – Rachel has had her baby, too, a little girl called Daisy who has gorgeous red hair, just like her mother. Three women, three small children, three babies. A gang of nine.

Nicky is also my conduit into art and culture. Freya is six months old when Milo is born, and she and Harper do manage to have nights, and even weekends, out and about in London or Brighton – or even further afield. At the end of 1989, when the wall comes down, they head off to Berlin to celebrate the end of the Cold War with the rest of the ravers. Plus, Nicky is very interested in fine art, and thinking of applying to University of Sussex to do a History of Art degree. So on those afternoons where I find myself going to Nicky's for lunch and staying till dinner time, I catch up on what's going on out there in the world.

For example, there are interesting things happening in contemporary art following on from an exhibition called Freeze, put together a year earlier by a couple of young artists called

Damien Hirst and Angus Fairhurst, recent graduates from Goldsmiths. They are calling themselves – or being called, more likely – the YBAs (Young British Artists) and amongst them is a woman called Sarah Lucas, who on this occasion had presented a pile of scrap material as her exhibition, but would soon go on to make ironic commentary on the female nude using raw chickens and fried eggs.

We talk about what's going down in the pop world, with my Icelandic friends The Sugarcubes really making their mark, and interesting new combo S'Express reinventing disco. Foz and I have both moved away from playing in bands (although for Foz this is only a temporary blip), but Harper is still very much in the thick of it, working as a manager and press agent for Cherry Red, Rough Trade and Factory, amongst others. So I get to hear who's doing what and where and when – although it feels like missives from some strange, distant galaxy that I can never get to. The Pixies, Primal Scream, Inspiral Carpets, Red Lorry Yellow Lorry, Wonder Stuff, Wedding Present – most of it is lost on me, just names, names, names that I'm vaguely aware of. But I do raise my head above the parapet for long enough to buy the Stone Roses album, mostly because they have a track called 'She Bangs The Drums', my one concession to the recent explosion of UK guitar-based bands.

The airwaves and TV screens are full of my friends from a previous life – scores of people I knew in the early days of punk or played alongside as a post-punk drummer are now pop stars. There they all are: Adam Ant and Marco, Siouxsie and Steven Severin from the Banshees, Steve Strange and Rusty Egan, Marc Almond, Boy George, Human League, The Cure. Even Malcolm McLaren is a pop star, recording with hip hop artists and opera singers – seems he was interested in the music after all. His former partner Vivienne Westwood is now a lauded designer, a queen of the catwalk, listed in John Fairchild's book *Chic Savages* as one of the top six designers in the world, up there with Yves Saint Laurent and Christian Lacroix. She's moved on from pirates to puffballs to *Commedia del'Arte*, the latest collection featuring Harlequin and Columbine – but I've never been to her new Mayfair shop, and am sticking resolutely to my World's End squiggly shirts, which have seen me through two pregnancies and years of breastfeeding.

And there's more. Weekend Swingers and El Trains singer Jay Strongman is now a world-renowned DJ, spearheading the whole warehouse party thing in London before going on to conquer the world via Kiss FM. Others are less well-known, but still 'faces'. Out there, doing stuff. Blitz girl 'Princess' Julia, and my former hairdresser James 'Cuts' Lebon, for example. My hair is now down to my waist and henna'd red. Pre-Raphaelite cascades on a good day; an unruly wild-woman mess on a bad day. James would not approve.

My former bandmate Genesis P-Orridge is still using the name Psychic TV, although co-founder Alex Fergusson has left, and there's an ever-changing roster of band members coming and going – it seems more like Gen and Paula's thing rather than a proper band. They're now playing around with acid house and techno, helped by an American electronic musician called Fred Gianelli. My Rema Rema bandmates Mark Cox and Mick Allen have made their mark with Wolfgang Press, still signed to 4AD. In an interesting coincidence, Dave Harper's brother Simon works for 4AD, and I get the occasional missive via Dave about how everyone is doing. Doing very well, it would seem. On one occasional, Simon turns up in Brighton with an envelope full of used banknotes, which is apparently my royalties for recent sales of Rema Rema's one and only record release, *Wheel in the Roses*.

I could, I suppose, reach out and make contact with people, but it feels pointless. My life is so very, very different – what would we have in common? I stay in touch with Andy – he comes down to visit us regularly, staying for the weekend, building fabulous Duplo-brick towers with Gabriel and coming on the beach outings. I keep up with Marco and Adam's derring-do's via the Pirronis, who visit regularly (they are Gabriel's godparents, after all). I occasionally see Marco in person. On one occasion, a while back, before we'd moved out of London, we'd been for dinner at the Pirronis' restaurant on Tottenham Court Road, and then headed off afterwards to see Marco's lovely new flat in Baker Street. I remember manoeuvring Gabriel's buggy into the lift and arriving in that fabulous pink-and-black pop art show-flat, decorated with jukeboxes and sassy sofas and, of course, gorgeous guitars. And I had to suppress the thought that leapt up: this is what I'd chosen, motherhood on a tight budget rather than life as a pop star's girlfriend, and this was OK. Well, wasn't it?

I suppose it was, but with the move to Brighton, the arrival of a second child, and a further step away from the old life, there were times when I wondered. I seemed to have become a kind of earth-mother figure – how did that happen? Extended breastfeeding, the family bed, attachment parenting. Trips to the Steiner School mother and toddler group. Running arts and crafts sessions at Earth Spirit festival. Leading post-natal support groups with La Leche League. Rock and roll!

But life wasn't all milk teeth and Moomins. There was something new emerging – a seed sown, a tiny shoot peeking up. It's not an offer to join a band, it's something else altogether.

In spring 1990, when Milo was about nine months old, I'd heard about a class at the Brighton Natural Health Centre run by Ginny Farman, one of the performers in Liz Aggiss'

Divas Dance Theatre company. I knew of Liz as a dancer of the German Expressionist ilk – someone blazing the trail as a postmodern performance artist honouring the Expressionist tradition but also mining the cabaret and vaudeville tropes. She and another choreographer called Lea Anderson – who had a company with the unlikely name of The Cholmondeleys (and a brother company, with the even more unlikely name of The Featherstonehaughs) – were the leading lights of this new trend in contemporary dance, which in many ways had more in common with experimental theatre companies like Lumiere and Son than with most dance companies. I'm really interested in all this – it's a world away from the often po-faced and over-serious contemporary dance scene.

Ginny had recently graduated from the Visual and Performing Arts course at Brighton Polytechnic (which is still fondly called 'the art school' by most), taking the dance strand led by Liz Aggiss. This course was gaining a reputation for itself as the market leader in experimental performance art. Although students were signed up onto one of three different strands – dance, theatre or music – everyone was encouraged to mix and match, using whatever worked best for them in making their art.

Guest lecturers that included Helen Chadwick (who I'd known a decade earlier when she lived on Beck Road, opposite Throbbing Gristle's HQ), the Brothers Quay, and Forkbeard Fantasy – all working artists using a wide variety of media – were drafted in to inspire and mentor. The term 'Live Art' has just started to be used, a handy term that knocks on the head the tedious argument about whether the work is 'dance' or 'theatre' or 'performance'. Ginny has been a member of Liz's Divas troupe for quite a while, but is thinking of branching out into her own work as a choreographer.

Her classes, which I'm now enthusiastically going to regularly, are great – a long way from the usual contemporary dance repertoire, inspired to a great extent by the playful work of Pina Bausch, with a fair bit of Limon release technique thrown in for good measure. Like her heroine Bausch, and mentor Liz Aggiss, Ginny is always happy to include popular music and dance motifs in her work – a dash of twist or jive or samba working its way into routines.

Ginny is currently making work with a writer called Graham Duff, creating experimental theatre works under the name Thumb Culture – though she now has something else in mind. She wants to create a Pina Bausch inspired dance troupe that will perform in nightclubs rather than on theatre stages. She has a slogan for this new venture: High Art in Low Places. Soon there's also a name – Disco Sister.

Ginny has been invited in as choreographer for a new event at Brighton's Zap Club, a monthly night called Pow Wow. Would I like to be part of this group? You bet! It's been a long time since I'd done any performance work, but now the time is right.

Time to step up and step out.

YELLOW MUMMY BIRD

The two little creatures are delighted
to have woken up to a naked and adorned mother
in place of the usual plain one in a cotton nightie. As if by magick!

hiG,
ar.
in
Low
RaC

disco Sister.

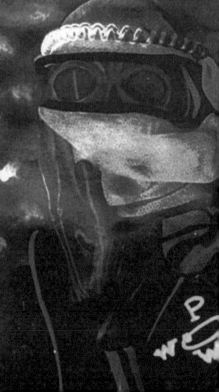

A small body nestles in. I try to go back to sleep, but little hands are pulling and prodding, tugging my ear lobes and twisting strands of my tangled hair. My? Are they mine? Ha! There's no me and you anymore, just us. I'm half-in half-out of sleep, dreaming of golden eagles and wide-eyed owls soaring around me when the baby voice breaks the dream.

"Lellow Mummy."

I look down at baby Milo who is lying across my belly, which is – yep – yellow. I look at the clock. 5.30am. Two hours after I'd gone to bed.

"Mmm, yellow mummy," I say, "Let's go back to sleep."

An hour later, Gabriel joins us in the bedroom. "Why have you got all those feathers in your hair?" he asks.

"Because I'm a bird."

"Lellow Mummy. Bird." says Milo, and the two of them roll around the bed laughing.

I give up on sleep. I go to the bathroom, passing the full-length mirror on the way. There I am, covered in yellow body paint – even though I'd had a late-night shower at the Zap Club, very little of the paint seems to have come off – hair backcombed and stuck with discarded feathers of spotted this and speckled that. I turn around and smile at the faces peeping out from the wrong end of the duvet – two little creatures delighted to have woken up to a naked and adorned mother in place of the usual plain one in a cotton nightie. As if by magick!

Despite the lack of sleep, the day goes well. In the afterglow of last night's adventures on the frontline of performance art, nothing seems to matter too much. The housework is ignored and we go down to the beach – just five minutes' walk away. On days like this everything feels easy and relaxed, and I'm basking in the post-show relief – pleased to have got it all done after weeks of planning meetings and rehearsals that somehow got squeezed in between breastfeeds and teatimes.

"God, I don't know how you manage," wide-eyed Atlanta had said.

I find myself almost apologising for my children. You get used to it, it's fine really, I say. There aren't many people to confide in; people who can handle the truth that it is ridiculously hard work looking after these two small human beings, and that trying to do anything in the way of art-making is a struggle, sometimes hard to justify. People will help, but that comes with its own baggage.

For example, my mum will happily babysit when I'm teaching my dance classes, glad to support me in earning what she calls "a bit of pin money", but she doesn't understand why I am doing performance work that I don't even get paid for.

"So how much do you get for doing this, then?" she'd asked last night before I left her to it, heading off to transform myself into the Yellow Mummy Bird. She already knew the answer, of course.

"Well, nothing really," I say. "Just expenses."

"But don't they pay you? That doesn't seem right."

Who's *they*? There is no *they* – we're doing it ourselves, I tell her a bit testily. This is a repeat conversation, and one I'm bored with.

I tell her that we've taken over the Zap one day a month with this new venture called Pow Wow, bringing Live Art into a nightclub setting – performance, dance, film, whatever.

Of course, this is just met with, "Well, I still think they should pay you". It irritates me more than it should because, if I'm honest, I do actually think 'they' should pay me, but just haven't quite worked out who the elusive 'they' might be.

The Pow Wow Posse, as it is called – we are in the days before 'posse' becomes a word so sullied by the Ibiza-frenzied-Danny-Rampling-Radio 1 wrecking crew that you wouldn't be able to use it without irony – the Pow Wow Posse circles around Mark Waugh the writer and philosopher and his partner Ivo, a young marquis or some such thing. There's the stupendously beautiful Sidonia, and wild child Atlanta. Ginny Farman is choreographer, her boyfriend Daniel is lead DJ, and then there's a bunch of performers – me and Steve Lacey and Helen whose surname I don't know, and many more – plus more DJs and filmmakers and God knows who else, enough to fill the place even without an audience. The Zap had been packed the evening before, but it was difficult to know if there was anyone who'd actually paid to get in – the crew list and guest list were pages long.

The theme for the evening was Alchemy and the performance had been based on an exploration of the elements – water, earth, fire and air. I'd been air: yellow, feathers, birds, wings, angels, mercury, breath, wind. Blowing up balloons and releasing them into the audience; climbing up on balconies, swinging, singing... In other words, spending my time away from the children playing the sort of games they played daily.

Pow Wow fills Spring and Summer 1991 with games: a Pina Bausch inspired procession through the club wearing pointy hats and painted rubber gloves, gestural arm movements played out whilst singing 'Dream a Little Dream of Me'; an Egyptian sand dance; a tango for 12 people, danced in two groups of six who work in traverse, stomping towards each other like gladiators. All accompanied by DJs and VJs mixing and matching sounds and visuals, the walls and floors a montage of moving images stolen from advertising and TV – Space Raiders and Skittles, Metal Micky and Sonic the Hedgehog, disembodied hands and lips and legs in rabid yellows, UV violets and gobstopper greens – merging with symbols nabbed from new age magickal mysticism – pyramids, triangles, infinity symbols, evil eyes, pentangles – all delivered with a post-pop-art Warholian sensibility; the speakers booming out the Bingoboys, De La Soul, and A Tribe Called Quest.

High Art in Low Places, Ginny's slogan for her dance troupe, Disco Sister, perfectly· captures the mood of the moment. Punk had paved the way, and rave culture drove the down-home DIY ethos forwards. Now, this new club culture/ performance art thing that has sprung up of late – inspired, perhaps, by New York clubs like Danceteria programming performance artists such as Karen Finley – playing a punkish postmodern game of 'spot my meaning by reading between the lines', teasing out a multitude of interpretations that could be ascribed to any one action or image that is presented outside of its usual context.

Humour and an appreciation for all popular culture tastes and styles, from all eras, are at the heart of this newest of new waves. There is no longer any punk versus hippy, 1950s versus 1960s versus 1970s versus 1980s divisions. Everything coexists. Here at the Zap Club, there are people in tie-dye and people in zipped leather. People in Zoot suits or flowery tea-dance dresses, and people in latex onesies. Knuckle-dusters, bovver boots, neon vests, feather boas, Adidas, PVC mini-skirts, denim shirts, bandanas, boilersuits, kaftans, crinolines, curtains. Is there anything that people won't wear? Philip Sallon really does have a lot to answer for. Leigh Bowery, too – he seems to be here, there and everywhere at the moment, with Ted Polhemus in hot pursuit, camera in hand.

This world was one that I'd only just moved into. I'd been to a couple of the early warehouse parties that sparked off the rave scene, such as Dirt Box where friend Jay Strongman DJ'd, but had missed all of those legendary late-80s smiley-badged day-glo'd all-nighters in fields – too busy having babies. I'm at least ten years older than Ginny – now in my mid-30s – and worried that I was maybe too old for all this. But Ginny is encouraging. She likes Psychic TV and other things I'd been part of, and is interested in hearing first-hand about the pioneering days of punk and post-punk, and especially about the Happenings (to use a term nobody uses any more) like the opening party for the *Prostitution* exhibition at the ICA, and PTV's *Fabulous Feast ov Flowering Light*, which had pre-empted the current fancy for cross-artform events, bringing bands and burlesque and live literature and performance and films and whatever else together.

```
        P
  W     O     W
        W
```

PRESENT

FYA Circus Irritant, Sweat Sound
System, DJ's Andy Crock, Shane,
Jamie, Budge, Tom. Performance by
Thumb Culture, Bomshelle & Les
enfants du Butoh. Psychedelic EYE
food, Phantasmagoria.

DATE 11th JULY
ORBIT 9.00 - 3.00
PRICE £5 & £5.50

It seems slightly odd that there is a whole new bunch of twenty-somethings interested in things that happened whilst they were just primary school kids – but no different, I realise, to my generation's friendships with the likes of William Burroughs or John Giorno and our interest in the artists, poets and experimental musicians who came before us.

For my part, I enjoy Ginny's reworking of contemporary dance. I liked the way she brought together disparate elements in her life and work: Ginny was interested in Buddhism and Barbie dolls, vegetarianism and House music, martial arts and pop art – embracing them all with a serious enthusiasm and a light touch. And she gives feminism a 1990s twist, making pink neon stickers that say things like 'God is a Girl'.

On the seafront the next day Gabriel and I throw a big beach ball to each other, shout into the wind, and dangle from the railings next to the Meeting House cafe, near the angel statue on the Brighton and Hove border. Milo sleeps in the pushchair with his back to the sea dreaming of yellow mummy birds, while the seagulls screech and circle in the sky.

Because children play all the time, it can be hard for them to understand the adult need to separate that play into little enclaves called art. When Milo is taken along to see me performing in an outdoor theatre show at Brunswick Festival, he bursts into tears and demands that I get off the stage, calling "Mummy Mummy" over and over again, arms held out, wriggling defiantly in his buggy, until wheeled away by his daddy. I was playing a bossy Thatcher-type lady councillor in the play. It was the hat I was wearing that upset him, apparently. That's Foz's view. But I think it was more likely the awareness of the separate space between us – and the refusal to be allocated the role of spectator rather than performer. Even when there's no obvious fourth wall, being in performer mode means that a kind of bubble is created around you, a barrier that can't be crossed. That must be frightening if you're a baby watching a mummy who's there but not there.

The summer draws to a close, and the very last Pow Wow leads the audience out onto the beach for a ra-ra girl swirling of neon tubes, and the arrival of flare-bearing sportsmen in a motor boat. I'm leading off the ra-ra girls – Ginny has opted out by now, as she feels the whole thing is going in a direction she's not interested in. And I kind of wish I had too when Mark brings on the topless female boxers – postmodern performance eats itself and suffers indigestion... Oh well, it ran its course and now Pow Wow is done and dusted. Time for the next thing.

So, what'll it be? What now?

+

The Zap has seen a lot of things coming and going over the past near-decade. It was started by Neil and Pat Butler in 1982, and right in there from the start were performance artist Ian Smith, and one Roger Ely – the Jeff Nuttall protégé who co-created *The Final Academy*, also in 1982. Before that, Roger and Neil Butler had launched the first Brighton Festival of Contemporary Performance, 1977 to 1979, which had programmed Throbbing Gristle alongside experimental theatre company IOU and performance artist Roland Miller.

The first Zap shows were at the Oriental Hotel, aiming to "mix radical art with down-home entertainment". Ian Smith hosted *Performance Platform* on Tuesdays, and later the *Silver Tongue Club* on Sundays. Both nights mixed up cabaret and performance art – and some things that sat between the two. With choreographer Liz Aggiss, Ian and Neil were also part of a group called The Wild Wigglers who appeared regularly,

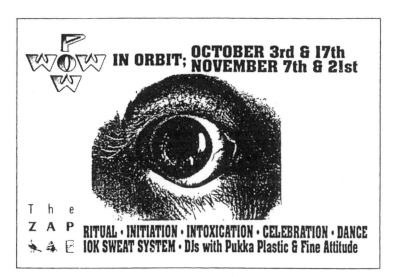

WOW IN ORBIT; OCTOBER 3rd & 17th NOVEMBER 7th & 21st

The ZAP
RITUAL · INITIATION · INTOXICATION · CELEBRATION · DANCE
10K SWEAT SYSTEM · DJs with Pukka Plastic & Fine Attitude

presenting beautifully absurdist little dance vignettes in which (say) they hopped up and down on the spot for five minutes non-stop, dressed in clownish stripy all-in-ones.

After try-outs at a few other venues, by October 1984 the Zap finally had its own space in the King's Road Arches on Brighton Beach.

My first trip to the Zap was in 1985, as a member of Psychic TV – just months after the move to the arches. We actually went twice that spring: once in March for a video art event in which Hilmar and Monte played behind a screen showing the harrowing *SXXX-80* video; and once in May, with the whole band playing a full set as a warm-up to *Thee Fabulous Feast ov Flowering Light* at Hammersmith Palais. On this occasion, the sun is still shining when we arrive in Brighton, and the arch next to the stage is opened up, so as we do the soundcheck we look out over the beach and sky and the beautiful old West Pier, the circling starlings joining in with the PTV tunes.

There are return trips over the years. *The Taboo Festival of Eroticism* in 1986 is another Roger Ely initiative, billed as an exploration of sex, art and the erotic. Cosey presents a live performance called *Ritual Awakening* and a film with the great title, *Pussy Got the Cream*. Also taking part are Marc Almond, Kathy Acker, Lydia Lunch, and John Maybury. The gang's all here, then! A lot of the performances at this festival take place in the 'second arch' bar rather than on the stage.

Although I get to the occasional event, a lot of the late 1980s is a bit of a hazy sleepwalk, due to pregnancies and those endless days caring for teeny humans. So I miss out on Zap gigs by the likes of Nick Cave and Pere Ubu. I miss the famous beach gig by Sonic Youth, and the pioneering club nights of Chris Coco and Paul Oakenfold – but I know they're there!

By 1989, when we'd moved to Brighton, the Zap had grown, extending out and back from the original two small arches into a much larger space, occupying five arches.

Later, an upstairs space and a balcony are added. It's bigger, but not too much fancier – there is still water running down the walls of the dressing rooms.

The new decade dawns and now that I'm starting to venture out a bit more, I get to the Zap to see performances by companies like Forced Entertainment and Nigel Charnock, who in their very different ways are twisting expectations of what 'theatre' might be. In May 1990, the Brighton based Yes/No People stage a preview of their show *Stomp*, ahead of the show's official premiere at the Edinburgh Fringe the following year – a show featuring exuberant percussion using dustbins and scrap metal, a bit like Test Department but less shouty. And, of course, there's the perennial favourite, Wild Wiggler Liz Aggiss who is one half of Divas Dance Theatre, with composer Billy Cowie, Their first show, *Grotesque Dancer*, premiered at the

Zap in December 1986 (although I missed it then, I do get to see it eventually, as it's revived many times). Other Divas shows included *Dorothy and Klaus* in 1989 – good name, I think, when Ginny tells me about it a year later. *Drool and Drivel They Care,* 1990, is the first show by Divas that I get to see live. It features Liz and a team of five or six other dancers, including Ginny and someone I know from the London post-punk scene, Maria Burton. The piece uses soundbites from speeches by Margaret Thatcher, which the performers lip-synch to, all dressed in matching Thatcher drag, creating fabulously distorted dances – a brilliant parody that is a far stronger political commentary than a more straightforward piece of agit-prop theatre would be.

+

Autumn 1991 sees a new performance night at the Zap, which is continuing to lead the way in the clubland performance art explosion, boundaries breached nightly. Anything could happen, and often did. Set upstairs in the smaller space, *Andy Walker's Fame Frame* features – yes, Andy Walker, in sharkskin suit and slicked back hair. The Frame is just that: a small stage framed in silver cardboard. On the opening night there's a man who wraps himself in Sellotape, then rips it all off to the accompaniment of painful squeals from the audience. Over the weeks, a clutch of regulars appear. Performance poet Yvonne Holton has a beat-girl type punchy delivery of her surreal lines. Stella Starr, a local burlesque queen cum performance artist (who happens to be the daughter of legendary artist and filmmaker Jeff Keen), comes on as a harem-girl belly-dancer – worrying about cultural appropriation is not yet a thing. Sidonia performs a dead-pan – actually, stony-faced would be a better description – reverse striptease. Ginny shaves her legs to a recorded soundtrack of

Louise L Hay inviting her to 'Love her Body'. Is it art? Is it cabaret? Is it ironic pastiche? Who knows.

There's a video of me performing at the *Fame Frame* with Ginny, which I don't get to see until a few years later. Ginny's choreography plays on the gestures of everyday life. There are six of us nodding along to a cheesy piece of muzak, walking forwards, backwards and sideways in robotic harmony, turning, always nodding, like Stepford Wives at a disco. At one point, I go the wrong way, and my wide-eyed look as I try to mask my confusion is an interesting moment. There is a close-up shot of me at the end of what would be my last performance for quite a while, capturing a version of me that would soon dissolve.

I'm not to know it, but I'm on the cusp of a new phase of life that will be the most difficult yet. It'll be a couple of years before I'll perform again.

But the me on screen is oblivious, she just nods and smiles her nonchalant smile, her eyes meeting the viewer's gaze.

THE ART SCHOOL DANCE
GOES ON AND ON

Time to throw off the Madonna's cloak
and get back in to the world.
Time to do things a little differently.

Three children? But really – am I the sort of person who has three children?

Looks like I am. This time, for the first time ever, I've taken a pregnancy test and know early on. I get through the nine months without invasive tests or internal examinations. I have no scans, and don't even visit a hospital. Jill the midwife – formerly an 'independent' but now back with the NHS – uses an old-fashioned little trumpet type thing to listen to the baby's heartbeat; and as she is a highly experienced midwife she knows exactly which way the baby is positioned. I wouldn't abort a Downs Syndrome child, so why would I want to have the test to find out if the baby is Downs? As Robert Anton Wilson and Jon Savage and whoever else would say, late-20th century life is all about information wars: who has it and what it's used for. If the information provides no benefit, nothing you'd act on, then you don't need it. And why give away intensely personal data about your body to other people?

This one will be a girl, says just about everyone. I grit my teeth. I can't stand this assumption that I'm pregnant again because I'm desperate to add a girl to my two boys. I mean, I would like a daughter so that the line back to Eve or Lilith or whoever will be continuous and intact and will carry forward – and also so I have somebody to give all the 50s frocks, cabaret costumes and ballgowns to. But even if you do have a daughter, you can't assume she'd want to have babies herself, and you certainly can't assume she'd want to wear ballgowns. Besides, once you're pregnant there is no point *wanting* one thing or another. Whoever is on the way is already here.

Our third son, Francis – later known as Frank, my father's name – is born in August 1992. The birth is straight out of a Hollywood farce. Like Milo, he's born at home. Unlike Milo, who arrived after a labour that progressed through the night in an orderly textbook fashion, baby arriving in morning sunshine with everyone who was supposed to be there present and correct, Frank bursts into the world in a flurry just an hour or two after big brother Gabriel's sixth birthday.

The first weird thing is that I don't realise I'm in labour. Yes, yes – I've had two babies already. You'd think I'd recognise the signs. But each pregnancy is different, and each labour is its own thing. With this one, I was too busy marching a gang of pirate children down to the beach – all dressed in stripy T-shirts and carrying the large cardboard boat that Foz had made – to notice what my body was doing. Then, back to the flat to shove pizzas in the oven. Then, bringing in the cake. Then, opening the fizz for the grown-ups. I was aware of a backache. I'd had a cranial osteopathy treatment that morning and practitioner

Rex had said, "This'll ease things up and make the birth smoother." Hmmmm...

So come 10pm I'm in bed, exhausted, my back killing me. A few minutes after midnight, I'm woken up by a massive, hellish contraction. Feeling like I'd been floored by a knock-out punch in the boxing ring, I somehow stagger downstairs alone. I lie in the dark on a cushion on the living room floor, surrounded by deflating balloons, empty champagne bottles, and scraps of cake. Time stops working – I've no idea how long I lie here for. Jesus, if I am actually in labour, and it hurts this much already, what's it going to be like further down the line? I phone the labour ward to check in with the community midwife team. The person I speak to is saying strange things to me. Am I on my own? No? Then wake up your husband. We've sent someone out immediately. They are on their way. If the baby comes before the midwife arrives, don't worry, it'll all be fine. Leave the cord attached, and wrap a blanket around yourself and the baby.

What *is* she talking about, I think. I'm just phoning to say I might possibly be in labour. But the experienced nurse at the other end of the line can read the signs, and knows I'm in transition – which is midwife-speak for entering the final stage of labour.

The next bit is a blur. I must have woken Foz, because I'm now upstairs in the bedroom, and it would seem that he has let the midwife in, sadly not my dear Jill who has just gone off duty, but a rookie – someone hardly out of her teens who had never attended a home birth before. The more experienced second one (you get two midwives when you have a home birth) was hot-footing behind, I learn later. So whilst this girl flaps around trying to find the 'home birth kit' – a bin bag full of plastic sheets and rubber gloves and other unnecessary junk – I reach up to pull the (flimsy, totally inadequate) curtains closed, and that's it – whoosh. "Oh my God it's a baby!" I say as Francis hurtles to the floor, and Foz leapfrogs over the midwife to catch him. I kid you not. I used to hear my mother's tales of Auntie Mary giving birth on the kitchen floor because she hadn't realised the baby was on its way, and I sneered to myself thinking *that can't really happen, surely*. But here I was – a shocked third-time mother clutching a slightly surprised but very awake and unfazed baby who is gazing at me with steadfast eyes. Welcome to our world, third-born son. You'd clearly picked your moment. Waited until it was your day, not your big brother's, and then gone full steam ahead.

It's what they call a precipitous labour. Aren't you lucky to have had such a fast birth, people say. But without wanting to sound ungrateful, when there are women out there who have laboured for days before having all sorts of horrible interventions to get the reluctant baby out, I do actually feel a bit stunned by it all. I much preferred the properly-paced timings of the previous birth, where there was the chance to adjust to each new phase.

People present at the birth: me, baby Francis, daddy Foz, the rookie assistant midwife. People not present: the senior midwife, my birth companion Mags, newly six-year-old Gabriel, three-year-old Milo, and our friends Steve and Sally, who'd been booked in to take care of the other children during the birth.

They all arrive in due course. The senior midwife first, overseeing the messy after-birth stuff. I don't let her take the placenta away, as I don't want my insides used to make luxury cosmetics (yes, this happens). We don't have a garden, nor a car, so the placenta sits in the fridge in a plastic bag for a while until I persuade a friend who drives to take it away and bury it under a tree in some woods. Next, my friend Mags who arrives at 3am with fresh pastries – no idea where she gets hold of those. She's also my acupuncturist, so that's handy. At 6am, Gabriel runs in. He'd really, really wanted a baby sister, as he was fed up with his little brother and didn't want another of those. We hand him Francis and break the news that it's a boy. That's OK, says Gabriel, clearly smitten – he's the right baby for us, the best baby we could have wished for. Milo is less sure. He clutches his bottle of apple juice and looks very worried when the interloper latches on to feed.

By 9am, Steve and Sally have arrived. They are two artist friends, in their twenties, who we spend a lot of time with, and who often babysit for us. I'd met Steve Lacey when I performed with him as part of Ginny Farman's troupe at the Zap's PowWow Club. He's mostly an experimental musician and performer, but also a sculptor. He makes interesting pieces from scrap metal, and assemblage 3-D paintings that incorporate keys and animal bones. Sally Noele Johnson is another performer, fresh from the legendary Visual and Performing Arts course at Brighton Poly, but also a painter. Although she uses a conventional form, her large canvases are strikingly different – filled with beautiful colours, alchemical symbols, and snatches of poetic text. We've purchased paintings and sculptures from both Steve and Sally, and these are dotted around our flat. Gabriel and Milo love both of them dearly, but are especially fond of Steve, who plays wild tumbling games, takes them off to the woods to climb trees, and helps them build fabulous dens.

So after a certain amount of tea drinking and admiring of the new-born, Steve and Sally head off with Gabriel and Milo in tow. Foz decides – somewhat bizarrely – to go to his studio around the corner and paint the walls. Some sort of displaced male thing about needing to nest, I suppose. This leaves me and a now-sleeping Francis with Mags, who observes that I'm clearly in shock, and gives me an acupuncture treatment.

This will be the last baby, I decide. I give away the name I was keeping for a daughter, Frances or Francesca. It's a name that has followed me around. I was called Francesca for the first month of my life; my confirmation name is Frances; Gabriel was perhaps going to be Francesca; Milo was possibly going to be Liberty Frances, as he was born July 1989, the two-hundred-year anniversary of the storming of the Bastille that kickstarted the French revolution. So, Francis it is.

As for the size 10 ballgowns and cabaret costumes, they get squirrelled away in the loft for a future granddaughter (although one nice flouncy frock made of ruby red taffeta will get nicked years later by Milo for a Can-Can routine in which he wants to be a Moulin Rouge dancing girl, not a boy waiter). Some of the 'exotic dancer' accoutrements find their way into the children's dressing-up box. A rabbit-fur g-string gets turned around to be used as – well yes, a bunny tail. There are photos of three small boys dressed in lace bodystockings, armpit length satin gloves, and feather boas, but those will remain in the closet.

+

1992 sees another birth in the family – this one a band, not a baby. And this one, although conceived around about the same time, had a shorter gestation, and burst upon the world in time for the Brighton Festival in May 1992.

It's a convoluted conception, so bear with me.

Foz had been out of the music loop for while, focusing on his graphics work. After a couple of years commuting to London, he has managed to persuade his employers that it would make sense for them to rent him a Brighton design studio.

This has now materialised, at an artists' space called Pen and Ink, in Middle Street in the Lanes, the oldest part of Brighton – and Foz has achieved an odd ambition, which was to be able to paddle to work. Well, he needs to walk one block down from our flat in Montpelier Road to the sea, and one block up when he reaches Middle Street – but other than that, he does indeed paddle to work.

Now that Foz is working in Brighton, it's a lot easier to see and do things here together – like going to the degree shows at the art school. There's a post-grad course, an MA in Narrative and Sequential Art, which has some particularly good stuff. We note an artist called Mikey Georgeson, whose project is called something like *Miscellaneous*, with rather lovely drawings of random everyday objects; and someone called Emma Carlow, whose work Foz likes so much that he offers her a job in his new design studio.

Foz's design work involves lots of photocopying of hand-drawn illustrations layered on acetates to get multi-coloured prints. At the local copy shop, round the corner from Pen and Ink, Foz is standing in the queue behind someone – he notes this young man's fringed Wrangler jacket – who is holding some illustrations that look familiar. Oh, says Foz – did you do that big mural in the car park by the swimming pool? Turns out that he did indeed do this wonderful mural (called *Everyman*), which features a giant man with a donkey's head; and that he was also the 'Miscellaneous objects' artist we'd noted at the degree show. Foz asks if he can buy one of the booklets Mikey is making, and they swap phone numbers. Oh, you're Foz, says Mikey...

A while back, when round at Harper and Nicky's house for dinner, we'd met *NME* writer and features editor James Brown, and his girlfriend Julie Jackson. James would go on to co-found and edit *Loaded* magazine, but not yet – and that's not the important bit of this story. What's important here is that his girlfriend was a student on the MA in Narrative and Sequential Art. Oh, she says, on meeting Foz, there's this guy on my course called Mikey, who likes The Monochrome Set and wants to form a band. You two should meet.

A week or so later, Foz is once again back in the photocopy shop, as is Mikey. Foz realises that this Mikey, apart from everything else, is the person Julie was talking about. Everything fits into place. Yes, Mikey is indeed trying to get a band together,

with another guitarist called Graham. Would Foz meet up with them and give them some tips?

Mikey and Graham turn up at our flat with their guitars, looking like a pair of budding young Country and Western singers. They play some songs – I hear the first one, and I do like the sound of Mikey's voice, which has something of an

Anthony Newley twang to it – but then give my apologies and head out to the Zap for my show, leaving Mikey and Graham in our front room, serenading a slightly bemused Foz with their acoustic guitars. Later, I ask Foz how it went and what they want from him, exactly. They want me to be a sort of godfather-cum-manager, says Foz, who has decided to take the bait. He also discovers that Emma, the new junior designer he's about to employ, is Graham's wife. Well, well, well...

So now someone in Brighton is having a party and Mikey and Graham have been invited to play. But they can't do it as a two-piece, so Foz agrees to play guitar; and Graham is the drummer for the night, bringing along a snare drum, a bass pedal and a suitcase.

Next thing we know, Graham has bought a drum kit, and Foz is the band's lead guitarist. So now they are three. I'll stay in the band if we only play weddings, bar-mitzvahs and parties, says Foz, who post-Monochrome Set has had it with record companies and deals and the whole music biz rat-race, and doesn't want to go there again. The party host, Jem, had liked what they were doing, and wants to join the band. That's Jem Egerton, a classically trained violinist who happens to be engaged to Esther, sister of Mark Anthony Turnage. The band need a bass player – and violin and bass are pretty much interchangeable, right? So Jem takes up the bass. And then there were four – a proper beat combo.

Someone called Andy Perry is putting together a venue for Brighton Festival, upstairs at The Rock in Kemptown, just round the corner from where Emma and Graham live. He's looking for something that's more theatrical than a straightforward band. Foz agrees to add theatre and cabaret events to his will-do list. They are booked in for May 1992 –

festival month – committed to making a show. But what are they going to be called?

Mikey says "I did this painting a while back – David Devant and his Spirit Wife." So then comes a song of the same name, and the band devise a whole act around the notion of collectively being the reincarnation of a Victorian magician who conjured up and communed with his dead wife.

Now they have a name and a concept, and a few songs. Together, they create a show telling the story of David Devant, which features live music, a set and props built from cardboard, and 'fake magic' performances and audience interactions – balloon animals and all. There's a model of Brighton Pier, replete with little lights, and cardboard signs urging the audience to applaud or dance. There are Spirit Specs, which will magically enable the audience to see the Spirit Wife when she materialises – through the medium of one of Emma's nighties, pinned to a long stick. Two assistants cum performers, dubbed the Spectral Roadies, are now on board – both called Nick, the dark-haired one a filmmaker, and the blond one a trumpeter.

The band rehearse in Pen and Ink, in the PMT machine room, where the giant black plastic tubes that the Rubylith masking film comes in (this used in the printing process) get repurposed. With white paper added to the ends, they become giant magic wands. Mikey and Foz do most of the songwriting in the classic sense of that term, getting the ball rolling with lyrics and tunes and all that; and Graham initiates much of the prop and set making – but everyone contributes to all aspects of the work, from start to finish, music and artwork.

The theatrical conceit is that Mikey is the vessel through which David Devant's wishes are projected from the afterlife and brought to fruition, and thus adopts the stage name The Vessel. The rest of the band also assume new names: Jem

"For one night only"

The Paganini Room
Old Ship Hotel
Kings Road
Brighton
Saturday 16th May
from 9.00pm
Tickets £7.50

becomes The Colonel, Graham is Professor Rimschott, and Foz, somewhat confusingly, is called Foz? (pronounced 'Foz Questionmark').

Costume is crucial. The band go for a distressed time-warp lounge lizard look. They dress a bit like a showband that hoped for Las Vegas but only made it to the Watford Empire. Mikey wears an Elvis-inspired bouffant wig, and all the band sport exaggerated sideburns. They wear tartan three-piece suits or tuxedos that have seen better days or leopardskin jackets with satin lapels, these teamed with frill-fronted dress shirts or wide-collared lurex numbers.

And thus David Devant and His Spirit Wife launches onto the world...

Meanwhile, back in the jungle:

Well, having three small children is hard work, but in a way two was the big shock and three is just more of the same, with an extended amount of years in the baby zone. There are, after all, limited resources. Only 24 hours in each day. Only two hands to fetch things or to hold on to little ones. Only one pair of legs to chase after someone running away. Oh well, they'll probably come back, you find yourself thinking as two of them tear off in different directions.

A nervous first-time mother comes round to our flat with her precious only child. Francis is sitting on the floor amongst the debris of his brothers' toys, happily foraging. Oh my God, says the friend, your baby has Lego in his mouth. Oh, I say, I expect he'll spit it out in a minute.

I'm reminded of a line in my favourite, unorthodox, childcare book – *The Baby*, by Warhol superstar Viva. She's relating an incident where her overburdened Irish Catholic mother is trying to calm her brood of noisy children sitting in the pews of the church, with the people in the seats behind tutting at her. When the priest gets to a part in his sermon about the blessed Holy Trinity of Jesus, Mary, and Joseph, Viva's mother is heard to be muttering "Huh. Them and their one..."

One child, two parents – easy peasy. Two children, two parents – fine if you're both on duty with a child each as your allotted charge, and don't expect to be able to talk to each other. One mother and three children? Total immersion. Chaos.

I'm on my own with the kids more and more these days as Foz is away so much of the time: paddling to work at his design studio in the Lanes on weekdays; or playing weekend gigs with David Devant and His Spirit Wife; or going on business trips to America for design briefing meetings, where he stays in the Four Seasons in LA and has lunch with Klingons on the studio lot for *Star Trek*. It takes hours and hours for the Klingons to get their drag and slap on, and there's no way they can take it off for lunch, so bizarrely there they are in the canteen, he reports in a long-distance phone call – a cluster of Klingons. Or sometimes it's a works outing to Las Vegas, or a conference in Atlanta, Georgia. This is the 1990s and there is money in Foz's world of graphic design and branding – lots of it, splashed about generously by the bosses on endless trips to Soho bars or joy rides to foreign cities. It's a whole other life, and it passes me by. All of that hedonistic clubbing and boozing and networking and buying and selling. Not that I'd want it – at least, that's what I tell myself.

Meanwhile, I'm at home, cooking porridge and lentils. It won't last forever. My time will come. I'll get my body/soul/mind/creativity back soon enough, I say – although some days this earth mother life feels like a trap I've unexpectedly fallen into and now can't escape from. I have my hair braided and beaded, and I'm dressed in Thai fisherman trousers and silk tunics. I can't remember the last time I wore high heels – it's

Birkenstocks or die these days. I'm an ardent Green Party member and hoping Caroline Lucas will eventually get elected as an MP. I support women who choose to breastfeed, and advocate attachment mothering. I campaign against Nestlé the babykillers, with their aggressive marketing of breastmilk substitutes (aka 'formula'), and their appropriation of water supplies that deny access to clean water for people in what are called Third World countries. Right on!

I see dear friend Nicky Harper now and again, but whilst I had a third baby, she took herself off to the University of Sussex, where she studies History of Art, and she and Harper now spend a lot of weekends in London going to gigs and partying – so our lives veer off in different directions. I see Rachel sometimes, and she has had another child, called Syd (after Syd Barrett), but she is splitting up with Captain Sensible, and heading out of Brighton to live in the Sussex countryside. I'm running various post-natal support groups, and involved with the Brighton Steiner School, where Gabriel and Milo both go, so a lot of the people I hang out with in the daytime are friends made through those two channels. But these are mostly people who have no connection to my life in music and art, and once again I seem to have duel identities marked by the name I use. To women who phone for breastfeeding support, or the people in the Steiner School kindergarten, I'm Dorothy. To the artists and musicians and dancers who are the friends that Foz and I share, or the rare few remaining friends from the punk days, such as Andy Warren, who still visits regularly, I'm Max.

But there are a few odd life-art-children crossover points. Genesis and Paula P-Orridge, for example, had moved down to Brighton a year or two before.

So let's back-track to Spring 1991.

Gen and Paula's daughters Caresse and Genesse are, like my two boys, at the Brighton Steiner School. Or at least, they are for a while. It's easy to understand how Gen would see the logic of sending them to a Waldorf School, as Rudolf Steiner's worldwide network of schools are called. The belief in the importance of the spirit world and the powers of nature; the distrust of television and awareness of the damage it could do to young brains (I remember Gen citing a study done in Portland Oregon that linked hyperactivity and ADHD in children with sleeping in proximity to TV sets); the Steiner belief that black clothing was inappropriate for children and for those who worked with them – in an interview with Tom Vague done for *International Times* in 1986, Gen had said, "Black is the colour of death. If you wear it all the time, you tell yourself death every day, you kill yourself, you eliminate your spirit". This could almost be Rudolf himself speaking!

But then the children leave abruptly, and when I'm round at their house, Gen tells me that the school is indoctrinating children with Christian ideas – brainwashing them, he says – eyes growing wider. Mmmmm, I say. Another weird Gen misunderstanding or misinterpretation, it seems to me. It's common knowledge that the Steiner philosophy, known as Anthroposophy, is based on a form of esoteric Christianity, with touches of Buddhism, Paganism and Animism here and there.

Closely linked to Madame Blavatsky's Theosophy, Steiner's Anthroposophy has connections to the Rosicrucians and the order of the Golden Dawn. It is loosely Christian, but the emphasis is on the magical, and the broader spiritual path of life.

In my mind, it ties in quite nicely with the ideals of the mid-1980s version of Psychic TV that I was part of: to reject boredom and negative attitudes; to embrace enthusiasm, colour, light, and happiness; to encourage each individual to find and honour their own path in life, rather than follow the herd. But no, Gen doesn't see it this way, and the children are pulled out of the school...

I'm not sure where the girls then go – perhaps to the state primary school closest to their house on Roundhill Crescent. Which, coincidentally – or perhaps it is planned not coincidence, and what is coincidence anyway other than celestial planning? – is the street that runs down to Woodvale Cemetery where Aleister Crowley's earthly remains are interred. Although Crowley lived the last few years of his life in Hastings, and died in a boarding house there, his funeral and burial was in Brighton – possibly favoured due to the auspicious ley lines of the town, or its abundance of sacred waters, such as St Ann's Well. Or maybe Hastings didn't want him. Who knows?

By the way, does anyone else think PTV's Alex Fergusson looks a lot like the young Aleister Crowley? Or is it just me? I digress...

Before Caresse and Genesse, who are a few years older than my Gabriel and Milo, leave the Steiner School – and indeed, afterwards too, throughout 1991 – we spend quite a few afternoons together in the Roundhill Crescent house. Genesse and Gabriel are the closest in age (and have a kind of psychic affinity in that my bonding with new-born Genesse triggered the maternal instincts I didn't know I had), so play happily together in the garden, sometimes inviting Milo into the game, if he's lucky. Caresse, being nine years old, tends to go off and do her own thing. In a couple of years' time, we'd be living in a similar terraced Victorian house very close to Roundhill Crescent, but for now we are still in the garden-less Montpelier Road flat – travelling daily up to the Steiner School on Ditchling Road. The

P-Orridge household is just a short walk from the school, so we visit often. Halcyon days.

Things change. That's one thing you can always guarantee – whatever is happening now, it will change. Suddenly, Gen and Paula and the girls are gone. And no one knows where...

On the evening of 19 February 1992, the long-running Channel 4 documentary series *Dispatches* had featured an episode called 'Beyond Belief', about Satanic ritual abuse. Presented by journalist Andrew Boyd, the show promised to deliver, for the first time, unequivocal evidence of Satanic abuse and ritual murder having been carried out in Britain. The show features the testimony of an alleged survivor of Satanic abuse, and had been trailed heavily with clips of a tape that the British police had seized which, the programme makers claimed, was a home-video recording of a Satanic ritual killing.

But after the broadcast, the footage is identified as an art video called *First Transmission*, made by Genesis and Sleazy for Thee Temple ov Psychick Youth. The show was denounced in the media over the following days and weeks as what some witnesses quite rightly called "a grotesque lapse of journalistic integrity". Amongst the voices of reason and anger was that of Derek Jarman, who very publicly criticised the programme and challenged any aspersions cast on Psychic TV.

But Gen and Paula were taking no chances. With a Scotland Yard raid on their Brighton home and the London HQ, in which not only PTV videos, tapes, artefacts and documents, but also hundreds of family photographs and personal possessions were confiscated (and never, to this day, returned), they chose to flee rather than risk having the children taken from them by police or social services while they were under suspicion. Actually, they didn't flee from England: they were on a family holiday in Nepal when the raids happened – so rather than return to

Brighton, they stayed away, heading off to California to take shelter with Timothy Leary, rumour had it.

This is all pretty frightening and worrying. It is highly upsetting to have people you know well and have worked with wrongly accused of the worst kind of sexual abuse – and possibly even child murder. It is terrifying to see how easily people are manipulated – the Channel 4 switchboards are inundated after the broadcast with people claiming to have been abused by Satanists, possibly by the very ones they'd just seen on their TV screens. And as a mother-of-two now pregnant with her third child, who is co-incidentally also a former member of Psychic TV, and therefore connected to Thee Temple ov Psychick Youth, I can't help worrying that the media and police might now be on the prowl for any known associates of PTV, TOPY and the P-Orridges.

So this odd shadow hangs over the second half of the pregnancy. I only learn about Gen and Paula's whereabouts through third parties. They are, understandably, lying low, and only communicating with a very small number of people in the UK. I hear nothing directly from either of them for many years – and when I do, they are divorced and living very different lives in separate parts of the USA.

But that is all to play out in future time. Let's go back to where we were: Spring 1993.

Things are changing again. I'm emerging from the blur of early motherhood, exacerbated this time round by what is euphemistically called a 'health scare' – six months in, around Easter time. Gory gynaecological stuff. Biopsies, invasive treatments, and a *Hammer House of Horror* night when, alone with baby Francis, I haemorrhage two pints of blood and end up in intensive care. The paramedics on the scene are reassuringly stoic: always looks worse than it is, blood loss, they say. There's plenty more inside you. You'll live. In the hospital, Francis (who was brought in with me, naturally) is given his first solid food – a portion of mashed potato, fed to him in the NHS staff canteen by a friendly nurse. Foz, who was doing a David Devant gig in London, where he'd deposited the older two with his mum in Pimlico, has been summoned back, and arrives at my bedside looking rather shocked.

It feels like another notch on the 'being an adult' belt, a brush with death. I later find out that my father was taken ill around the same time, so my poor mum was dashing between two hospitals. With her usual tact, she takes one look at me – on a drip, and off food – and says, "Oh well, it'll do you good to lose a bit of weight."

I'm out of hospital within the week, and on the road to recovery. In my dad's case, it's more serious – a heart condition that'll see him off within two years. More adulting, as it'll come to be called in future years. For now, it's just called life, as in "Oh, that's life" said with a sigh over a cup of tea, or overheard on a bus. Or repeated endlessly by Esther Rantzen on her TV show of the same name. Life and more life, which contains death.

But these two interweaved events – my health crash and my dad's – have given me an injection of new life. I've been hippy earth mother for long enough, I decide. Time to throw off the Madonna's cloak and get back in to the world. Time to do things a little differently.

In between babies two and three, I'd built up a bit of work in Brighton as a dancer, teacher and choreographer. I performed with Ginny at the Zap numerous times, and did some other things here and there. Liz Aggiss gave me some teaching work on the Dance with Visual Arts course as an occasional visiting lecturer, where I'd befriended many of the students, including Adrian Court, Jeremy Diaper, Adelle Carroll, and Marisa Carr

(soon to be rising star of Live Art, Marisa Carnesky); and I'd worked as a guest choreographer with some of the students on their degree shows. There was, for example, a tango for a rather marvellous immersive piece called *Journey to the Red Bed* staged in the Zap, in which audience members are sat at tables decked in white linen, and fed delicacies prepared by a gourmet chef, before an abundance of dancers and circus performers take over the space. It's a forerunner of the sort of performance work that'll come into its own in future decades, with the arrival on the scene of the likes of Duckie and Punchdrunk.

Everything had then ground to a halt as the final stages of pregnancy, post-natal exhaustion, and illness took their toll. But now, I'm here – ready and waiting. You just have to decide you are open to possibilities, and they will come to you.

And it happens. Liz calls me and says she's been offered a choreography job with veteran theatre company The People Show – who I'd first seen at the ICA in 1976 – which she feels is more my sort of thing. And yes, it's right up my alley. They are creating a piece called *For One Night Only* and need a choreographer, and a dance troupe to play – well yes, a dance troupe – in a show about the ghosts that act out the fading echoes of their lives in an old dancehall that's about to be reborn as a disco.

I cobble together a makeshift troupe from the students at the art school. We create a great batch of distorted dance numbers. There's a couple dressed in evening wear, covered in cobwebs, with numbers pinned to their backs, who sleepwalk their way through a wonky waltz. There's a conga-dancing line who erupt in the space at regular intervals, dancing a frantic samba, whooping and screeching and waving cocktail glasses in the air. And there's a twisted tango – of course there is. It's the first of a number of commissions from companies to use ballroom and popular dance in a contemporary theatre setting.

As well as the choreography work, I'm now running classes in all sorts of things, from Cuban beat to street samba. Liz Aggiss gets me teaching her students how to cha-cha and how to do the line dance from *Saturday Night Fever*. Word gets round that I'm the go-to person for anything related to social and popular dance. I also teach vaudeville and music hall routines, and I can step in to create a Can-Can, a cowboy polka, or a Charleston. You name it, I'll teach it or choreograph it for you. It's an odd niche to occupy, but it's mine.

I do still perform myself, now and again. I take part in a few dance shows made by other people, and occasionally make a small piece for the Brighton Dance Collective evenings, which are held regularly at the Pavilion Theatre. These evenings are a magnificent hotch-potch that could, and often would, include anything and everything from serious contemporary dance from graduates of The Place, to ironic and challenging performance art work. On one occasion, I have a now seven-year-old Gabriel with me, seated in the middle of the front row – perfectly placed to witness Marisa Carnesky enact a wild burlesque number that includes a grotesque striptease and the massacre of a whole menagerie of cuddly toys. He watches wide-eyed but takes it all in his stride.

Meanwhile, David Devant and His Spirit Wife have been going from strength to strength since their auspicious debut the previous year. One of the two Nicks (the dark-haired one, filmmaker Nick Curry) is still on board as a Spectral Roadie, with the stage name Iceman. He's now joined by Gaz Smith, aka Cocky Young 'Un, who gained his spot as a Spectral Roadie by winning a competition at one of the gigs. Which may or may not have been rigged. Visual and performance art elements continue to be a vital part of the show – video projections onto paper screens that are then jumped through, a cabinet of swords, a spooky disembodied head-on-a-platter, Gilbert and

George masks for the song 'Pimlico' ("*it's got a lovely gallery!*") and giant cardboard signs extolling the audience to Go Wild.

Our work comes together when Foz suggests I bring on the dancing girls (and boys) to the new David Devant show being planned. Once again, the art school crew are approached. As ever, they're up for anything suggested. We rehearse a vaudevillian Egyptian Sand Dance wearing Tutankhamen masks; and a jerky jive to Foz's version of 'Dead Cats Don't Swing' – the song that had grown out of a conversation with Monte Cazazza during a drunken supper at our flat in Wandsworth, back in 1985. Monte had done his own version with his band The Atom Smashers, and there is a third one somewhere with me singing on it.

Standing in the wings as the opening notes to 'Dead Cats Don't Swing' start up, and the dancers leap-to, I think: Monte would find this very funny – I must write to him and tell him about it. I never do.

Meanwhile, the dance goes on.

POSTSCRIPT:
A LETTER TO MONTE

4 July, 2023 Seville, Spain

Woke up this morning and Monte Cazazza was still dead.

I suppose I was hoping it might be one of Monte's terrible pranks. I wouldn't put it past him. A desire to separate himself from the world, so a faked death. Yeah, go Monte! But no. I don't think his girlfriend Meri St Mary would go along with that. I think – really, can it really be? – that Monte is dead.

It's been four days now. Meri posted on the morning of Friday 30 June, so perhaps he died the night before. The wording of the post is ambivalent. I can't help speculating: Did he choose to take himself off on the voyage out of this life? Which would be so like Monte. Ill and in pain – time to go.

I'd last been in conversation with Meri – and through her, Monte – in late 2022. In recent decades, I've only communicated with Monte through intermediaries: Meri, Fred Gianelli, Cosey Fanni Tutti, a few others. I'd sent a copy of my book, *69 Exhibition Road*, to Meri (and therefore, by default, to Monte too). I'd heard back through the grapevine that Monte had read it, and Fred said he'd spoken to him about the 'I Confess' chapter, which documents my involvement with Industrial Records and the beginnings of our friendship, and a typically self-effacing Monte had said "Max too complimentary!"

Meri and I agree to a radio interview on her KVMR show, assuming we can sort out the transatlantic technical stuff – and she says Monte might take part too. His only reservation was what were described as "acrimonious feelings towards GPO even though he's dead" – so he's reluctant to discuss his relationship with Genesis P-Orridge. I reply and tell her and Monte that ambivalent feelings about Gen and those PTV times are par for the course – and that I'd recently been to Iceland and had had a pretty deep de-brief with Hilmar. Then comes another message: "Monte says hello and speaks highly of you and Hilmar. He will definitely join us!"

Great, I say. But follow-up emails get no response – and now I understand why. Or I think I do.

Just a few days ago, here in Seville writing the remaining stories for this volume, I was thinking how much I needed to speak to Monte – right now. Because writing about him has put him at the front of my mind. Because I wanted to ask him how he felt about me using *Sex is No Emergency* for the title of this book. Because I wanted to ask his permission to quote from letters he sent me, keen not to upset him or breach confidence. I was on the point of writing to Monte. The time's right, I reckon.

But now Monte is dead.

For the past four days, I've heard his voice constantly – that odd mix of gentleness and scathing humour. Tender and

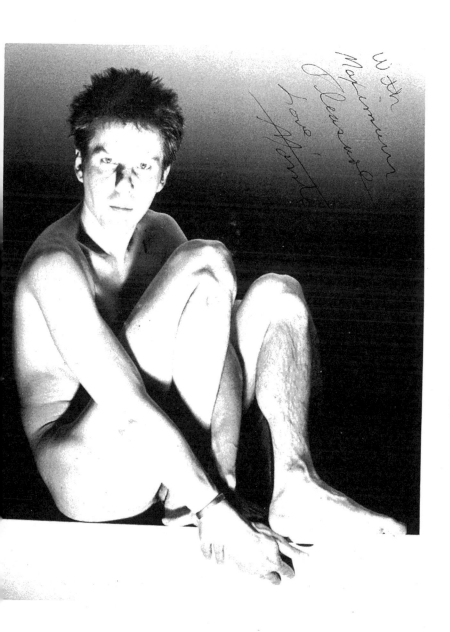

wild, so raw and open to being hurt. Oh Monte, dearest Monte. How can you be dead?

In the story 'Baby Love', I write about the time I was on my way to see Monte: April 1986, a year after he'd left the UK, escaping the wrath of Gen, the financial worries, and the complications of relationships "both inside and outside of PTV".

After Monte had left town on 22 April 1985, we'd started an intense exchange of letters back and forth. Monte's letters were usually handwritten, often on the back of one of his collages. They started cautiously, but built to a more confessional mode over the year.

Re-reading those letters now, I'm quite shocked at how easily they veer from playful flirting, to declarations of love, to upfront detailing of extreme distress and anxiety. The Trickster and the Bleeding Hearted Lover vie for the upper hand. Sometimes there were two letters written within one week, and sometimes months would go by. The flirty ones say things like "Sweetheart, thank you so much for the wonderful letter. I love your big bow [in the Xmas photo]. You look like a luscious present come alive. Wish that you were under my Christmas tree." Sometimes there is a kind of Victorian love letter vibe: "I have a photo of you on my wall and people keep asking who the hot redhead is – and of course no one believes we haven't consummated our relationship." In that same letter, he says: "There's nothing to report about San Francisco. I just want the earthquake to hit the place and swallow everything up. I wish I could stay drunk all the time, but it doesn't make me forget anything, in fact I just remember everything even more... I guess I'll sign off for now and see you in my dreams."

In Spring 1986, I'd bought a plane ticket to San Francisco, on what was supposed to be a triangular trip of West Coast

USA, Canada, then New York. I ended up going straight to Canada – Monte saying in a phone call that he couldn't see me, he needed to go into the desert and have time by himself. Just that, nothing more.

A couple of weeks later, a letter arrives. It is dated 18th March 1986, and thus written four days before our phone conversation:

"I was sad when I left London, but in one way it was good that I left when I did or else I would have been in ten times the trouble I ended up in, if we had gotten more emotionally involved. I miss you bunches. You don't know how much I had to keep myself under control… it was torture. Write more as you don't know how much I appreciate your letters. Miss you immensely."

Forty years on, I'm astonished at my own stupidity. What on earth made me think it'd be OK to go and stay with him, five months pregnant with someone else's child, after he'd put his heart on the line in his letters? What was I expecting? What did I want of him? I have no idea. I just know that I wanted to see Monte, to talk things through properly. But really – what *was* I thinking? The whole idea was so preposterous – so lacking in awareness of what Monte might think and feel, and what Foz might think and feel. And what on earth was going on in my own head and heart?

A day or two later…

In the days after Monte's death, Meri posts a lot of photos of them together: hanging out at the radio station, out and about with friends, making music together – they had a Duelling Theremin thing going on, which sounds magnificent. Her

grief is tangible, although her posts are kind of upbeat, and celebratory. Look, Monte in all his magnificence!

I'm not sure how long Monte and Meri were together. I think around 14 years. I hear from other people that Meri was good for him, and that he was happy – and seeing her many social media posts on various platforms in recent years, this seems to be so. This is corroborated by mutual friends such as Cosey, who stayed in regular contact with Monte, and writer Jack Sargeant, who met with Monte and Meri on various West Coast of America visits in the past decade. She clearly loved him deeply, and he loved her with all of his heart. I am pleased that this nurturing relationship happened for him, and saw him through to the end of his life.

I had, of course, responded to Meri's posts, expressing condolences and sending love, but now I write to her. I write quite a long email, and get a short one back. Understandably, there are a lot of us making contact with her about Monte, and I am sure she has enough to deal with, wrestling with her own grief, without having to worry about our distress.

A week on...

There come posts on social media correcting the false information about Monte's life and death that has been floating around the internet. Apparently, he was born on 23 January 1949 – his date of birth on Wikipedia had been previously given as November 1954. I was born May 1955, and I'd always assumed he was round about my age. But no, he is, was, six years older. Aged 74 at the time of death. Oh, and apparently he died on the 27th June 2023, not on the 29th. I start to wonder about his death. Where and how did he die? I push back the

morbid desire for more information. Why do I need to know? What the hell does it matter? Monte is dead.

A few months later...

No news of a funeral. Months after his death, it would appear that Monte is in limbo. The morbid thoughts return, and the questions resurface: How did Monte die? What has happened to his body? It's a mystery – and one I have no right to try to solve. All is unnecessary and unhealthy speculation. The 'earthly remains' – such a haunting phrase. I push away the thought of a mangled Monte in a morgue, and let my mind drift back to early 1985, just after I'd joined Psychic TV.

I hadn't seen anything much of any of the TG/PTV crew for a couple of years – I was working day and night in two different dance schools, and there was hardly a moment for anything else. I'd started going out with Foz in 1983, and we moved in together in early 1984, so that was also a whole new all-consuming thing.

When I joined Psychic TV, I gravitated towards Monte and we formed a kind of mutual appreciation society.

On 14 February 1985, whilst rehearsing for our DJM recording dates, Monte gave me a copy of that famous *Vile* magazine Valentine's Day cover. You know the one – Monte holding a bleeding heart out to the viewer, seemingly torn from his chest. Musing now on this image, I reckon it could be read two ways. You could see it as a schlock-horror gesture celebrating all things gory and gruesome. Or you could see it as a gesture of extreme love: Here, take my heart, which I have torn out for you. I think it's both, at one and the same time.

In a way, Monte reminded me of Andy Warren. Both had cynical exterior selves with easily-hurt interiors; soft creatures who live in hard shells made of caustic humour. Both were appalled by most of who and what constitutes this world, but always ready to alleviate the distress with a clever quip. I'm very different – an optimist, mostly, who tries to see the good in everyone and everything. Maybe pessimists find me reassuring to be around, a safe harbour and a beacon of hope, I speculate. I'm also someone who famously doesn't get jokes and hates being teased – but Monte, like Andy, traded in the kind of ironic black humour that I liked and understood. And he was, actually, a really sensitive soul who, once he'd decided he liked you, would do anything for you. Random acts of kindness were routine.

It turns out I was right about the optimist/pessimist thing. In a letter received August 1985, Monte wrote: "As always, all I seem to do is get into more hot water wherever I am. In fact, it's the temperature of a nuclear meltdown, but that's the way it goes… I hope I do get to see you in the autumn… You know what I love about you most is your sense of optimism, which even to a totally sarcastic bastard like myself is still an endearing quality above all others."

So yes, I was in a relationship with Foz, and not free to give my heart to anyone else, and yet, and yet – in a parallel universe…

Unconsummated love stays pure and perfect, unsullied by the messy business of having to accommodate the other person whilst living everyday life together. The fantasy other-life the sliding doors close on. What would that have been? Nothing that can be sensibly imagined.

This weird, intense, friendship-plus – a Brief Encounter for the Blank Generation – lasted just three months, before Monte ran away at the end of April 1985. And then came the year of letters to and fro, and the plan to visit in April 1986. Which didn't happen – and that is that. I didn't see him then, and I haven't seen him since.

From then on, the letters arrive less frequently, and have a cheerier, more distanced tone. They describe visits to Japanese temples and tea-ceremonies and Monte's forays into rap music. My replies, as far as I can remember them, document the strange unchartered land of early motherhood.

He sends me City Lights books, photocopies of his interview with Andrea Vale for *RE/Search*, a zine called *Pain* that he's made with Lydia Lunch, more hand-made collages, and an LP by his new band, the Atom Smashers, featuring their version of 'Dead Cats Don't Swing'.

The letters go back and forth for a few more years, then stop. I think it was me who stopped writing back, but I can't remember exactly when. By the time I'd moved to Brighton and my second, and then third, baby was born, I was so far away from my old self, and in such an earth-mother fug, that I didn't really feel I had anything much to write about, I suppose. And those PTV times felt a lifetime away.

Every so often – maybe once or twice a decade – I'd look at the letters with the Berkeley PO Box number on the back and think: well, he has probably kept the address. Maybe I should write. Hope he's OK.

Somewhere along the line came the Internet and social media, and contact with people who knew Monte. I still didn't try too hard to make contact with him, just vague "Max says hello" messages, via Fred or whoever, that sometimes prompted a "Monte sends you his love" back.

Then, eventually, the connection to Meri, the radio show date, and the resolution to write that long overdue letter to Monte.

But too late – Monte is dead.

Well, time goes by, and time heals. Everything changes, always. It's a new year, it's a new day. A new beginning.

The shock has passed. Life goes on. The living can't hang about in the land of the dead. There is food to be eaten, wine to be drunk, dancing to be done, music to be played, shows to be seen, people and places to visit – here, there and everywhere.

When someone you haven't seen for close to four decades dies, what are you mourning, exactly? You're mourning an imaginary person, an echo of someone you once knew, a memory. You're mourning your own past, and the image of yourself that the dead person held, intact – because that image of you in your prime, age 30, stayed frozen in their imagination, unsullied.

A photo or two, cassettes of a few recordings made together, some Xeroxed magazine articles, a bunch of letters tied with red ribbon. The earthly remains. I close the suitcase. This is how it ends.

DISCOGRAPHY
FILMOGRAPHY
BIBLIOGRAPHY

Sex is No Emergency

In Every Dream Home...

Discs
'In Every Dream Home a Heartache', Roxy Music, 1973
'In Heaven' (Lady in the Radiator Song), Peter Ivers and David Lynch, 1977/1982
'Minnie the Moocher', Cab Calloway, 1931
'Knock Me a Kiss', Louis Jordan and His Tympany Five, 1941
'Quizas, Quizas, Quizas', Perez Prado, 1959
'Honeydripper Mambo', Alfredito, 1953
'Oyá Diosa Fé', Celia Cruz and Sonora Matancera, 1954
'Mi Buenos Aires Querido', Carlos Gardel, 1934
'Feelings', Morris Albert, 1974

Dirk Wears White Sox, Adam and the Ants, 1979
Strange Boutique, The Monochrome Set, 1980
Love Zombies, The Monochrome Set, 1980
Eligible Bachelors, The Monochrome Set, 1982

Film/TV/Video

Eraserhead, David Lynch, 1977
Flesh for Frankenstein, Andy Warhol and Paul Morrissey, 1973
Blood for Dracula, Andy Warhol and Paul Morrissey, 1974
Jubilee, Derek Jarman, 1978
Zelig, Woody Allen, 1983
The Draughtsman's Contract, Peter Greenaway, 1982
Educating Rita, Lewis Gilbert, 1983

Theatre/Performance/Art

Just what is it that makes today's homes so different, so appealing?, Richard Hamilton, 1956
Photo-portraits of nudes and flowers, including images of Derrik Cross and of orchids and arum lilies, Robert Mapplethorpe, 1983-1984
The GBH Series, Derek Jarman, 1983-1984

Tango'd

Discs
'A Night to Remember', Shalamar, 1982
'Night Fever', Bee Gees, 1978
'Cuba', Gibson Brothers, 1978
'You're the One for Me', D Train, 1981
'Three Times a Lady', Commodores, 1978

'La Cumparsita', Juan D'Arienzo y Su Orquesta Tipica, 1935-1939

'Blue Skies', Tommy Dorsey Orchestra with Frank Sinatra, 1941

'Bei Mir Bist Du Schoen', The Andrews Sisters, 1937

'Whatever Lola Wants', Della Reese, 1961

'Olé Mambo', Edmundo Ros and His Orchestra, 1967

'Cherry Pink and Apple Blossom White', Perez Prado, 1954

'La Maricutana', Beny Moré, available on A Night in Havana compilation released 2003

'Oye Negra', Homero Y Su Combo, available on the Cartagena! 1962-1972 compilation album.

'Tico Tico', Ethel Smith, 1950

'Deep Purple', Victor Silvester, 1939

'Can-Can' from Offenbach's Orpheus in the Underworld

'Wedding of the Winds', Richard Whitmarsh

'Baby Elephant Walk', Henry Mancini, 1962

'Bambah', Baligh Hamdi, 1975

'Young Guns' (Go For It), Wham!, 1983

'Malambo No 1', Yma Sumac, 1954

'Masochism Tango', Tom Lehrer, 1959

'So Many Men, So Little Time', Miquel Brown, 1983

'Ain't Nobody', Chaka Khan and Rufus, 1983

'No Parking on the Dance Floor', Midnight Star, 1983

'Jump' (For My Love), The Pointer Sisters, 1983

Film/TV/Video

Cabaret, Bob Fosse, 1972

Saturday Night Fever, John Badham, 1977

Jason and the Argonauts, Don Chaffey, 1963

One Million Years BC, Don Chaffey, 1966

Clash of the Titans, Desmond Davis, 1981

Books

Fahrenheit 451, Ray Bradbury, 1953
Something Wicked This Way Comes, Ray Bradbury, 1962
The Illustrated Man (short story collection), Ray Bradbury, 1951

Dorothy and Toto in New York

Discs
'Sexual Healing', Marvin Gaye, 1982
'Cha Cha Gua', Tito Puente,
'Mambo Infierno', Machito and his Afro Cubans, 1954
'My Baby Just Cares For Me', Nina Simone, 1957
'Blue Train', John Coltrane, 1958
'Body and Soul', Coleman Hawkins, 1939
'It Don't Mean a Thing (If It Ain't Got That Swing)', Duke
Ellington with Ivie Anderson, 1932
'Respect', Aretha Franklin, 1967
'Annie I'm Not Your Daddy', Kid Creole and the Coconuts,
1982
'Billie Jean', Michael Jackson, 1982
'Everybody', Madonna, 1982
'The Message', Grandmaster Flash and the Furious Five, 1982

Film/TV/Video
The Dark Crystal, Jim Henson and Frank Oz, 1982
The Wizard of Oz, Victor Fleming, 1939

Theatre/Performance/Art
One Mo' Time, a vaudevillian musical play by Vernel Bagneris,
presented at The Village Gate 1979-1982

How to Talk Dirty and Influence People, Lenny Bruce, an autobiography published in serial form in *Playboy* 1964-1965, and then in book form, 1965. Based on material performed at the Village Gate, 1960s

A Grapefruit in the World of Park was the first live performance work by Yoko Ono, Village Gate 1961

Andy Warhol's Exploding Plastic Inevitable featuring music by Nico and The Velvet Underground, with dancers Gerard Malanga and Mary Woronov, and performance artist Barbara Rubin, presented at Dom's in St Mark's Place, 1966-1967

Christmas on Earth, a film/video art piece made by Barbara Rubin in 1963 and incorporated into the Exploding Plastic Inevitable, 1966-1967

Keith Haring's early 1980s drawings and murals can be seen in the Keith Haring Foundation archive at haring.com

Louise Bourgeois, then age 70, had her first major retrospective at the Museum of Modern Art (MoMA) November 1982 – February 1983

Nightclubbing

Discs

'Antmusic', Adam and The Ants, 1980

'Stand and Deliver', Adam and The Ants, 1981

'Ashes to Ashes', David Bowie, 1980

'No G.D.M.', Gina X Performance, 1979

'Insomnia', Yellow Magic Orchestra, 1979

'Nightclubbing', Grace Jones, 1981

'Dance Away', Roxy Music, 1979

'Moskow Diskow', Telex, 1979

'The Model', Kraftwerk, 1979

'To Cut a Long Story Short', Spandau Ballet, 1980

'Just Can't Get Enough', Depeche Mode, 1981

'Spellbound', Siouxsie and the Banshees, 1981

'Release the Bats', The Birthday Party, 1981

'Bela Lugosi is Dead', Bauhaus, 1982

'The Hanging Garden', The Cure 1982

'Kiss Kiss Bang Bang', Specimen, 1983

'Relax', Frankie Goes to Hollywood, 1983

Fifi, Yip Yip Coyote, 1985

Wheel in the Roses (EP), Rema Rema, 1980

Garlands, Cocteau Twins, 1982

From Her to Eternity, Nick Cave and The Bad Seeds, 1984

Teenage Jesus and the Jerks, Teenage Jesus and the Jerks, 1979

Queen of Siam, Lydia Lunch, 1980

8-Eyed Spy, 8-Eyed Spy, 1981

Torment and Toreros, Marc and the Mambas, 1983

JG Thirlwell's prodigious 1980s output under the name Foetus (or variations thereof) includes the LPs *Deaf* (1981) *Ache* (1982), *Hole* (1984) and *Nail* (1985); the EP *Custom Built for Capitalism* (1982) and the singles 'Wash It All Off' (1981) and 'Tell Me, What is the Bane of Your Life?' (1982).

The Immaculate Consumptive existed for just three days and consisted of Marc Almond, Lydia Lunch, Nick Cave, and Clint Ruin aka JG Thirlwell. Their one performed song/track was 'Body Unknown'. See YouTube for evidence.

Film/TV

The Hunger, Tony Scott, 1983

Wings of Desire, Wim Wenders, 1987

Riverside, BBC TV series, 1982-1983

Books/Magazines

Pop Styles, Ted Polhemus, 1984

Ambit magazine was founded in 1959 and published until 2023

Albion Village Press, various by Iain Sinclair, including *The Kodak Mantra Diaries*, 1971

Take Foz

Discs

'The Monochrome Set' tracks and albums: Take Foz, 1985, Andiamo, 1984-1985, Alphaville, 1979, The Monochrome Set (I Presume), 1980 Ici Les Enfants Du Paradis, 1980, Jacobs' Ladder, 1984, Wallflower, 1985

The Lost Weekend, The Monochrome Set, 1985

Volume, Contrast, Brilliance Vol 1 & 2, The Monochrome Set, 1983

Pillows and Prayers, featuring The Monochrome Set, Eyeless in Gaza, Tracey Thorn, Thomas Leer, Five or Six, Marine Girls, Quentin Crisp et al, 1982-1983

'Reach for Your Gun', Bid, 1986

'Goodbye Joe', Tracey Thorn, 1982

'Shy Boy', Bananarama, 1982

'Stephen', Gene Loves Jezebel, 1984

'Smiling Faces', Pigbag, 1983

'Smooth Operator', Sade, 1984

'Rock and Roll Pt 2', The Gary Glitter, 1972

'Cleopatra', Adam and the Ants, 1979

'Waterloo', Abba, 1974

'The Bushes Scream While My Daddy Prunes', The Very Things, 1984

I BloodbrotherBe, Shock Headed Peters, available on *The Ruling Class – The Very Best of El Records*, 1986, which also features The Would-Be- Goods, King of Luxembourg, Momus, Vic Godard et al

...In Wooden Brackets, Lemon Kittens, on *Perspectives and Distortions*, Cherry Red Rarities 1981, which also features Matt Johnson, Lol Coxhill, Virgin Prunes, Mark Perry, Kevin Coyne, Robert Fripp et al

'Things That Go Boom in the Night', Bush Tetras, 1981. This and other early Bush Tetras tracks available on *Boom in the Night – original studio recordings 1980-1983* compilation album, 1995

'Yon Yonson', Dave Howard Singers, available on the compilation album *Control I'm Here: Adventures on the Industrial Dancefloor 1983-1990,* which also features Screaming Trees, Alien Sex Fiend, and Laibach,

'Good Vibrations', Psychic TV, on *The Magickal Mystery D Tour* EP, 1986

Seven Songs, 23 Skidoo, 1982

The Second Annual Report, Throbbing Gristle (Fetish Records re-issue), 1978-1979

Workforce to the World – Live! On Site, Devo (although their name doesn't appear on the record), 1978

The Bone of Desire, Simon Fisher Turner, 1985

Caravaggio, Simon Fisher Turner (film soundtrack), 1986

The Eye, Kukl, 1984

Uncarved Block, Flux, 1986

Soul Possession, Annie Anxiety, 1984

'Paperback Honey' can be found on *Island*, by Hilmar Örn Hilmarsson aka HOH and Current 93, recorded 1986 released 1991

'Crystal Daze' also known as *Crystal Daze* can be heard on Rose McDowall's 'Don't Fear the Reaper' 12", and on her solo album *Cut With the Cake Knife*, recorded 1988

How to Destroy Angels (EP), Coil, Zos Kia, Marc Almond, 1984

The Aryan Aquarians Meet Their Waterloo, Aryan Aquarians, 1986

Film/TV
The Lost Weekend, Billy Wilder, 1945
Nosferatu – a symphony of horror, FW Murnau, 1922
Cleopatra, Joseph L Mankiewicz, 1963
Eastern Eye, TV series, 1982-1985
The Tube, TV series, 1982-1987
MTV, cable TV channel, launched 1981

Books/Magazines
TransFM – Canadian magazine edited by John Tobin, linked to Radio CKCU Ottawa
RE/Search – San Francisco based counterculture publication, edited by former *Search and Destroy* editor/City Lights Bookshop worker V. Vale, who founded it in 1980.

Theatre/Performance/Art
Concerto for Voices and Machinery, Einstürzende Neubauten with guest performers Stevo Pearce, Genesis P-Orridge and Frank Tovey, ICA January 1984

The Fabulous Feast of Flowering Light

Discs
Psychic TV recordings cited:
Thee Fabulous Feast OV Flowering Light, recorded live 19 May 1985 (Vinyl album, CD and cassette versions, various release dates, of varying quality)
Force the Hand of Chance, 1982
Mouth of the Night, 1985

Dreams Less Sweet, 1983

Thee Starlit Mire, working title of the 1985 PTV album, eventually released under a new title in 1988

'Godstar', numerous versions released, recorded 1984/1985

'Just Drifting', 1982

'Roman P/Neurology', 1984

Holidays in Europe (The Naughty Nought), Kukl, 1986

The Moon Looked Down and Laughed, The Virgin Prunes, 1986

A Re-animated Corpse, 1982-1985, The Death and Beauty Foundation

Moral Rearmament, Zahgurim, 1985

Under a Glass Bell, Simonics, 1984

Death is Bigger (1984-1985), The Process /Bee's work under the name Getting the Fear, released on Dais, 2021

'Softness'/'I Confess', Dorothy w/ Alex Fergusson, 1980 'Stormy Weather', Elisabeth Welch, 1979

'We Hate You Little Girls', Throbbing Gristle, 1979

'Love Lies Limp', ATV, 1977

'Knife Slits Water', A Certain Ratio, 1982

'Jane B', Jane Birkin and Serge Gainsbourg, 1969

'Children of the Revolution', T.Rex, 1972

'She's a Rainbow', The Rolling Stones, 1967

'Jolene', Strawberry Switchblade, 1985

Monte Cazazza recordings cited:

'To Mom on Mother's Day', 1979

'Something for Nobody', 1980,

'Stairway to Hell/Sex is No Emergency', 1982

Monte Cazazza Live at Leeds Fan Club | Scala, London | Oudle School, cassette-only release on Industrial Records, 1980

A compilation album *The Worst of Monte Cazazza* features many of his recorded works

Heathen Earth, Throbbing Gristle, 1980

Scatology, Coil, 1984

Nature Unveiled, Current 93, 1984. Featuring David Tibet, Steven Stapleton, Annie Anxiety, John Balance et al

Transparent, Zos Kia / Coil, 1984

The Beating of Wings, Andrew Poppy, 1985

Laibach, Laibach, 1985

Nova Akropola, Laibach, 1986

Film/Video

The Tempest, Derek Jarman, 1980

Brazil, Terry Gilliam, 1986

SXXX-80, Monte Cazazza and Tana Emmolo, short film, 1980

Towers Open Fire, Antony Balch, Brion Gysin and William Burroughs, short film, 1963

Bill and Tony, Antony Balch and William Burroughs, short film, 1971

Catalan, Derek Jarman, short film made for Spanish TV, 1984

Unclean, John Maybury and Cerith Wyn Evans, short film, 1984

Godstar, Akiko Hada, promo video, 1985

Thee Fabulous Feast ov Flowering Light was filmed by Akiko Hada, but the video tape disappeared – possibly into the basement vaults of Scotland Yard.

The Psychic TV 1985 Red Ronnie Italian TV interview at 50 Beck Road, featuring Gen, Paula, Caresse, Monte, Max, Hilmar and Jym Daly, was retrieved and posted unedited on Vimeo by Thee Media Shaman.

Other PTV videos cited: *Terminus* and *Soul Eater* (both 1983-1984)

Books/Magazines

Blood and Guts in High School, Kathy Acker, 1984

The Story of O, Pauline Réage (Anne Desclos), 1954

JG Ballard books cited: *Crash*, (1973); *Concrete Island*, (1974); *High-Rise*, 1975

JG Ballard short story 'Answers to a Questionnaire' was first published in *Ambit* magazine, 1985

Sjón, aka Johnny Triumph, is a renowned Icelandic poet, lyricist and novelist. He was a founder member of neo-surrealist group Medusa, and has collaborated with The Sugarcubes and Bjork. His first novel, *Stalnott (Night of Steel)* was published in 1987.

Stabmental, fanzine 1979-1982, founded and edited by Geoffrey (Geff) Rushton aka John Balance

TransFM magazine Psychic TV interview by Gabriella Bregman, 1985

Theatre/Performance/Art

Bow Gamelan Ensemble, 1983-1990. Founded by Richard Wilson, Paul Burwell, and Anne Bean. See bowgamelan.com

Survival Research Laboratories (SLR) founded in 1978 by Mark Pauline, with numerous contributors/performers including Monte Cazazza. See srl.org

Jym Daly, visual artist and PTV associate, went on to found leading Irish aerial dance/circus company Fidget Feet. See fidgetfeet.com

Burning Man originated as a summer solstice event in San Francisco in the 1980s, subsequently moving to Black Rock Desert in Nevada, 1990-present. See burningman.org

Mouth of the Night, Mantis Dance Company, choreography by Micha Bergese, music by Psychic TV, design by Derek Jarman, 1985. Presented at ICA, *Thee Fabulous Feast ov Flowering Light*, Riverside Studios.

Lulu Unchained, with text by Kathy Acker, music by Jeremy Peyton-Jones, and direction by Pete Brooks, was performed at the ICA in July 1985. Reviewed in *Performance* magazine issue 36, Aug/Sep 1985.

Torvill and Dean performed at the Olympic Games in Sarajevo in 1984, winning gold with their ice dancing routine to Ravel's *Bolero*. They toured throughout 1985, including to Wembley Arena July-August 1985.

Europe Endless

Discs
'Europe Endless', Kraftwerk, 1977
'Half Past France', John Cale, 1973
'Smoke on the Water', Deep Purple, 1972
'The Third Man Theme' (aka 'The Harry Lime Theme'), Anton Karas, 1949
'Vienna', Ultravox, 1980
'Die Fledermaus Waltz', Johann Strauss II
More/High Noon', Klaus Wunderlich, 1971
'Being Lost', 1985
Beating The Retreat, Test Dept, 1984
Psychic TV recordings cited:
Allegory and Self, Psychic TV, recorded 1985, released 1988
Live in Bregenz, Psychic TV, recorded 1985, released 1990
Psychic TV

Film/TV
The Italian Job, Peter Collinson, 1969

Books/Magazines
Len Deighton's 'spy procedural' novels include *The IPCRESS File*, 1962; and *Funeral in Berlin*, 1964

The Discovery of Orgone Vol 1: The Function of the Orgasm, Wilhelm Reich, 1942

The Berlin novels: *Mr Norris Changes Trains* (1935) and *Goodbye to Berlin* (1939), Christopher Isherwood

The Devil Rides Out, Dennis Wheatley, 1934

The Confessions of Aleister Crowley, Aleister Crowley, 1929

International Times (IT), established 1966, ran till 1996, with a gap in publication in the early 1980s. *IT* Vol 86/1: extensive article on Psychic TV by Tom Vague, plus Hyperdelic article by Genesis P-Orridge

Sukia, a vampire-themed Italian comic, ran 1978 to 1986, seemingly inspired by the American comic *Vampirella,* which ran 1969 to 1983.

Ten Years After

Discs

'Anarchy in the UK', Sex Pistols, 1976

Never Mind the Bollocks, Sex Pistols, 1977

Duck Rock, Malcolm McLaren, 1983

'Rubber People', Adam and The Ants, Decca Demo, 1977-1978

'Ligotage', Adam and The Ants, John Peel Session, 1979

Both the above tracks were released on *Antbox* (2000), a three-CD collection of early Ants demos, singles, early versions and radio sessions.

'Go Wild in the Country', Bow Wow Wow, 1982

'Oh Bondage Up Yours!', X-Ray Spex, 1977

'Living on the Ceiling', Blancmange, 1982

'Say Hello, Wave Goodbye,' Soft Cell, 1982

'Sweet Dreams are Made of This', Eurythmics, 1983

'Double Dutch,' Malcolm McLaren, 1983

'Welcome to the Pleasuredome', Frankie Goes to Hollywood, 1984 'Sleep', Fad Gadget, 1984

'Truck, Train, Tractor', The Pastels, 1986

'Son of a Gun', The Vaselines, 1987

Run DMC 1986 singles: 'Walk This Way' and 'It's Tricky'

Hot, Cool and Vicious, Salt-N-Pepa, 1986

Licensed to Ill, The Beastie Boys, 1986

Easy Listening for the Hard of Hearing, Frank Tovey with Boyd Rice, recorded 1981, released 1996

Full Circle, Holger Czukay, Jah Wobble, Jaki Liebezeit, 1986

The Covenant, The Sword, and The Arm of the Lord, Cabaret Voltaire, 1985

Psychocandy, Jesus and Mary Chain, 1985

Strawberry Switchblade, Strawberry Switchblade, 1985 (features the singles 'Trees and Flowers', 1983; and 'Since Yesterday', 1984)

Nova Akropola, Laibach, 1986

Horse Rotorvator, Coil, 1986

Life's Too Good, The Sugarcubes, 1988

Berlin:

Bowie Berlin Trilogy, made in collaboration with Brian Eno and Tony Visconti, and recorded in whole or part at Hansa Studios, Berlin: *Low*, 1977; *"Heroes"*, 1977; and *Lodger*, 1979. Iggy Pop's *The Idiot*, 1977, and *Lust For Life*, 1977, co-written and produced by David Bowie, were also recorded in the same place/time period.

Einstürzende Neubauten 1980s releases include *Kollaps*, 1981, which features the single 'Jet'M' (a reworking of the Serge Gainsbourg/Jane Birkin hit 'Je' t'aime'; and *Halber Mensch*, 1985 Neubauten's Blixa Bargeld also played with Nick Cave and the Bad Seeds, including on the 1985 album *The Firstborn is Dead*.

Malaria! 1980s tracks include 'How Do You Like My New Dog?', 1981; 'New York Passage', 1982; and 'Beat the Distance', 1984.

Xmal Deutschland's releases include albums *Fetisch*, 1983; and *Tocsin*, 1984; and the single 'Incubus Succubus' 1983.

4AD bands referenced:

Xmal Deutschland, as above.

The Wolfgang Press, formed in 1983 by former Rema Rema members Michael Allen and Mark Cox: 1980s albums *The Burden of Mules*, 1983; *Standing Up Straight*, 1986 (featuring 'I am the Crime'); and *Bird Wood Cage*, 1988.

It'll End in Tears, This Mortal Coil (features Cinder singing Rem Rema's 'Fond Affections'), 1984

Filigree & Shadow, This Mortal Coil, 1986

'L'esclave endormi', Richenel, 1986

Belgium artists cited:

Jacques Brel: too many classic albums to namecheck, but see for example *Ne Me Quitte Pas*, 1972.

'Dominique', The Singing Nun, 1963

'Ça plane pour moi', Plastic Bertrand, 1977

'Maximising the Audience', Wim Mertens, 1988

Classical meets Contemporary in the USA:

Laurie Anderson 1980s recordings include the albums *Big Science*, 1982; and *Home of the Brave*, 1986. single 'O Superman' was released in 1981.

Meredith Monk 1980s releases include *Turtle Dreams*, 1983; and *Do You Be*, 1987.

Steve Reich 1980s compositions include *The Desert Music*, 1983 (set to text by William Carlos Williams); *Sextet* for percussion and keyboards, 1984; and *New York Counterpoint*, 1985.

Philip Glass 1980s output included the album *Glassworks*, 1982; the score to *Koyaanisqatsi*, 1982; choral and orchestral work *Akhnaten*, 1984; and a collaboration with experimental theatre-maker Robert Wilson on the opera *CIVIL warS*, 1984.

Film/TV

Repo Man, Alex Cox, 1984

Sid and Nancy, Alex Cox, 1986

Caravaggio, Derek Jarman, 1986

Sebastiane, Derek Jarman, 1976

Performance, Nicolas Roeg and Donald Cammell, 1970

The Man Who Fell to Earth, Nicolas Roeg, 1976

David Cronenberg's body-horror films include *Shivers*, 1975; *Rabid*, 1977; and *Scanners*, 1981

Kenneth Anger short films include: *Inauguration of the Pleasure Dome*, 1954; *Scorpio Rising*, 1964; and *Lucifer Rising*, 1972.

Swimming to Cambodia, Spalding Gray with Laurie Anderson, 1987

Books/Magazines

Howl and Other Poems Allen Ginsberg, 1956

The Handmaid's Tale, Margaret Atwood, 1986 *84*

Charing Cross Road, Helene Hanff, 1970

The View Over Atlantis, John Mitchell, 1973

The Adventures of Sweet Gwendoline, John Willie, first published as a serial in *Wink* magazine, 1947-1951. Artwork appropriated by Adam Ant and used in the band's promotional materials.

Atomage magazine, edited by John Sutcliffe, celebrating all things rubber, leather and vinyl, 1972-1985. Much of the magazine's stock and printing plates were destroyed in a police raid and prosecution in 1983.

TransFM magazine featuring regular column 'Letter From London', originally authored by Andy Warren aka John Bull, then Dorothy Max Prior, aka Jane Bull, 1985 to 1988.

The Face magazine, founded by Nick Logan, in print 1980 till 2004.

ZigZag magazine, founded by Pete Frame, ran 1969 to 1986. Editors: Pete Frame, Kris Needs, Mick Mercer.

ZG magazine, founded by Rosetta Brooks, 1980-1986.

International Times (IT), had a checkered history from 1966 to 1986, when the magazine was revived, but only three print editions were published January to March 1986, these being the final ever print editions of the magazine.

Theatre/Performance/Art

Jamie Reid exhibition, showing the No Future series and designs for the Sex Pistols records, posters etc: Hamilton's, Bond Street London, 1986.

Ad Reinhardt, *Abstract Painting no.5*, part of the 'black' series which the painter described as 'the last paintings that anyone can paint', 1962. Seen as part of the Tate exhibition *40 Years of Modern Art*, 1986.

Cosey Fanni Tutti is a visual and performance artist, musician and writer. For more about her, see coseyfannitutti.com.

Annie Sprinkle is an ecosexual performance artist, sexologist, former sex worker and pornographic film actress who continues to make inspiring and boundary-challenging work. See her Instagram account@anniesprinkled.

Baby Love

Discs

Sahara Elektrik, Dissidenten, 1983

Stop Making Cheese, Look People, 1986

Rockin' and Romance, Jonathan Richman and the Modern Lovers, 1985

Euronova classics:

'Fred Vom Jupiter', Andreas Dorau, 1981

'Einsamkeit hat viele Namen', Die Zwei, 1982

'Paul Getty's Ohr', Herman Koop, on the album *Pop*, 1983

'Prefazione di Pompei', Die Form, 1982

Film/TV/Video

Mean Streets, Martin Scorsese, 1973

West Side Story, Robert Wise and Jerome Robbins, 1961

Four American Composers, Peter Greenaway, 1983

La Belle et La Bête, Jean Cocteau, 1946

My Beautiful Launderette, Stephen Frears, 1985

Letter to Brezhnev, Chris Bernard, 1985

Paris, Texas, Wim Wenders, 1984

Troll, John Carl Buechler, 1986

Alien, Ridley Scott, 1979

The Ballad of Sexual Dependency, Nan Goldin, 1985

Rapture, Blondie – video featuring Jean-Michel Basquiat, 1980

Books

William Burroughs novels include *Junky*, 1953; *Naked Lunch*, 1959; *The Wild Boys*, 1971; and *The Western Lands*, 1987.

Anna Kavan novels include *Ice*, 1967; and *Sleep Has His House*, 1947.

Rosemary's Baby, Ira Levin, 1967

Theatre/Performance/Art

Composer Dave Brubeck and choreographer Murray Louis in collaboration, National Arts Centre Ottawa, May 1986

Beehive, a 1960s-inspired musical, created and directed by Larry Gallagher, Village Gate Upstairs, 1986

Andy Warhol and Jean-Michel Basquiat collaboration: around 160 works made between 1984 and 2985. See basquiat.com

Naked/Nude exhibition at MoMA, featuring Jasper Johns, Robert Rauschenberg, Claes Oldenberg, Roy Lichtenstein et al, 1986

Guerrilla Girls protest poster art, 1985 onwards, including: 'Do Women Need to Be Naked to Get into the Met?' and 'The Advantages of Being a Woman Artist'. The anonymous feminist art collective is still going strong! See guerrillagirls.com

Better an Old Demon than a Young God

Discs

Better an Old Demon Than a Young God, John Giorno et al, 1984

A Diamond Hidden in the Mouth of a Corpse, John Giorno et al, 1985

Raspberry / Pornographic Poem LP, Giorno Poetry Systems, 1967

You're a Hook, 15 year anniversary of Dial-a-Poem 1968-1983, John Giorno, Lenny Kaye et al, featuring Giorno's 'Last Night I Gambled with My Anger and Lost', 1983

You're the Guy I Want to Share My Money With, Laurie Anderson, William S Burroughs, John Giorno, 1981

Paradise Lost, Urban Sax and Pierre Henry, 1982

Fraction Sur Le Temps, Urban Sax, 1986

'Shouting Out Loud', The Raincoats, 1981

'The Pink Panther Theme', Henry Mancini, 1963

Books/Magazines

Books by the prolific Charles Bukowski include the semi-autobiographical novels: *Post Office*, 1971; *Factotum*, 1975; and *Women*, 1978. Short story collections include *Notes of a Dirty*

Old Man, 1969; and *The Most Beautiful Woman in Town*, 1983. Poetry collections include *Burning in Water, Drowning in Flame,* 1974; and *Love is a Dog from Hell*, 1977.

City Lights Booksellers and Publishers in San Francisco was founded by beat poet Lawrence Ferlinghetti and Peter D Martin in 1953. Its first publication was Ferlinghetti's poetry collection *Pictures of the Gone World*; a year later came *Howl and Other Poems* by Allen Ginsberg.

My Secret Garden: Women's Sexual Fantasies, Nancy Friday, 1973

The Final Academy brochure published by TOPY, 1982

Film/TV/Video
Sleep, Andy Warhol, featuring John Giorno, 1964

And the Ship Sails On, Federico Fellini, featuring Pina Bausch, 1983

The Final Academy Documents, video, 1982-1983. Published on DVD, and currently (2024) available on YouTube.

Theatre/Performance/Art
Giorno Poetry Systems: the chocolate bar poems, silk-screen poem prints, window-curtain poems... ephemeral events, 1960s onwards.

Dial-a-Poem, 1967 onwards, featuring John Giorno, Allen Ginsberg, Patti Smith, Laurie Anderson et al.

'Suicide Sutra', John Giorno, presented on Dial-a-Poem.

John Giorno and guest musicians live at the ICA, January 1986. Poems performed included 'Cancer in My Left Ball', and 'Eating Human Meat'.

The Final Academy tour took place 1982-1983, including four nights at the Ritzy in Brixton, South London, 29 September to 2 October 1982.

Urban Sax – composer/director Gilbert Artman and his team of 65 saxophonists – performed outside County Hall London on 3 August 1985.

Shouting Out Loud, choreographed by Gaby Agis, 1984. Score by The Raincoats.

Human Sex, LaLaLa Human Steps, 1985

La Fura dels Baus, the groundbreaking immersive company from Barcelona who created 'guerrilla theatre' in unusual sites, appeared in London in 1985 and 1986 with *Accions*, created 1984; and *Suz/o/Suz*, 1985.

Kurt Schwitters retrospective, Hayward Gallery, 1986

Eduardo Paolozzi's *Lost Magic Kingdoms*, Museum of Mankind, 1985-1986

Les Levine's *Blame God, Billboard Projects*, ICA 1985

Krzysztof Wodizcko's *City Projections* came to London in 1985 and included the infamous projection of a swastika onto South Africa House in Trafalgar Square.

Cirque du Soleil, contemporary circus company formed in Montreal by street performer Guy Laliberté, in 1984. Now the biggest producer of contemporary circus in the world, with numerous constantly-touring shows, and many supported or aligned companies.

Archaos, anarchic French contemporary circus company founded by Pierre Bidon in 1986. Now based in Marseilles and producer of the world's largest contemporary circus festival.

Pina Bausch/Tanztheater Wuppertal shows referenced: *Kontakthof* and *Viktor*, presented at Sadler's Wells at various dates in the 1980s/1990s.

The Neo Naturists live art collective was formed in the early 1980s by Christine Binnie, Jennifer Binnie, and Wilma Johnson. Grayson Perry appeared in many of their early performances.

Brighton Rock/s

Discs
'Happy Talk', Captain Sensible (with Dolly Mixture), 1982
'Miss Candy Twist', Dolly Mixture, 1983
'The Carny', 1986 and 'From Her to Eternity', Nick Cave and The Bad Seeds, 1984
'*EastEnders* Theme Tune', Simon May/London Theatre Orchestra, 1985
'Theme from S'Express', S'Express, 1988
'She Bangs the Drums', Stone Roses, 1989
'Dig for Fire', The Pixies, 1990
'Deep in Vogue', Malcolm McLaren, The Bootzilla Orchestra w/ Mark Moore et al, 1989
'Mama Told Me Not to Come', Wolfgang Press, 1991
Here Today, Tomorrow Next Week!, The Sugarcubes, 1989
Jacques, Marc Almond, 1989
Jack the Tab/Tekno Acid Beat, Psychic TV, 1988-1990

Film/TV/Video
The Last of England, Derek Jarman, 1987
Wings of Desire, Wim Wenders, 1987
Street of Crocodiles, animated short by Brothers Quay, 1986
The Cabinet of Jan Svankmajer, animated film made in homage to Jan Svankmajer, Brothers Quay, 1984

Theatre/Performance/Art
Young British Artists aka YBAs first exhibited together in 1988, beginning with *Freeze*, led by Damien Hirst, Angus Fairhurst, and Tracey Emin. Other YBAs, many of them graduates of Goldsmiths, include Sarah Lucas, Gillian Wearing, Anya Gallaccio, Gary Hume, and Sam Taylor-Wood. 'Second

wave' YBAs include Gavin Turk, Jane and Louise Wilson, and Tacita Dean.

Helen Chadwick, sculptor and photographer, famous for her 'Piss Paintings' and other works using organic materials, taught at both Goldsmiths and Brighton Polytechnic.

Brothers Quay are sculptors, animators and theatre designers, who have worked on numerous films and theatre shows, including work for Complicite, Pere Ubu, and Jonathan Miller.

Forkbeard Fantasy mix surreal live performance and film to create extraordinary works that include *The Fall of the House of Usherettes*, 1995; and *The Barbers of Surreal,* 1998.

Lea Anderson, choreography: dance companies The Cholmondeleys (female) and The Featherstonehaughs (male). Early works include *Flesh and Blood*, 1989; *Cold Sweat*, 1990; and *The Show*, 1990.

The Wild Wigglers, an anarchic post-punk electro-pop dance combo, existed from 1982 to 1990 and comprised: Liz Aggiss, Neil Butler, Ian Smith.

Thumb Culture theatre company with Graham Duff (writer) and Ginny Farman (choreographer).

Yellow Mummy Bird

Discs

'Dream a Little Dream of Me' The Mamas and The Papas, 1968

'How to Dance', Bingoboys, 1990

'Can I Kick It?' A Tribe Called Quest, 1990

3 Feet High and Rising, De La Soul, 1989. Featuring 'The Magic Number',

'Transmitting Live from Mars' and 'Eye Know'

Rising Above Bedlam, Jah Wobble's Invaders of the Heart, 1991, featuring 'Visions of You' (vocals Sinead O'Connor and Jah Wobble), 'Bomba' and 'Soledad' (with vocals by Natasha Atlas).

Film/TV/Video
Pussy Got the Cream, Cosey Fanni Tutti, 1986

Books
Anarchic Dance, Liz Aggiss and Billy Cowie, 2006
Performance Cleaner, Roy Barfield, published by Triarchy Press, is a brilliant account of working (as performer and cleaner) at the Zap Club in its 1980s–1990s heyday.

Theatre/Performance/Art
Pow Wow at the Zap Club, a monthly multimedia extravaganza throughout 1991. Curated by Mark Waugh, choreographed by Ginny Farman, with a cast of thousands.
Andy Walker's Fame Frame at the Zap Club started late 1991/ early 1992. Inspired by Andy Warhol's infamous quote, Andy Walker's take was that 'in the future everyone will be famous for 3 minutes'. Andy was aided and abetted in this venture by Stella Starr.
Divas Dance Theatre, founded in 1980 and led by choreographer Liz Aggiss and composer Billy Cowie, created very many live performances, dance works, films, installations and performance actions, including *Grotesque Dancer*, *Drool and Drivel They Care*, *Falling Apart at the Seams*, and *Men on the Wall*.
Disco Sister, led by choreographer Virginia (Ginny) Farman, started life as a live art intervention at Pow Wow, then went on to be a leading contemporary dance company throughout the 1990s and beyond.

Forced Entertainment early shows included *Nighthawks*, 1985; *200% and Bloody Thirsty*, 1987; and *Emmanuelle Enchanted*, 1992.

Dead Dreams of Monochrome Men, Nigel Charnock/DV8, 1990
Stomp, Yes/No People, 1991

The Art School Dance Goes On and On

Discs
David Devant and His Spirit Wife
Many early David Devant and His Spirit Wife songs are featured on the unofficial album *Don Spirit Specs Now*, 1993: 'Miscellaneous', 'Madame Devant', 'Don't Tell Me/ Slumberland', 'Monkey's Birthday', 'David's Coming Back' – and the band's only cover song, 'Look What They've Done to my Song, Ma'.

Other early (or second-wave) songs include 'David Devant and His Spirit Wife', 'Ballroom' 'Pimlico', 'I'm Not Even Gonna Try' and 'Goodnight', many of which eventually found their way onto the band's first album, *Work, Love Life, Miscellaneous*, 1997. 'Pimlico' was released as a single in 1997.

'Dead Cats Don't Swing', The Atom Smashers featuring Monte Cazazza, 1986

Film/TV
Star Trek, TV series, 1967. Featuring longterm antagonists the Klingons, a brutal race who feature in every subsequent series, and in most of the *Star Trek* films.

Dispatches, 'Beyond Belief', Channel 4, a discredited special investigation into ritual satanic abuse, presented by Andrew Boyd. The alleged documentary material used was soon found to be a Temple of Psychic Youth art film, *First Transmission*. Broadcast 19 February 1992.

First Transmission, 1982 – short film by TOPY, with contributions from Peter Sleazy Christopherson, Genesis P-Orridge, Monte Cazazza, Tana Emmolo, David Tibet, and Cosey Fanni Tutti; and using archive material from Jim Jones and Brion Gysin.

That's Life! BBC TV, a satirical consumer affairs programme that ran from 1973 to 1994. Written and presented by Esther Rantzen et al.

Books/Magazines

'The Art School Dance Goes On and On' is a title semi-stolen from *ZigZag* founding editor Pete Frame, who used 'The Art School Dance Goes on Forever' for one of his Rock Family Trees, featuring Adam and The Ants, The Monochrome Set, Bow Wow Wow, Rema Rema et al.

The Complete Rock Family Trees, Pete Frame, 1993. Combines previously published *Pete Frame's Rock Family Trees*, Volume 1 and Volume 2.

The Baby, Viva, 1974

Rudolf Steiner's books include: *Theosophy: An Introduction to the Spiritual Processes in Human Life and in the Cosmos*, 1904; *The Education of the Child*, 1907; *Reincarnation and Immortality*, 1970.

Madame Blavatsky's books include: *The Secret Doctrine: The Synthesis of Science, Religion and Philosophy*, 1888; and *The Key to Theosophy*, 1889.

Theatre/Performance/Art

David Devant and His Spirit Wife, a magical and theatrical performance art and music show, premiering at The Rock, Kemptown, for Brighton Festival Fringe, 1992.

For One Night Only, The People Show, Old Ship Ballroom Brighton, 1993

Journey to the Red Bed, multi-discipline immersive performance, Zap Club, 1993.

Brighton Dance Collective, regular presentations at Brighton Pavilion Theatre, various dates through the 1990s.

AFTERWORD

Sex Is No Emergency follows on from previous memoir *69 Exhibition Road* – although in some ways pre-dates it. Or at least the title does: between 2015 and 2020 I was using it as an umbrella for a whole bunch of autobiographical writings and cultural commentary about the 1970s and 1980s, some of which got published in a nascent form and some of which lay languishing in bottom drawers or on my laptop.

Originally, I thought I'd just put together one book about it all. Maybe a book about what it was like to be a girl drummer, including all musical adventures from 1976 to 1986. Or a more journalistic kind of book about punk and all the other and various aspects of counterculture London in the 1970s and 1980s.

It was in 2020, during lockdown, when I finally knuckled down to get 'the book' done, that the idea came of framing the book – well 'a book' anyway – within the time spent in that legendary house in South Kensington, 69 Exhibition Road, and thus mostly confining it to the years between 1976 and 1982 – a memoir of that time and place.

With that one done and dusted, there was, I felt, room for more. By ending it in 1982, with the departure from 69 Exhibition Road, there was a lot that hadn't been covered. My evolving friendship with Andy and ongoing relationship with The Monochrome Set. Meeting that new TMS guitarist, Foz (reader, I married him). The evolution of the relationship with Genesis P-Orridge, and finally joining Psychic TV on drums, having refused to do so years earlier (reader, that ended in tears). The extraordinary and intense friendship/romance with Monte Cazazza, whose song title 'Sex Is No Emergency' I've nabbed for the title of this book. All of the musical galaxies that sprung out of, or revolved around, Rema Rema/4AD on the one hand, and Psychic TV on the other. The fragmenting of 'youth culture' into the post-modern supermarket of style that defined the 1980s, as new club nights, lifestyle magazines, TV shows, record labels and clothes shops sprung up to feed the growing horde of hungry consumers of culture, and underground went overground.

Oh, and then there's ballroom dancing, babies, breastfeeding, and moving to Brighton to become a performance artist. Yep, quite a wondrous mix of experiences as girl becomes woman – hence the subtitle *Adventures in a Post Punk Wonderland*. The 1980s saw me hurled from one odd landscape to another. Changing shape and size. Playing strange games. Encountering a whole load of mysterious talking animals. Finding life to be ever more surreal and bemusing. An automated Alice?

As quite a few of the stories had already been started even before the first memoir was published, *Sex Is No Emergency* came together pretty quickly. Or at least, a first draft did. A good second draft was a bit of a struggle. There was a lot of rejigging, and a lot of shifting things from one story to another. I had my doubts about bringing such a strange collection of shapeshifting experiences together in one volume, and it took quite a while for everything to settle into its rightful place. But I got there with the helpful encouragement of Mark Pilkington from Strange Attractor Press. When Mark read the ballroom dancing story 'Tango'd' and loved it, I was sure everything would be OK. Another Mark – Mark Cox from Rema Rema/ The Wolfgang Press – read 'Baby Love' and gave enthusiastic feedback. I knew that there would, of course, be an audience for the two Psychic TV stories, 'The Fabulous Feast of Flowering Light', and 'Europe Endless', and for The Monochrome Set story 'Take Foz'; but to know that other stories were liked was reassuring. As it happens, the relationship with Genesis P-Orridge and PTV is a thread that weaves its way through the whole book, from the first story, 'In Every Dream Home', to the last, 'The Art School Dance Goes On and On.'

I originally intended the book to end in 1989, with the move to Brighton – but that somehow felt wrong. I think because I didn't want to abandon my younger self in a new city, knowing no one, with no creative outlets, bogged down in the mire of early motherhood. A starlit mire, but a mire none-the-less. The three Brighton stories that follow the move from London, with their tug between trying to be a 'good mother' and trying to be an artist, making new friends and discovering new means of expression, felt necessary. It also felt weird to reference two of the children and not the third, so we go to 1993 and end with Max in her late-thirties with three children and a new life as a Live Art performer, dancer and choreographer. Taking it to the early 1990s also meant winding up the Psychic TV story properly, with a new stage of friendship with Gen and Paula when they moved to Brighton, and the subsequent terror of the trial-by-TV 'satanic abuse' scandal and the P-Orridge family's hasty departure from the UK.

The process of writing this book was a little different to *69ER* in many ways. I had far more to draw on. Personal memories, of course, but also diaries, Psychic TV ephemera, my own writings from the 1980s, and a wealth of information out there as the world started to become endlessly documented.

Back copies of *TransFM* magazine, for whom I'd written a regular column in the 1980s, proved vital as a source not only of factual information, but an indication of my voice as a culturally engaged but slightly disenchanted 30-year-old. The choleric years, according to Hippocrates. Or perhaps that's William Shakespeare. Or maybe Rudolf Steiner. Anyway, someone or other said that not only do we each have a prevailing temperament, but in life we move through the four temperaments. Our thirties are all about being choleric: driven, motivated, and often a bit arrogant and angry. Yep, I can see that in the old me...

I tried to be true to that voice in these stories, and not impose too much of the 'me here-and-now' into the narrative. So, for example, when I write, in the story 'Ten Years After', about my disillusion with encountering Jamie Reid's work in a Bond Street gallery, that's very much the 30-year-old me talking. I've now got used to the fact that punk has become something historic, to be written about in learned journals; and that underground and transgressive artists have, inevitably, been embraced by the mainstream. *C'est la vie.*

I also had the support of numerous people who were there, too, and willing to be interviewed, or to have a more casual conversation, or to read stories in progress – to give additional factual information or supportive feedback. These include husband Foz, former wife and co-conspirator Andy Warren, dear friends Hilmar Örn Hilmarsson and Drew McDowall from the 1984-1985 line-up of Psychic TV, Mikey Georgeson from David Devant and His Spirit Wife, and Mark Alleyne who was The Monochrome Set roadie before forming Mark Antony and the Centurions.

The big empty space is Monte Cazazza, who died whilst I was writing the book, before I could talk to him. I decided that this great black hole needed to be acknowledged in the text – hence the final mini-story 'Postscript: A Letter to Monte'. Which raised some ethical dilemmas about how much personal material relating to someone who had recently died should be included. I had this parcel of letters (although his to me, not mine to him, which is interesting in itself) and I included some of the hand-made collages and a few direct quotes from his letters, weaved into a personal wail of anguish...

As for the title: there is, of course, an irony to *Sex Is No Emergency* as sexual intrigues and tensions certainly caused havoc 'within and outside of Psychic TV' as Monte put it; and rocked the boat for a while in The Monochrome Set. *Sex Is No Emergency* also flags up the furore that was the AIDS pandemic, a killer disease weaponised in the 1980s by Thatcher in the UK and Reagan in the USA to terrorise LGBT+ people – see Clause 28 and more. And *Sex Is No Emergency* points to the weirdly retrogressive views on sex and gender that emerged in the late 1980s and early 1990s as many of the gains won for women, gay and trans people during the punk revolution seemed to evaporate. It also signals the exasperation I felt as a pregnant woman when almost everyone seemed to have an opinion on what the sex of my babies might be or should be, and how those babies should be raised.

I'll also say here that whereas *69 Exhibition Road* was pulled together during the peaceful lockdown days of 2020, when I had the luxury of a room of my own to work in, and few distractions, *Sex Is No Emergency* was mostly written either in concentrated bursts during writing retreats abroad in Spain or Portugal, or at home perched on an armchair in the living room with a small grandchild sat next to me watching *Teen Titans*. Which, when it came to writing the latter stories about trying to balance out (ha!) being a carer of little ones and being an artist, felt somehow appropriate.

The dedication for this book is 'to sons and lovers', and goes out with infinite love to husband Foz, and sons Gabriel, Milo and Frank who are at the heart of this story.

Former or lost or almost lovers I'd like to acknowledge, with much love and appreciation for just being there and informing these stories, include Andy Warren, Marco Pirroni and Hilmar Örn Hilmarsson, who are still very much with us; and Monte

Cazazza, Genesis P-Orridge and Jamie Reid who have moved on to the heavenly spheres.

Love is eternal.

Tanti Baci, Max

Dorothy Max Prior
July 2024

ACKNOWLEDGEMENTS & CREDITS

This book's title references the Monte Cazazza song 'Sex is No Emergency', released with 'Stairway to Hell' on Sordide Sentimental, 1982. RIP dearly beloved Monte.

The very last line in the book, 'This is how it ends', is a quote from *The Years*, a memoir by Nobel-prize-winning Annie Ernaux. How wonderful that a memoirist has achieved such an accolade in the literary world!

Now for some words of thanks:

A big thank you to Foz (James Foz Foster) for creating the cover artwork and processing photos for this book; and for agreeing to be interviewed about The Monochrome Set, David Devant and His Spirit Wife, and other matters. Oh, and for reading the final manuscript.

Thanks go to dearly beloved Andy Warren for his input on The Monochrome Set and other sections; and to Bid of The Monochrome Set for sending me photos from Foz's time in TMS, 1983-1985. Thanks also to Mayfair Charm School alumnus Mark Alleyne for his contributions to the 'Take Foz' story and TMS additional information, and for his attentive reading of that story.

Muchas gracias Mikey Georgeson aka The Vessel for corroboration about the early days of David Devant and His Spirit Wife, and providing the lovely long-lost images of the band's first year.

Thanks and gratitude to former Rema Rema bandmate Mark Cox for ongoing support, and for reading 'Baby Love' and reassuring me that stories about babies cut the mustard!

Much appreciation to Hilmar Örn Hilmarsson for the in-person meeting in Reykjavik, two lengthy Zoom sessions, and the careful reading of the Psychic TV stories; and thanks also to Drew McDowall for his time and support on the Psychic TV material.

A big thank you to Ted Polhemus for providing so many wonderful photos from the 1980s and early 1990s clubs and events; and of street scenes and shop windows in London and New York in the early 1980s.

And another big thank you to John Marchant – gallerist, archivist and representative of Jamie Reid in this earthly dimension – for providing a conduit to Jamie before he died (sadly, we didn't re-meet), and for providing the scans of Jamie's artwork and permission for their use.

Thank you kindly dear Val Denham for providing the original artwork for the *Fabulous Feast of Flowering Light* T-shirt, reproduced in this book.

Molte grazie John Tobin, editor of *TransFM*, and journalist Gabriella Bregman, for use of the magazine's 1985 Psychic TV interview.

Salut to Thee Media Shaman aka Eden 123 aka Boris Hießerer who rescued the Red Ronnie Italian TV interview

(Beck Road 1985) video footage from the jaws of Scotland Yard and posted it on Vimeo.

Thank you to Simon Woodgate and anyone who has provided images, or helped me to source images, for this book. This includes the late Andrew Rawling, who kindly sent me his photos from the Psychic TV European tour; and the also-late Berlin-based photographer Norbert Bauer, who captured so many great images of Psychic TV at The Loft in October 1985.

Many, many thanks to Lee Oliver for scanning endless numbers of photos and all those fiddly bits of print ephemera (club membership cards, PTV set lists et al) for this book; and for contributing some of his own archive material.

Thank you to Kim Oliver, Jack Sargeant, Alex Fergusson, Paul Reeson, Matthew Levi Stevens, Jay Strongman, Tony D, and Tom Vague for additional information, support and encouragement.

Thank you Anna Goodman, Stephen Pastel, Isobel Smith, and Zoe 'Girl Shit' Bailey for the friendship, artistic suss and listening ears.

An enormous thank you to Cathi Unsworth for her friendship – and for reading the final manuscript, giving hearty encouragement, and doing such a careful and attentive line edit.

Thanks also go to Alena Zavarzina for the book design and layout, and to Richard Bancroft for proofreading.

Last but not least, a big thank you to Mark Pilkington and Jamie Sutcliffe of Strange Attractor Press for your continuing support as editors and publishers. I'm so very happy to be on this journey through a post punk wonderland with you!

LIST OF ILLUSTRATIONS

Annie Sprinkle, from the Total Theatre Magazine archive.

217 Sigurjón Birgir Sigurðsson aka Sjón aka Johnny Triumph, original artwork, courtesy of Sjón.

Baby Love

222 Clockwise from top left: Polaroid: Foz serenades baby Gabriel, photo by DM Prior, 1986; Gabriella Bregman and Dorothy Max on air at CKCU radio station, Ottawa Canada 1986, photographer unknown; Foz, Max and Gabriel, wedding day 3 Sep 1986, photo Andy Warren; Sharon D'Lugoff in Central Park, NYV 1986, photo DM Prior.

231 'Gay Uncle Ian', Ottawa Canada 1986, photo by DM Prior.

241 CKCU/TransFM friends and family, Ottawa Canada 1986: Sylvie, John Tobin (editor, TransFM), Gabriella Bregman, Will. Photo by Lorenz Eppinger, from DM Prior's archive.

246 Heathrow airport, en route to Iceland: back row, Drew McDowall and Foz; front row, Rose McDowall, Akiko Hada and Keri McDowall. Photo DM Prior.

251 Top: Foz and baby Gabriel; bottom, Max and Gabriel. Montreal Canada Xmas 1986.

Better an Old Demon Than a New God

254 Photomontage original artwork by Monte Cazazza, made for Dorothy Max, 1985-1986.

Colour Section

1   Montage of record sleeves owned by Dorothy Max: Psychic TV, The Monochrome Set, plus various on Cherry Red, él records, Blanco y Negro et al.

2   Mambo Mania: Polaroid of Dorothy Max with dance partner Joe, AKA Dorothy and Toto. Taken at Arthur Murray's Dance Studio in Kensington, 1982. Photographer unknown.

3   Arthur Murray's Dance Studios, Kensington: Dorothy Max and others performing at themed party nights, 1982-1983.

4   Polaroids of Dorothy Max taken at The Nursery, 50 Beck Road, 1985; used as inspiration for Psychic TV The Fabulous Feast of Flowering Light PR. Photos by Genesis P-Orridge.

5   The Fabulous Feast of Flowering Light painting used for T-shirt and postcard design. Original artwork by Val Denham, 1985.

6   Psychic TV poster for The Fabulous Feast of Flowering Light at Hammersmith Palais, May 1985.

7   Clockwise from top: Sharon D'Lugoff in Manhattan NYC, 1985; Andy Warren and Gabriella Bregman, 1985 or 1986; Heathrow airport departure to Iceland with Rose McDowall, Foz, Max, David Tibet, Mel Jefferson, and (front) Keri McDowall, 1986; Drew and Rose McDowall, 1985 or 1986. All photos by DM Prior, except the group shot, photographer unknown.

8   Polaroids 1985-1986, from top left: early pregnancy, late pregnancy, the blushing bride breastfeeds (Max on her wedding day), father & son (Foz and Gabriel).

9   Nursing toddler in red, 1987: Max and Gabriel. Polaroid by Foz, artworked on a Xerox machine by Max.

10   Top: PTV on tour, October 1985: Andrew, Genesis, Max, Drew & Alex. Photographer unknown.
        Bottom: Max on drums (left); Genesis on vocals (right). Photo by Norbert Bauer (AKA Noirbert), taken at The Loft in Berlin, 10 October 1985.

11   Psychic TV on tour, from the top: Max, Hilmar & Alex; Hilmar and (behind him) Drew; producer Ken Thomas and Drew. All photos by Andrew Rawling, October 1985.

12   Top: Aurelius performance company Dorothy Max, Deborah Hay, and Sally Noele Johnson, taken circa 1994. Photographer unknown.
        Bottom: David Devant and His Spirit Wife: Spectral Roadie Nick Curry and his signs, 1992 or 1993, photo courtesy of Mikey Georgeson.

13   Clockwise from top left: David Devant and His Spirit Wife brochure artwork by Mikey Georgeson, 1992; The Monochrome Set's Bid, Foz and Andy, 1984 or 1985, photograph courtesy of Bid; Propaganda artwork by Dorothy Max, 1986 or 1987; Pow Wow Club at the Zap Brighton, promo image 1991.

14   Nighclubbing, clockwise from top left: Hilmar, Max and Gabriella; Foz, Hilmar and Gabriella

outside Gossips at 69 Dean Street; Fiona Russell AKA Fifi Coyote (standing) with person unknown. Photos by Max and Foz, 1985.

15 Original artwork By Monte Cazazza, paint and photomontage, created for Dorothy Max, 1985.

16 Jamie Reid, self-portrait in red. Original artwork created by Jamie Reid, 1986. Reproduced with kind permission of John Marchant.

INDEX

Cuts Club

274

Meard Street, W. 1.

Strange Attractor Press 2025